W9-AQP-405

Welfare in America

Welfare in America

by Vaughn Davis Bornet

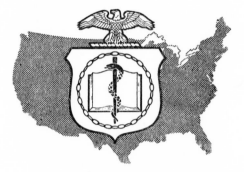

Norman
University of Oklahoma Press

By Vaughn Davis Bornet

California Social Welfare: Legislation, Financing, Services, Statistics (Englewood Cliffs, N. J., 1956)

Welfare in America (Norman, 1960)

The publication of this volume has been aided by a grant from the Ford Foundation

Library of Congress Catalog Card Number: 60-13482

Copyright 1960 by the University of Oklahoma Press, Publishing Division of the University. First edition, December, 1960; second printing, July, 1963. Manufactured in the U.S.A.

To John Earl Baker

a warm friend and wise counselor. Representative of the
humanitarian tradition of the United States, he devoted
his life to the administration of government and voluntary
agencies formed to help the starving and homeless.

A Preliminary Word

THE WELFARE OF EACH INDIVIDUAL in the United States has long been of deep concern to a large number of our citizens. Yet controversy has often accompanied the efforts of volunteers and social workers to organize and finance humanitarian services for children, women, and men. This is not surprising, for social welfare is an emotional area of activity. Involved in it are money, time, religious belief, the integrity of intentions, and other things which are known to divide ordinarily pleasant people, on occasion, into combatants. How far government should go in caring for the individual is an unsettled issue. Methods of supplying social service agencies with funds are heatedly debated.

Welfare in America is designed to bring into focus issues that have divided our people. It suggests others to which attention should be given without delay. Three years spent on an earlier social welfare book aroused my interest in further investigation of broad issues, with the result that fifteen months of full-time interviewing, research, observing, reading, reflecting, and writing went into the present volume.

There are fundamental points of view in these pages on which well-informed people who have read drafts of the manuscript disagree. Their differences seem quite irreconcilable. They do agree, however, that an entirely independent evaluation of this character needed to be written in order to present little known facts, sharpen issues, and invite open discussion.

I hope that the portrait of social welfare painted in these pages will attract the interest of leaders in our communities who share my concern over the present and future welfare of all the people who comprise our society.

VAUGHN DAVIS BORNET

Santa Monica, California
June 8, 1960

Contents

Illustrations

Welfare in America

The Path We Have Trod

Social welfare
In twentieth-century America:
An ever shifting pattern.
Charity; functional togetherness through organization;
Government payments, benefits, and services.
From Clara Barton to Mary Richmond,
From Carnegie to Girl Scouts to Cerebral Palsy,
From YMCA buildings to CARE packages,
From settlement houses to homemaker services,
From "paupers" to "clients"—
Here is
The Path We Have Trod.

AMERICAN SOCIAL WELFARE in the twentieth century has developed through six decades into a pattern derived from several basic forms of "doing good." Each form has served, on occasion, the interests of humanity. A vital part of the social history of the United States, therefore, is the story of how these several forms of social service activity clashed, built on one another, and finally emerged in an uneasy partnership.

The first "social service" reality in America was the individual caring for his own family, his close friends, and scarcely more than one stranger at a time. "Charity begins at home" was the outspoken motto of this individualist school, which rooted itself in such biblical statements as "Honor thy father and thy mother." Husbands and wives had primary responsibilities toward each other and toward their children. Younger brothers and sisters were often a lifelong concern of the eldest child. It was a disgrace to have a close relative cared for under the poor laws or living in an almshouse. Often the cloak of personal charity was cast over a total stranger, and neighborly concern could be expected in time of adversity. While some encountered social security in enslavement, many more discovered it in the diversity of opportunities for earning a living of one's choice on a new continent. The ministry then shouldered responsibilities that would one day become the province of social workers.

3

A new tendency in charitable activity, which had developed very slowly by the time of the Civil War, increased toward the turn of the century, and developed rapidly during the Progressive Movement, was the founding and growth of voluntary organizations. Largely urban in their origins, these agencies were often sponsored by religious bodies whose ministers found preaching and the business of running city churches quite enough to handle. Delegation of most charitable and protective work to subordinate groups, and to quasi-religious organizations, seemed the sensible thing to do. Laymen often founded and gave long hours to these new bodies, feeling that in organization there was strength. The late nineteenth and early twentieth centuries saw remarkable innovations in this new world of voluntarily organized social welfare work.

Gradually — and then suddenly — government entered the field. At local, state, and finally at national levels, government became a force in the fields of charity, recreation, and health. Soon it was possible to speak of "public welfare work." At length, with the extension of governmental payments to those in need, came "social insurance" programs financed by special taxes. With this step social welfare in the nation came full circle. Now the individual was being forced to provide for anticipated emergency needs of himself and his immediate family, paying on the installment plan in advance. On his employer was placed a parallel obligation.

Even though an apparently inexorable expansion of voluntary and publicly organized programs of social welfare had reached immense proportions by the middle of the twentieth century, many citizens clung to the belief of their forebears in the worth of personal responsibility for one's own and his family's well-being. Nevertheless, many of these same Americans also believed in the usefulness of voluntary organizations, no matter how large, seeing in them necessary solutions for social ills. Many citizens offered these agencies their time and their money. Yet the vast majority came at length to believe that only government, with its vast taxing powers and far-flung organization, could provide some of the expensive services that seemed needed. Particularly was this true of the problem of income maintenance in a complex society.

The ebb and flow of these tendencies or beliefs—some would

say faiths—is the essential story of social welfare in twentieth-century America.

What are some of the great changes that have taken place in social welfare since the days of Grover Cleveland and William McKinley? Over the years, even the words one uses to describe the assistance activities developed by Americans have changed to such a degree that two different descriptive vocabularies seem to be needed. The very nature of the motivation exhibited by our people in the nineteenth century now seems foreign.

For many who engaged in what was called "charitable work" at the turn of the century, motivations seemed quite clear and simple. It was God's will. It was right and proper to help one's fellow man. William Wordsworth wrote in 1822 lines that put charity in the light in which it was preached—if not always accepted—by the nineteenth century:

> Give all thou canst; high Heaven rejects the lore
> Of nicely-calculated less or more. . . .

Reformers who were inclined to do good for others could sing with heartfelt belief the final words from "Good King Wenceslas": "Therefore Christian men be sure, wealth or rank possessing; ye who now will bless the poor, shall yourselves find blessing." After the passage of a few decades of the twentieth century, however, the word "charity" would fall into disrepute in certain circles (particularly among social workers), although a few stalwart religious groups still found use for it. No longer did the nation have "paupers." Neither did it have "indigents," except now and then in the phraseology of legal enactments. Aid went to "recipients" and advice to "clients." The word "reliefer"—very common in the 1930's—simply disappeared in following decades. There remained "pensioners," even though a grave doubt remained in many a citizen's mind that old age assistance was properly, in law or in fact, a *pension*.

The role of government came in time to be infinitely greater than before. While it is true that the federal government has since the 1790's maintained hospitals for merchant sailors and benefits

5

for veterans are almost as old as our federal system, the major financing and leadership roles assumed by the government in Washington are phenomena of a much later day. The United States Department of Health, Education, and Welfare, the relatively new product of the fusion of many subordinate agencies and functions, had after 1955 more than 40,000 employees. The total was twice as great as in the Department of State and 10,000 more than in the Department of Justice. The employees were more than the combined total of the General Accounting Office, the Government Printing Office, the staff assigned to Congress, the Civil Aeronautics Board, the federal judicial branch, the Department of Labor, the Atomic Energy Commission, and the Selective Service System. By 1959, HEW had grown to 59,099 persons and had 584 district offices.

When one considers that the United States had by 1960 fifty-four secretaries of State, fifty-six secretaries of the Treasury, fifteen secretaries of Agriculture, thirty-seven secretaries of the Interior, and only three secretaries of Health, Education, and Welfare, the employment figures are all the more remarkable.

At the state level, the phenomenon of growth is also noticeable. The Wisconsin State Department of Social Welfare came to operate, in the 1950's, a dozen institutions, seven farms, three forestry camps, and ten district offices. Co-operatively it administered thirty-eight county mental hospitals, thirty-six county homes and hospitals for the aged, and seventy-one county welfare departments. Its annual budget exceeded seventy million dollars, exclusive of federal and county funds which passed through its hands. Its employee roster listed 4,010 positions.

There has been a great shift in the terminology and content of social work. The most obvious shift is exhibited in the change from "charity" to "social welfare." If these bare words do not convey the full change of emphasis, a few phrases will emphasize the contrast. What has happened to the expressions, "settlement worker," "orphan asylum," "poor farm," "benevolences," "easing the way of the immigrant," "child from the city streets," and "doing good"? These terms are seldom heard in social work circles or among our citizens. Today the phrases, "health, welfare,

6

and recreation," "character building," "psychiatric social work," "homemaker service," "recreation for the blind," "senior center," "rehabilitation," "adoption services," "united fund," "retarded children," and "social insurance programs" are continually used in social work literature.

Most Americans who read these pages would not be able to give the functions of an "overseer of the poor," nor would many know the purpose of the almshouse. "Outdoor relief" and "indoor relief" are expressions virtually extinct except in the most rural areas, and then only among old people. "Provident associations" and "associated charities" are gone, except where old names have been retained with more sentimentality than regard for current activities. To read the name of the Massachusetts state board which once handled supervision of certain institutions, that is, the State Board of Lunacy and Charity, is to rejoice that many aspects of the "good old days" are gone forever. Only a few Americans seriously press to have modern relief programs return to the distinction between yesteryear's categories of "the worthy" and "the unworthy," for enacting the concept of "need" into legal language has proved a hard enough task for modern legislators.

The path we have trod is marked, chronologically, by the emergence and growth of great national voluntary organizations. Why did certain ones come into existence at particular times? Why not earlier—or later? To choose one example, the American Humane Society was founded in 1877 to aid children and animals; the National Foundation for Infantile Paralysis was born as late as 1938. Why? The answer is the sum of many factors, ranging from the history of modern medicine to the tendency of individuals to sympathize with different groups in the population and to promote various "causes." It is not enough to say that "things were simpler in 1877," even though that may be true enough. Nor is it sufficient to point out that, in the case of the National Foundation, its birth, growth, and much of its success are traceable to the work and personality of a single individual, Franklin Delano Roosevelt, himself a victim of paralysis. But its remarkable growth in later years clearly rested on modern machine accounting, the development of fund-raising techniques, and the use of the mass media. What might the Humane Society have done with modern public relations techniques? Between these two organizations lies, in any event, a whole period of American history, a time of shifting loyalties, changing programs, and dramatic shifts in the processes of doing good. While the mere date of founding of organizations is not enough to tell so complex a story, a review of this subject is revealing.

The American National Red Cross, largest of all voluntary welfare organizations, provides an excellent starting point. It was in 1881 that the Red Cross had its first experience in relief work. Forest fires in Michigan had left many families homeless, and the Red Cross served. In 1884 there were floods in the Mississippi and Ohio valleys. Congress appropriated half a million dollars, and the Secretary of War made $50,000 in cash available for immediate distribution. The Red Cross, with Clara Barton in the lead, made a reputation for itself. It has been carrying a mighty load ever since, through major wars and a variety of disasters. Here is the foundation stone of American voluntary welfare, yet one on which the President of the United States, ex officio, keeps a watchful eye.

It is interesting that the Red Cross (1881) and the Salvation Army (1880) were founded at almost the same time. English in its origins, the latter came to make its helping role felt in cities across the American continent. The final decades of the nineteenth century saw also the spread of the YMCA movement, which, however, had been founded much earlier. The 1890's witnessed the beginnings of the American Public Health Association. An organization that would become the National Conference of Social Welfare also got its start at this time, and the Volunteers of America came into existence.

Soon Hull House began serving Chicago; Judge Ben Lindsay was creating precedents in the proper handling of children; and juvenile courts were taking the problems of the young out of the severity of the traditional courtroom atmosphere. The idea of philanthropy, as old as Benjamin Franklin and long considered a salient characteristic of the New World, took root in the minds of a Rockefeller and a Carnegie, with dramatic results. The leadership of Theodore Roosevelt in the White House was often important, as change seemed the order of the day. Blows were struck against child labor, although the results were discouragingly meager. Social casework had its beginnings. Important to reformers was the founding of the Children's Bureau by the federal government in 1912, after the White House Conference on Child Welfare (1909) evoked public sentiment in favor of the idea. The task of gathering information about the nation's children was soon accelerated as Julia C. Lathrop, and later Grace Abbott, led the new Bureau with enthusiasm and dedication.

Great organizations were born out of the creative spirit of the Progressive Movement, and names later to be familiar to everyone saw the light of day. Typical of the new groups were the National Tuberculosis Association (1904), Boys Clubs of America (1906), the National Recreation Association (1906), a National Association of YWCA Workers, the Camp Fire Girls (1910), the Boy Scouts of America (1910), Goodwill Industries (1910), the Family Service Association of America (1911), and in 1912 the National Federation of Settlements and the Girl Scouts of the United States of America. This was a period of tremendous activity in voluntary welfare; the excitement of the times must be emphasized. The Progressive Movement was deeply concerned with the welfare of young people, particularly in cities. Freedom of opportunity was beginning to be in jeopardy. Leaders not only sensed but could see what the congested cities were doing to the minds and spirits of children. They were deeply disturbed. And many organized to do what the personal charity of the nineteenth century seemed poorly suited to accomplish. Yet a long road lay ahead.

The Red Cross, as a national organization, was in those years only minute in size; one wonders how it accomplished anything under such a circumstance. The year's disbursements in 1902, for example, were $499.07; office space was rented for $45.00 a month; a part-time stenographer received $50.00 a month! When on January 5, 1905, the Red Cross obtained its charter from Congress, there were only 3,307 individual members in the entire United States. Yet by World War I the Red Cross had mushroomed to

250 chapters with 286,000 members. Such was the growth of this organization in less than a decade and a half.

The war in Europe, even before America's involvement, greatly affected public thinking. Four years of terrible holocaust, it was known, would leave a deep scar on civilization. American charitable organizations could not but be deeply and permanently affected. Especially significant was the impact of the war on the Red Cross, which won for a time the name "The Greatest Mother in the World." Vast sums of money were needed for relief work, and special ways of raising huge sums were developed.

In the meantime, the legal aid societies of the nation had organized a national association, and the American Cancer Society had been founded (1913). Yet these developments were little noted. The American Social Hygiene Association came into being in 1914 and the National Travelers Aid Association in 1917; still other groups entered for the first time on the American scene. Many of these came at length to play useful roles in society, living on for decades to serve some large or small need.

From April, 1917, to November, 1918, the United States was at war. On the home front, one of the most important of all American contributions to social welfare was gaining momentum: the community-chest movement. It was not a war-born idea. The Charity Organization Society of Denver had been founded in 1887, but it had inspired no imitators. From 1909 to 1917 a total of fourteen new groups were born and survived; yet six others died. The successful chests had been in Elmira, New York; Erie, Pennsylvania; St. Joseph, Missouri; Baltimore; Cleveland; Dallas; Oshkosh; Grand Rapids; and Milwaukee. The community-chest movement had expanded during those years, even though opponents within social work itself charged that the chests portended a time when financial interests could come to dominate social work and there might be some leveling down of services to a standard common to most member agencies. Still, the increased money was welcomed even though independent fund-raising campaigns survived. If chests were a sign that the soliciting of funds was becoming institutionalized, so was the founding, during the war, of the inquisitive National Information Bureau, which came in time to act as a watch dog for those with little time or facilities for making their own investigations.

The idealism attending America's entry into World War I had its effect on services rendered by government as well as on those rendered by voluntary agencies. Benefits were devised for servicemen and their families, especially when the man in uniform was disabled. The Home Service Bureau of the Red Cross was particularly active, and the training given to lay persons by this organization had lasting effects across the nation. Postwar construction of veterans' hospitals and the creation of a government life insurance program were important break-throughs by those anxious for government to remain aggressively interested in the welfare of the veterans who once wore khaki or navy blue.

Little attention was paid when the infant American Hearing Society was formed in 1919; the American Association of Social Workers and the National Society for Crippled Children and Adults emerged in 1921 without headlines. If the tiny Cancer Society had created little stir on its organization in 1913, the Heart Association was just another group when it was founded in 1924. Their days of giant size and national importance were yet to come.

We sense at once that things have not always been as they have come to be in the social welfare field. Change has been gradual. Yet the way in which change has developed was not inevitable. If the United States had not entered the conflict in 1917, the entire pattern of development might have been different.

Veterans of the first great war showed in the 1920's a group consciousness and eagerness to enlarge their benefits. They formed the Disabled Veterans and the American Legion; the veterans' lobby became a growing reality. In 1925 the Legion decided to establish its useful Child Welfare Division. Earlier, in 1920, the Child Welfare League of America had been founded, to the gratification of social workers. A different and unique type of pioneering took place in 1929, when in New Jersey the Seeing Eye, Inc., decided there was a way to unite a guide dog and blind man in a mutual-assistance team.

With the election of Herbert Hoover in 1928, many Americans discerned the arrival of "a new day." Yet the subsequent stock market disaster and the accelerating deterioration of the national economy meant that voluntary welfare would be tested to the breaking point. After October, 1929, there were many leaders who grasped for new ideas. Although "mothers' aid" had been a program of government for some years in most of the states and some public welfare activity was to be found in nearly all of them, it was not until 1930 that the American Public Welfare Association was founded.

The popular new president of the United States, Herbert Hoover, was a man noted for relief work in World War I. His opposition to the exploitation of children was well known. Soon he called a White House Conference on Child Health and Protection, which attracted widespread attention from both the press and the public. It had a lasting influence.

The Veterans Administration was a development of the year 1930 which would focus renewed attention on the continuing problems of those who had fought for their country on the high seas and in the trenches of France. Facing new responsibilities in the 1930's, the Red Cross was not idle. It had come out of the war at a great peak in membership, yet there was a peacetime decline in numbers (from twenty million to three million). The Red Cross faced the depression of the 1930's as the colleague of government—not willing or suited, perhaps, to be the vehicle for paying federal relief funds to the unemployed, but still a very powerful force in caring for the needs of many citizens affected deeply by the unhappy conditions of those troubled years.

Whole books have been written on the governmental relief agencies which arose and swung into action in the 1930's. But the Hoover administration early took aggressive steps, in the President's words, "to see that our great benevolent agencies for character building, for hospitalization, for care of children and all their vast number of agencies of voluntary solicitude for the less fortunate are maintained in full strength." The Reconstruction Finance Corporation (RFC) made funds available to the states in July, 1932, for unemployment relief. Its Emergency Relief Division made loans, not gifts, and states had to demonstrate that they lacked the means to handle their own relief problems.

The social welfare philosophy of the Hoover administration has been little understood, and where understood, little appreciated. It is true that the President hoped "to maintain the bedrock principle of our liberties by the full mobilization of individual and local resources and responsibilities." He also desired "to maintain as a pillar of unassailable strength" the credit of the government. The federal government, Mr. Hoover felt, "should not make direct charitable gifts to individuals." Nor should this be necessary, for the man who had won world-wide acclaim as a humanitarian had, at the outset, full confidence in "the spiritual impulses in our people for generous giving and generous service—in the spirit that each is his brother's keeper." Thinking of the traditional pattern in social welfare, he said:

> Personal feeling and personal responsibility of men to their neighbors is the soul of genuine good will; it is the essential foundation of modern society. A cold and distant charity which puts out its sympathy only through the tax collector yields a very meagre dole of unloving and perfunctory relief.

Even so, government action proved essential. The President told a Welfare Relief Mobilization Conference on September 15, 1932, that in addition to $300,000,000 in RFC loans to states, the federal government had speeded up its construction work during the year to $750,000,000 and had provided for loans of one and one-half billion dollars for the construction of public enterprises of a self-sustaining character. Employer and labor groups had been organized carefully to spread work and shorten the work week. Was all this enough? Many did not think so. Yet the administration continued to feel that the full power of the federal government should not displace, much less replace, the efforts of voluntary agencies and charitable individuals.

To the heads of great voluntary welfare organizations President Hoover delivered messages of constant encouragement. Over one thousand towns and cities, he observed in 1931, had "well-organized and experienced relief committees, community chests, or other agencies" for the efficient administration of relief and provision of work. States, counties, and cities would also do their

13

part, he hoped, for "the possible misery of helpless people gives me more concern than any other trouble this depression has brought us." In a vigorous plea by radio to the charitable instincts of the people on October 18, 1931, President Hoover reminded his countrymen of their heritage:

> No governmental action, no economic plan or project can replace that God-imposed responsibility of the individual man and woman to their neighbors. That is a vital part of the very soul of the people. If we shall gain in this spirit from this painful time, we shall have created a greater and more glorious America. The trial of it is here now. It is a trial of the heart and conscience, of individual men and women.

A year later, on October 16, 1932, he made his plea for donations to community chests in this way:

> The purpose of this appeal this evening is to summon again the great heart of the American people. We must make our material provision for the support of our charitable and character building institutions. We must provide to the utmost extent for the local community support to the increased distress over the country.
>
> I take profound pride in the fact that my countrymen have accepted the responsibility, each in his own community, to meet this need. That is the only way to meet it effectively—in the neighborhood itself, where the need is known . . .
>
> In closing let me say that no richer blessing can fill your own hearts than the consciousness on some bleak winter's evening that your generosity has lighted a fire upon some family's hearth that otherwise would be black and cold, and has spread some family table with food where otherwise children would be wanting. I wish my last word to you to be the word "give".

Out of charity, said President Hoover on another occasion, will come not only hope but faith. Nevertheless, as the Hoover administration came to a close, embroiled in political contests with a Democratic Congress, one of the eight measures the President urged the Congress to enact in the interest of economic recovery was the granting of authority to the Reconstruction Finance Corporation to increase the amount of federal loans to states and municipalities to relieve distress. Voluntary welfare had failed the President and those among the people who needed continuing financial help in large amounts. Perhaps the failure was inevitable. Clearly the nation's chief executive had asked for more than human nature in the mass was willing to give.

There can be no question, as it turned out, that the RFC became the entering wedge for further development of programs of federal aid. It paved the way for the creation of a multitude of later federal agencies which did not retain the lending principle to which the Hoover administration clung tenaciously. The stage was set in the autumn of 1932 for a new cast and, as it developed, a new play before a divided, but on the whole a highly receptive, audience.

As governor of New York, Franklin Delano Roosevelt revealed to a confidant his belief that, with regard to people in need, "the important thing to recognize is that there is a duty on the part of the government to do something about this—it just can't sit back and expect private charity or even local government to take care of it entirely." Feeling no fear of government, since it was to him "not the master but the creature of the people," the presidential hopeful preferred to call direct aid by government a "social duty" and not "charity." The Governor felt in April, 1932, that the nation was in "the midst of an emergency at least equal to that of war." In a commencement address that May, Mr. Roosevelt told the young people that theirs was the task "of remaking the world." He hoped that all would be granted the courage, faith, and vision to "give the best that is in us to that remaking." Whether or not most Americans wanted their world remade, the manner in which the future President had rebuilt a body wracked by infantile paralysis won him respect, and his bubbling personality served him well. The people were deeply frightened by an assassination attempt and a bank crisis that came on the eve of the Roosevelt entry into office in 1933, and the national mood as a result was expectant.

Roosevelt's first term quickly brought giant expenditures by the federal government. The Voluntary Way was swamped. From

May, 1933, to November, 1935, payments of direct relief by the Administration came to $3,700,000,000. Government bureaus designed to expend federal funds for the welfare and even the re-shaping of the depressed came and went. The Federal Emergency Relief Administration (FERA), under Harry L. Hopkins, op-erated on the principle of grants-in-aid to the states for the pur-pose of unemployment relief. It could seize control of relief ad-ministration in any state where inefficiency was thought to exist. Its share of federal expenditures came by June, 1936, to three billion dollars. A devoted friend of government welfare programs has nevertheless written in perspective that the head of FERA "had virtually unlimited discretion, and he utilized his broad powers without the counsel of an advisory board. The FERA was an independent agency and the President, therefore, was the sole check on this almost dictatorial power of the administrator." The agency was quickly staffed by men and women drawn chiefly from existing voluntary agencies and city and other governmental wel-fare organizations.

Still other agencies embodied the faith of the Roosevelt ad-ministration in centralization of power and in ample expenditures from federal tax funds. The Civil Works Agency (CWA) was created by executive order to provide work relief. It was this agency that became associated in the public mind with the opprobrious term "leaf-raking," because of the transitory nature of its projects, 95 per cent of which were repair and maintenance work. The CWA had few friends when it died in 1934 and was replaced by an Emergency Work Relief Program, which provided much the same class of work. This agency in turn was displaced by the fa-mous Work Projects Administration (WPA) in 1935. The WPA did not pay wages on the basis of family size or "need." Harry Hopkins declared that such scaling was not done in private in-dustry and should not be in government employment, either. Pay-ments for work with the WPA were normally higher than relief checks, however. In six years the WPA expended eleven and one-quarter billion dollars on a quarter of a million construction and conservation projects and on public buildings, utilities, highways, and programs of community service. It left its mark permanently on the face of the nation.

Far smaller agencies than these were the Civilian Conservation Corps and the National Youth Administration. They were particularly aimed at meeting some of the needs of young people on the city streets, in schools, and in colleges. In such organizations much work of value was performed, and services were rendered for the modest salaries that were paid. For this reason work programs like WPA were not, strictly speaking, "social welfare" or relief programs, even though personal "need" was a criterion for participation in them. "Work relief" was a contemporary label applied to such groups.

There were many other agencies and subagencies created during the Roosevelt administration in its patchwork efforts to remedy the needs of the nation. Yet, in 1938, five years after the beginning of the New Deal, the United States still had 9,796,000 unemployed—only 1,589,000 less than in 1932. The national psychology, however, was much improved. Soon the war in Europe placed new demands on the American economy. It brought to an end, in the years after our entry, nearly all the relief and work agencies of the earlier Roosevelt years, as European requirements produced an economic boom of nation-wide proportions. Yet dramatic departures from the past remained, chief among them a social security system comprised of federal grants-in-aid to the states for public assistance programs and various social insurance activities.

In the persons of Presidents Herbert C. Hoover and Franklin D. Roosevelt had long been personified—although in somewhat blurred image—the basic philosophies of the nation's social welfare scene. Each leader believed in voluntary agencies; both believed that government had active roles to perform. Voluntary agencies prospered under each, government was passive under neither. President Roosevelt, for example, was enough of a friend of the Red Cross to name his own law partner to be its national chairman; he was also the patron of what would become the best financed voluntary national health agency. Yet, as is well known, he tried to place government in a paramount role in social welfare when he was governor of New York State and during his twelve years in the White House.

Mr. Hoover, for his part, had performed great services during World War I as the talented agent of the United States government in starving Belgium. As President, Mr. Hoover placed great faith in the voluntary way, but he continually attempted to use his high office in government to further the policies in which he believed. Always he stressed the importance of organizing at local levels to meet local needs. Aware of many changes taking place on social work frontiers and anxious for additional improvement, he brought together the experts who produced the solid research study, *Recent Social Trends*, contributing greatly to national self-analysis. Few persons have surpassed Hoover's heartfelt eloquence then and since in support of the voluntary way in social welfare.

Franklin D. Roosevelt enlisted the masses of men behind his cause, and his successor in office, Harry S. Truman, still further enlarged the power of the Washington government over basic social programs and services. Both leaders saw social security legislation in political as well as human terms; many a politician of both major parties watched Roosevelt and learned much. The threats to party fortunes during his first term had their due effect on social welfare legislation. Roosevelt's strong leadership and his position at the center of the stage were guarantees that his name and personality would for all time be associated with the idea of federal action in social welfare matters. "FDR" did in many instances what the masses of the people wanted. True. But first he aroused in many of them a desire to possess in the world of reality, with or without great sacrifice, the vision he conjured up for them. In summarizing the effects of the Roosevelt leadership in social welfare matters, one must agree with the generalized view of Edgar Eugene Robinson in *The Roosevelt Leadership, 1933 to 1945*: "This personal leadership was pragmatic—an individual playing by ear. It was experimental—an individual using successive opportunities. It was intuitive—an individual sensing the popular desires."

President Hoover believed in the worth of voluntary welfare

organizations. Not born to wealth, from boyhood he had been deeply aware of man's hope to achieve security. As a citizen one year out of high office in 1934, he found that some suggested solutions to the nation's problems added up to a vital challenge to individual liberty. He wrote:

> Liberty conceives that the mind and spirit of men can be free only if the individual is free to choose his own calling, to develop his talents, to win and to keep a home sacred from intrusion, to rear children in ordered security. It holds he must be free to earn, to spend, to save, to accumulate property that may give protection in old age and to loved ones. . . .
>
> There are stern obligations upon those who would hold these liberties—self-restraint, insistence upon truth, order, and justice, vigilance of opinion, and co-operation in the common welfare.

In such a view lay reliance on neither voluntary agencies nor government programs. In the last analysis the individual would have to be the guardian of his own—and his family's—well-being. Only then would it be society's turn.

As citizens pondered their obligation to serve as individuals and through voluntary organizations—and considered the cost of government aid to "givers" in tax dollars and to recipients in the necessary sacrifice of clear-eyed independence—ideas new to the United States came to be expressed in federal legislation.

Set up by executive order, a Committee on Economic Security had studied, in 1934, the problem of social security legislation, including social insurance. Old age and unemployment were two of the major problems considered. To some extent the committee relied on experience in Great Britain and on the Continent. Congress held extensive hearings. The bill which emerged from the committee and was presented simultaneously in the Senate and the House was amended on the floor of both houses. There were many differences of opinion, even among experts in such matters, and when the bill that resulted from many compromises was finally presented to the President for signature, it was evident to insiders that the new legislation would certainly have to be modified from time to time in later years.

19

The Social Security Act of 1935 was called "An Act to provide for the general welfare by establishing a system of Federal old-age benefits and by enabling the several States to make more adequate provisions for aged persons, blind persons, dependent and crippled children, maternal and child welfare, public health, and the administration of their unemployment compensation laws . . . " While employers carried much of the financial load (a burden carried ultimately by consumers and stockholders), the basic idea behind social insurance was to have the possible beneficiary pay into a federal Trust Fund over a period of years so that under certain conditions of adversity or age he and his would be entitled to cash payments.

Constitutionality of the act was soon challenged, and the Supreme Court held in *Steward Machine Co. v. Davis* in 1937 that the taxes to be paid by employers to finance unemployment compensation were entirely constitutional. The states had not been coerced, it said, the tax was sufficiently uniform, and employment was not being "burdened with a tax." The allocation of these tax funds by the Secretary of the Treasury to a trust fund was thought by the court to be "an assurance of stability and safety in times of stress and strain."

In an equally momentous decision that year, in the case of *Helvering v. Davis*, the Supreme Court found valid the withholding tax on employees and with it the whole social insurance concept of the Old-Age and Survivors Insurance program (OASI). "Congress may spend money in aid of the general welfare," said the court, reflecting that "the purge of nationwide calamity that began in 1929 has taught us many lessons." One was that the problem of the aged was "plainly national in area and dimensions. Moreover, laws of the separate states cannot deal with it effectively." The court did not find the Social Security Act wise or unwise—only constitutional and not contrary to states' rights. "When money is spent to promote the general welfare," said the Supreme Court, "the concept of welfare or the opposite is shaped by Congress, not the states."

At cabinet meetings and in private conversation in 1934-35,

President Roosevelt had said of social security legislation, according to an intimate:

> You want to make it simple—very simple. So simple that everybody will understand it. And what's more, there is no reason why everybody in the United States should not be covered. I see no reason why every child, from the day he is born, shouldn't be a member of the social security system. When he begins to grow up, he should know he will have old-age benefits direct from the insurance system to which he will belong all his life. If he is out of work, he gets a benefit. If he is sick or crippled, he gets a benefit. . . . Cradle to the grave—from the cradle to the grave they ought to be in a social insurance system.

One must respect and weigh carefully the later judgment of the President's secretary of Labor, Frances Perkins, that Mr. Roosevelt "always regarded the Social Security Act as the cornerstone of his administration and . . . took greater satisfaction from it than from anything else he achieved on the domestic front." FDR, like many informed contemporaries, saw the public assistance parts of the act as temporary relief programs, which would be done away with as the social insurance provisions of the law were gradually extended so that there would be nearly universal coverage. At the time of its enactment, thirty states had laws providing some small payments to old people, half aided the blind, and mother's aid was reasonably common.

Many persons and organizations were responsible for the Social Security Act. There were the American Association for Old-Age Security and its director, Abraham Epstein; members of the President's cabinet—Frances Perkins in particular; the members of the Committee on Economic Security of 1934 and especially its director, Edwin E. Witte; Katherine Lenroot, Isador Lubin, and others; and members of the Congress, particularly Senator Robert F. Wagner and Representative David J. Lewis. The law was passed by the votes of both Democrats and Republicans. At the time, many conservatives saw in this innovation protection against extreme schemes of the Longs and Townsends.

The person of the President was clearly the central catalyst that kept many of these forces working toward their often dissimilar goals. An old-age insurance benefit program is essential, Roosevelt said to intimates:

> We have to have it. The Congress can't stand the pressure of the Townsend Plan unless we have a real old-age insurance system, nor can I face the country without having devised at this time, when we are studying social security, a solid plan which will give some assurance to old people of systematic assistance upon retirement.

As was so often the case, Roosevelt was in this instance that combination of humanitarian and what James P. Warburg called "Hell Bent for Election."

Former President Hoover watched closely the debates on the Social Security Act. Two months before its passage, in June, 1935, he told the graduating class at Stanford University:

> Over the century we have seen the vast development of insurance against the effect of fire, flood, sickness, accident, and death. The expansion of these principles to the remaining fields of human accident, that is, security against poverty in old age, to unemployment, must now be brought into action.

Less than two months after passage of the act, Mr. Hoover called portions of it "of right objective and wrong method." Six months later he thought that farmers as consumers were paying for a large part of the act but receiving little benefit. Nevertheless, in April, 1936, he found the social security legislation of the previous summer to be pointing "in the right direction." Mr. Hoover added, "We should be in sympathy with legislation to protect old age and unemployment." "Mighty revisions" in the Social Security Act would help, he thought, and he added a month later that, after all, "many states under normally Republican governments have given old-age pensions for years. We should approve of Federal subsidy to the states to strengthen and unify their efforts." Prophetically, he called for "radical revision" of OASI, toward which only 50 per cent of the public was directly contributing and from which the farmer would get nothing as things stood.

Even though, as Arthur P. Miles has written, "the enactment of the Social Security Act in 1935 made the federal government's role a permanent rather than a temporary one in public welfare," the act after amendment in 1939 won an increasing number of friends. The Congress of American Industry (NAM) announced in 1940 that "at the present time there should be no basic changes in the Social Security Program." Following a survey to determine the status of opinion regarding the act among conservative groups in the early 1940's, researcher Thomas Paul Jenkin concluded that "qualified support for the Social Security Act now in effect can be presumed." There had developed a "volume of favorable opinion," he discovered, and the program had become "acceptable." As war spread throughout the world, it became clearly evident that grants-in-aid to the states for relief of "need," an unemployment compensation system, and a "social security" program for old age and one's close survivors were on the statute books to stay for an extended period.

World War II brought new problems to the nation while seeming to help solve others. Before United States entry into the conflict, the Red Cross acted as an administrative agent of the executive branch of the government, distributing in this role supplies and clothing for the people of war-torn Europe, financed by nearly $50,000,000 in government funds. Gifts to the Red Cross during World War II, as a result of five fund-raising campaigns, finally totaled nearly $785,000,000. This has been called quite properly "the greatest free-will offering in history." About 150,-000,000 separate gifts were represented in this total, which was raised through the help of the Office of War Information, the War Advertising Council, and the War Activities Committee of the Motion Picture Industry. Industrial and trade-union groups also helped, especially the AFL's Labor League for Human Rights and the National CIO War Relief Committee. The labor press, eight hundred publications strong, backed the American National Red Cross in its fund-raising efforts.

The volunteer workers of the Red Cross, all unpaid persons,

put in 470,000 "man-years" of work during the war. These dedicated persons, most of them women, served 121,000,000 meals, drove 60,000,000 miles, transcribed the equivalent of nearly five hundred books into Braille, and made two and one-half billion surgical dressings. The Red Cross loaned $69,000,000 to servicemen and their families. The field directors and assistants on duty with it in April, 1945, totaled 3,520. Were all these services during World War II and the Korean War which followed accomplished with maximum possible efficiency? Who can say? Could more have been done with the dollars at hand? We will never know. But of the record of accomplishment we are sure. Meanwhile the work of water safety, first aid, accident prevention, disaster relief, and home service went on. The Salvation Army and the YMCA compiled enviable records of service, as did many other voluntary agencies. At home, social insurance was paying its first monthly checks, following payment of the first monthly old-age benefit to a Miss Ida Fuller of Ludlow, Vermont, on January 31, 1940.

One of the issues of the postwar years was "socialized medicine." All over the nation (particularly in urban areas), a great change was quietly taking place which seemed to weaken the position of those seeking federal legislation to provide for all age groups a medical program similar to that of Great Britain. From 1950 to the close of 1956, the number of people whose hospital expenses were covered in whole or in part by voluntary health insurance increased from forty to sixty-six million, or more than one-third of the whole population. Other coverage included surgical expense, sixty-three million; medical expense, twenty million; and major medical expense, nearly nine million. Although such "coverage" obviously could not take care of all expenses in most cases and the cost of long hospitalization in an inflationary period naturally seemed high to many Americans, the existence of this insurance was a mighty deterrent to aggressive planners seeking the entry of government into this field. Millions of individuals (workers and their dependents) thus came to have part of the expenses incurred through sickness or accident provided for by some form of medical benefit program. Annual benefit payments of voluntary health insurance climbed from $1,300,000,000 to $5,200,000,000 during the decade of the 1950's.

Contributions to nongovernmental group benefit programs, including group life insurance, in a single year (1954), were $6,-800,000,000 ($4,500,000,000 from employers and $2,300,000,-000 from employees.) The reserves of these benefit plans came to reach $20,000,000,000 to $25,000,000,000. Such pension fund reserves were "the largest single source of equity capital," according to the Securities and Exchange Commission. That these giant-sized programs cut across the hopes of those who had expected the federal government to develop universal medical benefit plans goes without saying. The existence of these programs, together with continuing medical accomplishments, accounted for much of the conservatism of voters who declined to permit unlimited federal activities in the medical field. Still, the government in the 1950's enlarged its medical budget substantially. A medical benefit program for those receiving public assistance payments was enacted in 1957. Another program was adopted for dependents of men performing military service in peacetime, the Medicare program. Research institutes got ever larger appropriations.

From the time of the Wilson administration to that of Eisenhower there existed conflicting points of view on the respective roles of government welfare services and voluntary activities. Extremists who overemphasized the abilities of people in trouble to solve their own problems without help could see little good in social welfare effort regardless of its sponsorship. Some social workers liked to pretend that the difference between "government" and "voluntary" was completely unimportant. In any case, the balance between these two areas of organized effort began to shift rapidly in the 1950's, thus accelerating tendencies arising in the Depression and emphasized in World War II. There was gigantic expansion in social insurance program payments; the Hill-Burton hospital construction program provided over a billion dollars to be used by private groups, including many religious organizations; disability amendments to the Social Security Act portended giant new government activity and there was some blurring as certain government agencies, such as those charged with vocational rehabilitation, transferred government funds to private welfare agencies. Unemployment insurance, meanwhile, moved into the mainstream of controversy as automation and other factors brought spot unemployment of long duration.

Units of government at all levels came to encroach steadily on the independence of private welfare organizations—supplanting them, subsidizing and orienting them, or regulating them in fund-raising, capital improvements, or even operations. Many who had once thought that the voluntary-agency way was no more than the old way of individual charity—only organized and planned—found these changes hard to take, but did not always speak out. The pattern of government regulation of fund-raising was uneven, and its effectiveness was variable; but, encouraged by better business bureaus and chambers of commerce, the regulatory bodies increased in boldness—always invigorated by the thought that the public was being protected from "charity rackets." And so it was, to some extent, but voluntary welfare was, in any case, subjected to government control of its ability to finance its own survival. Meanwhile, state and local licensing laws, framed to maintain or improve standards in boarding and nursing homes and other institutions, became ever more elaborate and rigorous, and this trend was furthered by scandals and disasters in various communities. Here again was government regulation of private institutions in which voluntary groups were trying to satisfy the needs of certain groups of children, the sick, or the aging. The number who could be housed, the construction of buildings, and the physical conditions therein, as well as the precise training required of those in charge—all fell under the control of a well-motivated but expansionist government.

Concerned over the rate at which the Protestant church seemed to be falling behind in its historic task of financing voluntary services for the welfare of the majority of the nation, the National Council of Churches held a meeting in Cleveland in November, 1955, to assess the standing of the church. Seven years earlier the group (then still the Federal Council of Churches) had made this announcement:

Within the past decades there has been a growing concern on the part of many churchmen, clergy and laity alike, that the increasing secularization of the welfare services and the high intensity of specialization has just about left religion out. Therefore there are denominational leaders, within our own constituency and without, who feel that the time may have arrived when the church, which was the originator of most modern social work, must reassert itself, and reclaim some of the ground it has lost.

The Cleveland meeting concluded, however, that "our complex and rapidly changing society now requires a network of private and public services — national, state, county, and local." Still, "Christian love must now find expression; not only in personal deeds of kindness, but in a highly organized system of social and health services as well. . . . Health and social welfare have become the responsibility of the whole community." As for the government programs which two decades had brought to full flower, the delegates passed a resolution:

> Support for these great human services by all is now of critical importance. The churches must give greater attention to these matters of public policy, including the use of public funds for health and welfare programs. If public programs are to operate on levels which Christians can support, the churches have a tremendous stake in the adequacy of appropriations, the quality of leadership selected for citizen commissions, the competence of judges, and the professional qualifications of staff.

In short, much Protestant leadership was prepared to recognize and often to accept what had come to be. Catholic and Jewish leaders, meanwhile, seemed more inclined to build and to finance sectarian social work agencies in such a way as to take care of their own—where such care was financially possible—and to rely on government where it was not.

Protestant, Catholic, and Jewish leaders alike continued to be united in opposition to government intervention in matters of pure religion. (The reports of the Cleveland meeting of the Protestants had contained the usual phrases calling for the continued

27

separation of church and state.) Yet Hill-Burton hospital construction money from the federal government was considered a
godsend to struggling and overburdened church institutions; its
acceptance, most religious leaders concurred, would do no permanent damage. Once buildings were built, would not the voluntary way take over again, operating the new structures for a
generation and more? And where were the donations that could
ever come to such giant totals? Here was the argument. Many
were persuaded.

It seemed clear in the late 1950's that government was in-
exorably upsetting whatever balance there had been among the
major tendencies in the nation's social welfare experience. There
was concern in some high places over this development. New
methods of financing voluntary agencies flowered in the 1950's,
and increases in available leisure time (and in the number of
healthy oldsters) seemed to portend more volunteering for community service. Would federated financing through united funds
save voluntary agencies? Or were payments of fees by those in
"need" to be the reluctant financial answer? Perhaps corporations
would come to the rescue, or labor unions would learn to use their
organized strength with maximum effectiveness. All was in flux.
It might be that from such elements, coupled with a rebirth of
spirit, an uneasy equilibrium between voluntary and government
activity in social welfare might result—at least for a time.

Meanwhile, citizens were reminded of the value of personal
charity in the traditional manner on Sundays and during the
Christmas season, and often through the mass media channels
during community fund-raising campaigns. Private benevolence
continued. Most citizens made sure, however, that, through their
income tax deductions each April 15, the federal and state governments would, in a sense, finance a percentage of even this char-
ititable activity.

Social service work by the 1960's had become amazingly institutionalized. Yet programs were sometimes fluid and subject
to sudden change, as legislators passed significant new laws from
time to time. Not much debated in a press concerned over world
developments and space accomplishments, their implications were

not always understood—except by insiders. Even to more thought-ful Americans, under such circumstances, the current status of social welfare, and the most fruitful attitude to be taken in order to mold it into more desirable patterns, came to be something of a mystery.

CHAPTER II

The Anatomy of Social Welfare

What is this thing, this "social welfare,"
    this strange juxtaposition of undefinable words?
It is charity, of course,
Yet something more, something different,
Something often better (yet sometimes worse).
All-embracing? No.

It is public aid and private charity,
Not one's wages;
Not fringe benefits supplied in lieu of wages.
Social services, yes; and sometimes—but
Not always—social insurance.

Not education, not the judge and jury,
Never four walls and bars and scowling faces;
Not the organized machinery or locale of
Sunday worship (though from this scene
Derives motivation to "do good.").

"Social welfare is special services supplied
And material assistance given
By all or part of society to
A human being
Thought to be in need."

FEW EXPRESSIONS in the United States are heard so often, written so frequently, and accepted so widely as the words "social welfare." They seem to communicate. Yet at the same time, few terms transfer ideas from one person to another so inexactly, can be made to cover so many irrelevant subjects, or arouse such explosive emotions.

When this is said, one must add in haste that many of the words in daily use in the field of social work are not to be found in the writings or conversation of leaders in public or civic life. The vocabulary of the social-service field, enlarged by its contact with psychiatry and even elementary abnormal psychology, is most alarming to the layman. However, this is not the place to get involved in the mysteries of social-work linguistics.

But the expression "social welfare" is different. The writer of a book or even an article on this subject must define this term. I will now try to show what ought to be included and what should be excluded from the field of "social welfare." A definition and criteria of this sort have long been needed by those who casually employ the phrase, as in newspapers, and even by some who write more formally in social-work journals. Here is my working definition of that term, arrived at after much consideration of social service and educational and religious activity in the United States. The definition is inherently simple, yet it is tightly worded:

> Social welfare is special services supplied and material assistance given by all or part of society to a human being thought to be in need.

This brief definition seems to be comprehensive enough and yet exclusive enough to serve as the basis for study, research, and even some statistical work in the complex, modern social-welfare field. The key elements appear to be present. Still it is necessary to clarify several things about the definition by quick dissection. We must know at once (so far as possible) what social welfare is —and what it is not.

With one eye on the formal definition, we find it to be "special services." One cannot include everything that society does to make it possible for human beings to live adjacent to one another, remain healthy, earn a living, conduct government, and educate their children.

Social welfare is both "material assistance" and something more. Material aid can be the payment of cash or payment in kind. Social welfare is supplied or given, as the definition indicates, by all or part of society. There is definitely an organizational implication in the definition. And in social welfare neither gifts nor services are in payment for the performance of work. There must be a free or part-pay element.

The final phrase of the definition expresses the thought that the recipient of social-welfare services and aid is a person "thought to be in need." All the children, youths, adults, and old people being aided may not really be in need, but all or a controlling part of society thinks that this is the case and has acted accordingly. Some people want to help others because they seem to be in need. The concept of "need," one may suggest, will never be developed with scientific exactness, in spite of all the words spilled on its behalf.

Once again, here is the suggested definition of our subject: "*Social welfare* is special services supplied and material assistance given by all or part of society to a human being thought to be in need."

Social welfare has long consisted chiefly of public aid and private charity. Here is a catchy phrase. But it does not satisfy the subject matter of social work or social welfare in modern America. Services are being rendered by many government employees and the men and women who labor for voluntary agencies. Such services are neither public assistance nor charitable giving. Then there is that sometimes quasi-welfare area known as social insurance, which will be discussed shortly. Our attention should be drawn instead to the giant area of aid payments called "public assistance."

Public aid has come a long way since the days when, under local poor laws, the person who was down and out could get a pittance from local government to avoid starvation. At the present, for example, old-age payments to many aging citizens have come to over one hundred dollars a month, while the blind get somewhat more, and fatherless families get two to four hundred dollars per month. Some people seek to raise these figures far higher. Medical benefits and other special privileges are accorded the aid recipient found to be in need of them, even though many such citizens on old-age rolls own their homes free and clear (while many a wage earner cannot pay his doctor's bills). Federal sharing in the costs of the Old Age Assistance program and the Aid to Dependent Children program has, since the passage of the Social Security Act in 1935, made such payments possible. Yet inflation has played an equally substantial role in forcing higher monthly checks and preventing recipients from being satisfied with them.

Public assistance programs financed by the federal and state governments (and many times by county governments) from tax funds include: Old Age Assistance (OAA), Aid to Dependent Children (ADC), Aid to the Blind (AB), and Aid to the Permanently and Totally Disabled (APTD). These programs provide for the payment of money to aid recipients from the federal government and from the states, prorated by complex formulas. In practice, the states often share their part of the burden with the counties and with some metropolitan cities.

Public aid programs like these have long historical roots. A number of the states were paying some kind of monthly sums to indigent old people when the federal government stepped in with its grants-in-aid plan in 1935. The custom of mothers' payments, made to keep a young child under his own roof in preference to sending him to an orphan's home after the death of one or both parents, has also been well known in America. But federal legislation has greatly extended both the coverage and the benefits of of such programs. Frequent amendment of the Social Security Act and innumerable changes in the laws of the states combined to make vastly different the pattern and the significance of tax-financed aid payments to the needy. The trend in payment totals has been ever upward, although in the normally prosperous 1950's, with the number of recipients stabilizing (and slightly declining in OAA), increases in gross expenditure totals were maintained only by the raising of average monthly payments and by adding a comprehensive medical benefits program.

While this was going on, county governments continued to pay general assistance, indigent aid, general relief, poor relief or whatever they chose, in their wisdom, to call local aid to the needy. These weekly or monthly payments in cash or grocery orders are a minor factor in social welfare today. They have been relegated to temporary care for families down on their luck, to often-transient unemployable males, and to aging persons or children soon to be eligible for Old Age Assistance or Aid to Dependent Children. This kind of temporary relief increased suddenly in the recession of 1958, however.

Social insurance programs have been moving into a field once occupied by private insurance, personal savings, family devotion, and charity. Federal Old-Age and Survivors Insurance, known to the public as "social security," has six categories of benefit payments, of which the most extensive types are "Old-Age" and the "Wife's or Husband's." Others, payable to dependents after death of the wage earner, are "Child's," "Widow's or Widower's," "Mother's," and "Parent's." Disability benefit payments began in the late 1950's. The OASI program has long been financed by withholding taxes on the salaries of employees and by matching amounts from employers. The self-employed pay extra percentages. Financing of the program remains constantly controversial.

Social security benefits are paid eligible persons only on application. While a needy person can gain social security and Old Age Assistance payments at the same time, the amount of the former is normally deducted from the maximum OAA grant which might otherwise be obtained.

With immense increases in the numbers of persons covered by social security, the United States Department of Health, Education, and Welfare has, through its Social Security Administration, exerted great efforts to publicize all aspects of social security. There is ample evidence that some headway has been made in public education on the matter as millions of leaflets have been distributed broadside, and public relations techniques have been exploited fully. Yet certain illusions were engendered and hard feelings created in the government's eagerness to popularize social security. Articulate enemies of all or parts of the program continue to make trenchant criticisms and predictions of trouble ahead— predictions that while not always well rooted, have in important instances proved correct.

Are social insurance programs "social welfare"? Can it be said, for example, that Unemployment Insurance (a social insurance program financed by payroll taxes on employers) is a welfare program? The answer is far from simple or clear-cut. Fact and intent clash. Consider social security for a moment. It is not a savings account—and it is not insurance. Persons may get back far more— or far less—than they pay in. If we could only say that all social insurance is actually paid for by the wage earner because otherwise he would get as salary the monthly amounts withheld, it

34

would greatly simplify the matter. But there is absolutely no as-surance of this. These sums might go to the stockholders. A fur-ther fact is that none of these programs has universal coverage in American society. This means that many consumers who have lacked "coverage" have for a generation footed a part of the social insurance bill for others through increased prices on things they have bought.

Ardent and extreme advocates of social insurance reject any thought of labeling social security (OASI) as "welfare." They went out of their way for years to persuade their fellow citizens that here was insurance per se. There was frequent and careless use of the word "insurance" and easy drawing of analogy to pri-vate insurance policies or to converted GI life insurance. Such analogies were not justified. Certain facts are pertinent. In 1959 the gross payment by an individual making over $4,800 was $124 from him and an equal amount from his employer. In 1960 it was $144. Yet a bachelor who dies at 64 or sooner will have got no annuity or other benefits and there will be no insurance bene-fits for his estate (except for a tiny burial benefit). What this indi-vidual paid during a working lifetime will simply enlarge the Trust Fund to permit payments to someone else—a stranger. Again, payments made into the Fund by uncovered individuals (women who work irregularly, for example) bring no returns. There were in the 1940's and 1950's, furthermore, many over 65 who got in-finitely more out of social security than they or their employers ever put in. In some instances, through extreme longevity, the dis-parity was shocking. And the older members of each *new* group taken into the system ("covered") during the years since 1935 have reaped a bonanza of extraordinary proportions. The point is that social security is not insurance. It is a "floor" of basic protec-tion. As such, it cannot avoid leading to all kinds of inequities and inequalities, at the same time that it does marvelous things for the young widow with three children and the couple who live on from 65 to 92.

In view of the various inequalities and outsized benefits, which are inescapable in the very nature of social insurance financ-ing and benefit structure, social security is "social welfare oriented." This is particularly true whenever society pays any part of the bill for the individuals who get far more than they put in. But it may be that the most glaring inequities are in the past. Frequently passed amendments to the 1935 act have patched holes. This was especially true of the amendments of 1954. Increased longevity for most persons, thanks to medical advances and dietary and environmental improvements, is responsible for some of the outsized benefits of the first two decades of the law. Rates, moreover, have gone up, and it is inevitable that they will continue to do so. Someday, forty-four years of payments followed by fifteen years of benefits will more closely resemble "insurance" than what has gone heretofore—which was often one to ten years of payments and ten years or more of benefits! The obtaining of much for little, and little for much—the past inequities of Old-Age and Survivors Insurance—will even out in time, provided our legislators refrain from tampering thoughtlessly with the basic system.

There is a general belief that a heavy percentage of social security will one day have to be financed through general taxation. Yet the higher tax rates passed in 1958, and others to come, will greatly increase revenue. Americans will just have to wait and see what penicillin, geriatrics, constant liberalization of benefit payments, lowering of eligibility age, pressure to allow payments to wage earners under seventy, and possibly postponed raising of withholding tax rates will do to trust fund economics. The annual more than 3 per cent interest income of the OASI Trust Fund (and the several other social insurance trust funds which hold social security receipts) already comes from general taxes. This is because funds invest their revenue in interest-bearing securities of the federal government which pay about that percentage. Compound interest on the billions involved will come to a tidy sum, and all interest paid on the public debt is a general charge to the taxpayers.

Both the social insurance programs and the public assistance programs are paid from tax revenues, be they from special or general taxes. Neither old age social security benefits for the aging couple retired in the semi-tropical sunshine nor OAA public assistance payments to a discouraged old man in a snowbound rooming house can be paid except from tax revenues. Neither benefit nor payment checks are gifts from outer space. There remains, however, a sharp difference in legislative intent. Social security is paid under law as a matter of "entitlement," because the individual involuntarily paid money into a fund when he was gainfully employed. He was joined in this by an employer.

Old Age Assistance, of course, is paid legally as a matter of "need." The need is administratively established in the light of legislation. Public aid payments clearly derive from the basic humanitarian decision of society to help the aging, lonely mothers and their needy children, and the blind when they are in financial difficulties.

It is submitted that the intention of society is that the public assistance programs be social welfare activities; conversely, such an intention is not present in the case of the social insurances, where the basic burden is supposed to rest on the person being helped and on his employers.

Sometimes called "private welfare," the field of voluntary welfare is the non-governmental part of social welfare. Here we find old and tried organizations: the American National Red Cross, the Salvation Army, the Young Men's Christian Association, and family service agencies bearing a variety of names. These and the multitude of other organized welfare groups, recreation and character building agencies, and free and part-pay medical clinics have been joined through the years by national health agencies such as the American Heart Association, American Cancer Society, the National Foundation, and others. All are properly termed voluntary welfare. All get their operating funds from contributions, often augmented (and sometimes substantially) by membership payments, fees, or profits from benefits or sales of merchandise. Tax funds sometimes end up in the hands of the voluntary agencies in reimbursement for specific services rendered, but this has normally been the exception rather than the rule. The heart of the voluntary field in America has long been gifts of money and gifts of time from citizens who desired, above all else, to help their fellow man achieve a better life.

Community chests were organized in some quantity during

37

and after World War I in an effort to co-ordinate more efficiently the fund-raising of voluntary agencies, raise more money, and enlist additional public support for these services. United funds came later, beginning in 1948. The united drives combined in one appeal the community chest agencies and one or more of the national health agencies and/or the Red Cross.

The united funds have borne original and catchy titles. One and the same in function are: the United Givers Fund (Washington, D.C. and Natchez, Mississippi), United Bay Area Crusade (San Francisco Bay Area), United Foundation (Detroit, Michigan), United Appeal (Brockton, Massachusetts), Heart of America United Campaign (Kansas City, Missouri), United Givers (Milledgeville, Georgia), United Success (San Diego, California), and United Good Neighbor Fund (Tacoma, Washington). These "give once" organizations are sometimes called "federated drives," and the whole movement is often nicknamed simply "federation" by professional fund raisers.

The raising of money for charitable and health purposes has often come under the scrutiny of city officials, and this area of activity is called the regulation of solicitations. New York State has been experimenting with regulation at the state level, while the best entrenched of the city regulatory bodies is in giant Los Angeles. Voluntary welfare has not been able to escape government regulation of its pleas to the public for financial support, for there have been charity rackets and profitable lotteries lurking under many a rock.

Foundations, which are tax exempt if established in conformity with federal and state laws, play an important role in the financing of voluntary welfare. I discovered after comprehensive research in records of the Internal Revenue Service that of $2,500,-000 in grants by the 92 foundations in Northern California in a single year, 59 per cent ($1,500,000) was given within the social welfare field, while the rest went to education, religion, and other causes. The role small-family foundations like these play in American charity has received too little attention, for these almost anonymous organizations can be found all over the nation, though they are concentrated in urban areas.

Social welfare can be more clearly understood by noting carefully what it does not normally include. Let it be agreed at the outset that there is a field of activity that all recognize as education, public and parochial, and that this area of daily activity cannot be included in a delineation of social welfare. Our schools and colleges perform a vital social role to be sure, and they contribute to the well-being of all of us. Yet it is not helpful to think of them as social work agencies, or to include teachers among those who are "doing good" or "relieving misery" or "dispensing aid to the needy." This is not their role. Public libraries, moreover, are part of the educational structure of society. Their business is the care of books and stimulation of reading. If libraries sometimes invade the field of pure recreation, providing "busy work" and other services to the aging and to children, we must pause and reconsider the general judgment that libraries, like schools, are not social welfare agencies as the term is defined here.

The vast area of corrections consists of prisons maintained by governments and the judicial machinery which upholds the supremacy of the law. This area should be excluded from consideration, even though it is generally agreed to be for the welfare of society that the violent man and the anti-social woman be tried, sentenced, and confined in institutions, with or without retraining, for months and years.

Society is, on the whole, both safer and better because of our correctional machinery—antiquated though it can be and often is—but our judges, police, and sheriffs—and the employees in the jails and penitentiaries—are not social workers. What they do is not normally social work. Active in the field, on the other hand, are the probation departments, the enlightened machinery of most juvenile courts, and various youth guidance activities. Here our dividing line becomes blurred and even disappears. Policewomen at their best, for example, are quasi-social workers.

The field of health is the special province of doctors and nurses housed in private offices, group clinics, and giant hospital buildings. These persons are uniquely concerned with medical diagnosis, treatment, and surgery. Despite widespread indoctrination of the public in the ways of "dread diseases" and the large

39

amounts of charitable work financed by government and by gifts from the public, one must be careful to exclude nearly all of the diagnosis and treatment in the medical field from the social welfare category. The payment of a child's tonsillectomy bill by his parents is a business transaction pure and simple. Services are bought and paid for. Part payment by an insurance company, by Blue Cross, or some other fee-supported group does not change the business nature of the transaction, which then becomes a private purchase on the installment plan. Physicians work for a living and are nearly always paid for their efforts. Few physicians would admit to being social workers; even a psychiatrist employed by a state mental institution would take a long look at his M.D. diploma on the wall before admitting to the label of "welfare worker." Dentists, wherever employed, even full-time by the Veterans Administration or part-time by a community chest supported clinic, would show the same reluctance to be embraced by a field on which many of these individualists look with suspicion or distrust. But we must not let all these self-exclusions stand without challenge.

Much of the "health maintenance field" has come to be financed—not by the individuals directly benefited—but by the tax dollars of city, county, state, and federal governments and the charitably contributed dollars of generous persons. Hospitals care for the indigent, and public health services have become accepted as necessary to the well-being of society. Research on dread diseases is heavily supported by government. Like these, the free and part-pay clinics for victims of accidents and alcoholism—or those giving free polio shots, for example, are properly termed social welfare. There would seem to be little doubt about it.

In summary, our schools, courts, and prisons ought not be called welfare activity if terms are to communicate ideas. But in the medical field, difficulty is encountered in the case of programs like the federal Medicare program for the dependents of servicemen. The new clinics and hospitals built and operated by labor unions for the use of their members (using in some cases union dues, and in others employer contributions to special funds) are difficult to classify, as are benefits deriving from membership in fraternal bodies. But most such activities seem to lack some of the aspects borne by bona fide social service activities.

How are we to classify employment benefits? There is wide difference of opinion about what constitutes "fringe benefits." One study, made by the U. S. Chamber of Commerce in 1957, found that computing these according to one set of criteria made them total 21.8 per cent of payroll, while another way made them total 25.7 per cent. The researchers concluded, "Differences of opinion regarding what constitutes fringe benefits and how they should be computed indicate the need for a generally accepted definition of fringe benefits, and for a uniform method of comparing fringe benefits with employee compensation." Fringe benefits seem to embrace such items as the following long list (when viewed from the standpoint of the employer): (1) Employer's share of payments to OASI (social security), employment and workmen's compensation, or if a railroad, equivalent payments. (2) Net cost of company payments to special pension plans; for life insurance and death benefits; for sickness, accident, medical-care, and hospitalization insurance; and for contributions to privately financed unemployment benefit funds and termination pay. (3) Discounts on goods and services purchased from the company by employees, and such items as free meals, extra compensation payments in time of personal disaster, tuition payments for education, and savings and stock purchase plans. (4) Money paid for rest and lunch periods, travel time, wash-up time, clothes changing, and time when getting ready to perform work. (5) Payments for employee time not actually worked, such as vacations, bonuses paid if vacations are skipped; wages paid for holidays, sick or military leave, and absence due to entirely personal reasons. (6) Bonuses at Christmas time, and gifts and awards for services or suggestions.

In addition to this long list of alleged fringe benefits, some employers would include profit-sharing payments and wage payments made after the loss of court fights, especially when payment is made retroactively even though no work was performed during the period in question.

Such lists of the possible fringe benefits, open to many employees of giant corporations and to some who work with businesses in metropolitan areas, are viewed with awe by self-employed persons, professional people, farmers, and many teachers and professors. To be covered by many, most, or all of these benefits— in addition to one's wages or salary—is truly to have security benefits that are remarkable in extent. When one adds the helpful role of skilled interviewers, personnel officials, and even ministers and social workers on the company payroll, one has to study the pages of books on social services to ascertain what else could be done for employees blanketed so thoroughly by services and special benefits provided as an adjunct to employment.

But are these fringe benefits properly included in the category "social welfare" as defined at the outset? Some are, perhaps, but most, it would seem, are not. The individual is served, beyond doubt, and so are his dependents in many instances. But is it not true that abolishing any or all of these benefits would allow an employer to raise wages? These are, indeed, benefits in lieu of wages and in most cases they came because of union pressure, the desire of an employer to prevent unionization of a plant, competitive necessities in the employment community, or the influence of modern industrial relations teachings on the relation between employee content and corporate profits. (The humanitarian desires of some management personnel or company owners cannot be ignored, of course.)

The abolishment of modern fringe benefits supplied by employers would result quickly in vast problems for bona fide social service agencies. So much is clear. The existence of these activities by American business must be borne in mind by all who study social welfare; for whatever these services may be called and however their "category" may be defined, they have a profound impact on the well-being of millions in the nation. There will be no further opportunity here to give them the attention they so richly deserve, whether they are "social welfare" or not.

It is contended in any case that fringe benefits agreed on jointly by management and unions around the bargaining table should not be called "welfare plans," a title they so often bear in newspapers. They are part of the wage structure of many industries, forestalling discontent or strikes, and easing the worries of workingmen and their dependents. They also increase the financial burden borne by consumers, who buy the products whose advancing price tags reflect every new fringe benefit offered by industry. Newspapers, radio, and television would be rendering a distinct service to the semantics of social welfare if they would gradually cease the practice of calling union-management agreements "welfare plans" and the union funds "welfare funds." They should call them something more nearly reflecting what they are, perhaps "fringe benefit plans" or "union health insurance" or, best of all, "employee benefit plans." The extension of the word "welfare" to cover loosely such things suggests that it could even be stretched, just as logically, to embrace wages themselves, particularly guaranteed annual wages. This recalls the days when wages, earned by the sweat of one's brow, were paid in some instances as if they were the consequence of employer largesse. Union benefit plans are earnings, not welfare. They are often won in lieu of wage increases at the bargaining table; they are seldom donated as charity.

In still another large area, the word "welfare" has been used to its semantic detriment. The expression "welfare state," very commonly heard during the Fair Deal presidency of Harry S. Truman, has been less often heard since his retirement from public office. Yet it is still a barrier to the transfer of thought, even though one sometimes encounters it in other lands. Consider it carefully for a moment. From one point of view, a "welfare state" is a society with a government that is benevolent rather than malevolent. This is hardly something to be cringed at. Such a label—or epithet—moreover does not convey any sense of degree; who can tell how many will be aided, how much, and by what method?

The absurdity of a term as sweeping as "welfare state" is well illustrated by the way it cuts across the entirely proper debate between advocates of social insurance on the one hand, and public assistance on the other. Are both of these programs part and parcel of a welfare state? One cannot ignore the fact that the aged or unemployed individual drawing social insurance benefits once paid some of the costs himself, with his own money. And he may

43

not be in any need. Is this welfare? Such concepts could cause us to give the pension plans of federal, state, county, and city governments shelter under the giant umbrella of a "welfare state," thus loosely defined. Or, to take an even more extreme example, uneven tax benefits in the Internal Revenue Code might, when beneficial to special groups, be termed "welfare." This would be satisfying to no one. Nor would teachers be happy to learn that a lifetime of heavy salary deductions, under retirement plans, had been no more than a beneficial service rendered by a "welfare state," whose every payment of funds to individuals could then be called an act of "welfare."

We are not sentenced to the term "welfare state." Should it not be abandoned? A state can have "positive government." It can be a "regulatory state," an "ownership state," a "laissez faire state," a "management state," or a "humanitarian state"—to name a few possibilities in the use of labels with some semblance of meaning. (Whether all such states would be democratic, republican, and benevolent are questions which need not be answered here.)

What should be said about veterans' benefits in a discussion of social welfare? This is a very touchy subject. Some critics would remind us of pertinent facts, to wit: A part of our people carried guns against the British and the Mexicans, struggled at Gettysburg, subjugated the Indians, stormed San Juan Hill, fought under Black Jack Pershing, and came through two bloody wars in our own day. Many of these men later drew pension checks. It is not begging the question to assert that these payments were made as rewards for services rendered. Veterans' pensions through the years have not been social insurance. Neither have they been public charity to persons who first established "need." The veteran has received his check regardless of whether or not he needed it. He paid nothing to the government to get it—nothing, that is, except a few years in a Philippine jungle, a leg severed at the knee, or the privilege of retaining a mind in which only happy memories of childhood and youth would dwell. The veteran paid a withholding tax for his benefits, paying the tax "in kind." Much that might have been his was withheld for a period of time, or forever: health, love, quiet contentment.

44

The chief trouble has been that all veterans have not paid in equal degree. Government has tried in vain to recognize this fact by a variety of benefit scales. Veterans' benefits, properly legislated and carefully administered, are not "social welfare." But in so far as there has been enactment of too liberal laws in some matters and loose administration in others, the whole veterans' program has been tainted in many minds and has some aspects of "give-away" about it. Properly delimited and tightly administered, however, benefits for veterans ought to be placed in a special category similar to fiscally sound social insurance. They are highly relevant to any discussion of public aid programs, primarily because men living on disability pensions are not candidates for county aid or Old Age Assistance.

The membership of the United States in the United Nations, with all it has meant in the appropriation of millions of dollars by the Congress for technical assistance under the banners of humanitarianism or self-interest, has led to statements that foreign aid through the UN is purely a "welfare" activity. At the same time, direct non-military gifts to other nations under the Marshall Plan, Point Four, and Mutual Security have sometimes borne the same label. One must hasten to agree that, in a general sense, the $30,400,000,000 pumped into foreign countries as foreign aid from 1948 to 1956 was for the well-being (welfare) of peoples and governments overseas. These expenditures were also for the benefit of the United States. Here were activities carried forward under guidance of the State Department and the Department of Defense. Their general justification was the strengthening of the nation without war, foreign conquest, or the erection of puppet governments. Seventy-seven cents of every dollar spent on foreign aid was spent directly in the United States for commodities and military goods. The Department of Health, Education, and Welfare naturally had little to do with such overseas aid. Nor was there the slightest indication that Americans wanted these programs to come under the wing of the same cabinet officer who administered their public assistance and social insurance programs. Call most foreign aid either a "give-away program" or "our first line of defense," but save the label "social welfare" for more precise usage, divorced from foreign policy and the preservation of the United States. It is a doubtful "charity" that benefits the giver equally with the recipient.

Police and fire protection furnished by local government are not welfare but protective services. The police do warn and advise juveniles, and firemen repair toys at Christmas and rescue children from iceboxes and get cats from trees—to say nothing of helping people from burning buildings. Policemen save lives and they contribute to our daily well-being, but so do plumbers, employees of water companies, food inspectors, and sanitation crews. All of these, together with highway crews, postmen, soldiers, sailors, airmen, and marines are in categories to be excluded from "social welfare" by all who seek to use broad terms with some semblance of precision.

Finally, the field of organized religion has to be examined tentatively to determine its "welfare" status. Shall the budget for paying a minister, heating the church, and replacing worn hymnals be considered similar in kind to payments of county relief or maintenance of the Boy Scout organization? One hesitates with some reason, but only briefly. The minister and the priest give spiritual, moral, and economic guidance to individuals. They or their staffs organize recreational activity for young people. Funds are gathered by them for missionary (i.e., religious, health, educational, and charitable) work overseas. All of this sounds familiar. And a special church fund sometimes meets mortgage installments on the home of a hard-pressed communicant until he "gets the breaks." Does this not sound very much like "social welfare"? That same church may help to operate a home for orphans, cooperate to keep a youth center open night after night, and help finance a part-pay home for the aging. Here is social work beyond any doubt, and the fact that we are so sure in these instances puts the major, purely religious work, of the ministry in its proper light. Ministerial and church expenses, parish expenditures, and the chiefly religious aspects of missionary work ought not be added into "social welfare" totals.

Let the categories of religion, corrections, education, foreign policy, and the rest be maintained separate from "social welfare" if possible, and thereby avoid the quite natural tendency to throw all well-motivated, humanitarian, beneficial, and constructive deeds into the social welfare category. It is not enough that one person benefits by the actions of another. The words "giving," "sharing," or "serving" are often useful tests to apply when one is in doubt.

Successively, if reader and writer are of one mind in the matter, there have been eliminated from the term social welfare the following:

(1) Education—that is, public and private schools, adult education, and public libraries. (2) Corrections—prisons, police, parole and probation officers, jurists, and courts. (3) Private hospitalization and clinical procedures, the services of physicians and nurses (except when free or part-pay) remembering that Blue Cross and similar pre-payment programs are insurance paid by individuals or by companies. (4) Union-management health and/or pension plans, which are to a large extent benefits in lieu of wages. (5) Civil service pension and retirement plans, for the government contributes in the capacity of employer. (6) United States overseas aid and technical assistance programs given through the United Nations structure or extended independently; these, it has been contended, are integral parts of our foreign policy.

Definition of terms is seldom satisfactory, but in this instance the effort to define is essential. Three well-known authorities in social work education agreed in the 1950's that "the scope and nature of social services have never been precisely defined, and it is doubtful whether they ever can be in a field so dynamic, so diverse, and one which by its nature forms border-line areas with so many others. . . . The frontiers of social work are fluid." Their position is a reasonable one. There will continue to be discussion of what social welfare includes and what it does not. And this is as it should be. Those who try to measure the services and costs of social welfare in our towns, states, and the nation must make their peace on inclusions and exclusions—much as has been done

47

here. Because the time for a degree of basic agreement on the American pattern in social welfare has come, we may hope that the analysis offered in this chapter will afford at least a point of departure.

CHAPTER III

Weaving a Pattern

Dollars:
  Multiple billions
  Gathered, distributed
  And gathered again.

Contributions:
  Freely given (and
  Not so freely).

Services:
  Accepted with thanks
  And without.

Payments:
  A matter of right . . .
  Or of charity.

Programs:
  Forever and a day, or
  Here today and gone tomorrow.

The Pattern:
  Fluid, like human tears, or
  Embroidered in red tape?

As THE UNITED STATES passed through the seventeenth decade since the writing of the Constitution, an institutional pattern in the handling of social welfare problems was emerging. A degree of stabilization seemed to have set in, even though the growth rates of varying programs differed substantially. There was a recognizable pattern—four decades after the spread of the community chest movement over the nation, two decades after the upholding of the constitutionality of the Social Security Act, and one decade after the founding of the first united funds.

It was possible as the 1960's dawned, therefore, to coin the phrase "the American pattern in social welfare" as something that might be identified and something that might be counted on to endure for an expanse of some years. Yet the pattern that

49

emerged remained dynamic. Its nature and some of the forces making for change in its fundamental outline will be the concerns of this brief discussion. The importance of the subject and the need for precision in treating it make the next half a dozen pages crucial to our understanding of much that follows. Here, certain basic facts must be looked full in the face.

Money paid out to finance social welfare in the United States must be seen in the context of the total expenditures made by government. These came to $71,800,000,000 in the fiscal year 1958—a $32,300,000,000 increase over 1949. Such a total, virtually incomprehensible, makes the social welfare portion of the whole seem small by comparison. Yet only the size of federal budget items earmarked for national defense and the furthering of our foreign policy keeps the social insurance, public assistance, health, and veterans expenditure items from looking gigantic indeed. And the federal is not the whole story.

Federal, state, and local governments together spend billions of dollars for social welfare and social insurance activities, deriving the money from general and special taxation. Each year the figures are added up. A typed carbon copy of the manuscript on which the key table is based was forwarded to me by Charles I. Schottland, then U.S. Social Security commissioner, and various computations that follow are based on it.

A brief summary of the large adjoining table will tell the minimum story in terms of billions of dollars spent by all governmental units in the indicated years.

	1950–51	1955–56	Per cent of Increase
Social Insurance and Related Programs	$ 6.9	$13.4	95
Public Aid*	2.6	3.0	17
Health and Medical Care	3.1	4.0	30
Other Welfare Services	1.2	1.3	12
Total	$13.8	$21.8**	58

* Includes some payments made on behalf of persons on public aid rolls to hospitals and private physicians.
** Figures here are rounded. The rounded total is 21.8.

Here are a few dramatic statements that derive from the statistics in this small tabulation and the larger table adjoining:

(1) The 58 per cent increase in total expenditures by government for social welfare and related programs in six years greatly exceeded the parallel growth in the population and inflation in the dollar. Still it must be remembered that the nation's gross national product increased substantially in those years, and far more people were employed than ever before. Their earnings made new records. Under these circumstances, those who pass judgment on

THE GOVERNMENT IN SOCIAL WELFARE
[IN MILLIONS]

Social Insurance and Related Programs	1950–51	1955–56	Per cent of Increase or Decrease
Old-Age and Survivors Insurance	$ 1,569	$ 5,485	250
Veterans' Pensions, Allowances, Burial Awards, Costs	2,132	2,826	33
Unemployment Insurance and Employment Programs	1,051	1,621	54
Public Employee Retirement Systems	923	1,556	69
Workmen's Compensation	702	975	39
Railroad Retirement	321	603	88
State Temporary Disability Insurance	139	232	67
Railroad Unemployment Insurance	28	60	111
Railroad Temporary Disability Insurance	29	53	83
Subtotal	$ 6,893	$13,411	95

Public Aid

Public Assistance (assistance to aged, blind, children, and mothers)	$ 2,261	$ 2,708	20
General Relief (County Relief)	324	314	-3
Subtotal	$ 2,585	$ 3,022	17

Health and Medical Services

Hospital and Medical Care	$ 1,758	$ 2,473	41
(Portion for Veterans only)	[585]	[730]	[25]

Other Community & Related

Health Services	744	1,117	50
Hospital Construction	550	351	−36
(Portion for Veterans only)	[106]	[27]	[−74]
Maternal and Child Health Services	34	104	206
Subtotal	$ 3,087	$ 4,044	31

Other Welfare Services of Government

Institutional and Other Care	$ 367	$ 524	43
Miscellaneous Veterans' Programs	663	233	−65
School Lunch Program	129	293	127
Child Welfare	6	146	. . .
Vocational Rehabilitation	31	52	68
Surplus Food for the Needy	. .	91	. . .
Subtotal	$ 1,196	$ 1,338	12
Total	$13,761	$21,815	59

Note: The 1955–56 figures for Public Assistance and General Relief both include sums paid for medical care, amounts that increased sharply in following years. Figures do not always add to totals and subtotals because of rounding.

Inclusion of a program on this table is not an indication that it was classified as "social welfare" in Chapter II of this book; the decision to include items in this tabulation was made by the Social Security Administration—the source of the data. Very lengthy footnotes accompany the original version of this table, and these may be seen in departmental publications.

Substantial changes made in these categories after 1956–57 destroyed comparability, in general. The recent figures appear annually in *Social Security Bulletin*, but the corresponding table given there for 1958 and 1959 wore the aspect of an "all-inclusive" philosophy. Many items not considered "social welfare" in this book have been added—apparently because education is, to some extent, the responsibility of the Department of Health, Education, and Welfare, for which Congressional appropriations for 1960 totaled $4,016,485,981.

the 58 per cent increase in social welfare expenditures by government are bound to be torn emotionally. Shall it be said in judgment that the six years "brought the nation entirely too much welfare activity," or should it be said instead that "so rich a nation ought to be spending more and more for human needs"?

(2) The total figure of $21,815,000,000 can be compared with three of the better known items of cash payments contained in it. The first is "social security" (Old-Age and Survivors Insurance), which totaled $5,500,000,000. Second, "public assist-

Photograph by the author

The first of all the registered Girl Scouts of the United States of America was Daisy Gordon Lawrence, of Savannah, Georgia, who is coauthor of a biography of Juliette Low, founder of the organization.

Social Security Administration

The first citizen to receive monthly old-age insurance benefits under the Old-Age and Survivors Insurance program, January, 1940, was Miss Ida Fuller, of Ludlow, Vermont.

ance" (aid and relief payments to the needy) which amounted to $3,000,000,000. Pensions for veterans, in the third place, came to $2,900,000,000. Adding together these famous expenditure areas, it can be seen at once that they are only half of the total "social welfare" figure on the adjoining table. Thus the "miscellaneous" social welfare and social insurance programs of government, some well publicized and others little known, have been totaling as much each year as social security, public aid, and veterans pensions put together. The miscellaneous programs include, however, most health activities, unemployment payments, and certain retirement programs. And unemployment payments rocketed in the recession year 1958.

(3) Social security, public assistance, and veterans payments were in shifting relationship to each other during these years. Their movement is readily seen:

	1950–51	1953–54	1955–56	1959–60 (Estimated)
Old-Age and Survivors Insurance	$1.6	$3.4	$5.5	$11.1
Public Assistance and General Relief	2.6	2.8	3.0	4.0
Veterans Pensions and Allowances	2.1	2.2	2.8	3.4

Such figures indicate that, if it was ever possible to speak of social security, public aid, and veterans pensions as a "big three" in government payments to individuals (meaning that all three were very roughly similar in annual payments), by the 1960's it was no longer possible to do so. Social insurance was leaving the other two far behind. It greatly exceeded their sum in 1959–60, having been only one-third their sum in 1950–51. It seemed possible that in the future, as disparity continued to grow, there might be growing pressure to amalgamate public aid and veterans payments into the social security system; yet the veterans' programs themselves might blossom in the event of a depression.

(4) Old-Age, Survivors, and Disability Insurance—and Unemployment Insurance—totaled $7,100,000,000. Veterans' benefits and public assistance were tied at about $2,800,000,000 each.

Public aid, however, no longer swelled its overall totals, except in seriously depressed areas. Public assistance, beyond any doubt, was becoming a junior partner among the immense social welfare activities of government. The unemployment insurance figure for 1959–60 was only slightly higher than it had been ten years before.

(5) Compared with the expenditures of state and local governments for social welfare and related programs, the federal percentage of the gross total came to stand at 62 per cent. Here was an increase of five percentage points in two years, and back in 1950–51 the federal share had stood at 54 per cent. So drastic a shift in less than a decade was chiefly due to the coming-of-age of the social security benefit payments programs.

(6) Vocational rehabilitation (outside the Veterans Administration) came to a mere $52,000,000, a sum large enough in itself, to be sure, but one not in the same class as the giant cash payments programs. Realizing this, the Congress doubled the amount by 1959–60 (to $103,000,000).

(7) The more than $4,300,000,000 spent by government for medical and health services, an amount rising sharply in 1958 in tune with the 1956 medical care amendments to public aid portions of the Social Security Act, came to more than either public assistance or veterans' cash payments. These revealing comparisons needed to be better known, since there was widespread opinion that American medicine was still an essentially private activity. Those who said with conviction that "government must be kept out of the medical field at all costs" did not seem to realize that much of their battle had long since been lost and that further losses lay ahead. The medical programs of government, including care of members of the military services, came to expenditure totals so great that all should have granted that care for these men, their dependents, the nation's veterans, persons on relief rolls, merchant seamen, and possibly other groups to be added (the aged, for example) attested to the fact of our government's involvement in the medical field.

One turns from a consideration of this $21,800,000,000 of annual expenditure from tax funds to a contemplation of national totals for charitable contributions. The figure commonly used in this connection varied in the 1950's from six to seven billion dollars. This included contributions for the work of religious, educational, medical, and philanthropic organizations; it was not a strictly defined social welfare total, by any means. Perhaps one-third of the seven billion dollars went for health and welfare purposes, if one included hospital construction and other capital improvements.

From such figures as these one could easily surmise that government expenditures were at a ratio of 10 to 1 with voluntary expenditures in the middle years of the twentieth century. But this is a shaky generalization. To the voluntary figure must be added income from fees, memberships, and endowments, and in some areas of the voluntary field this was vastly important. Then there should be a prorating, in cash equivalent, of the tremendous voluntary activity of men and women which makes the whole voluntary welfare field what it is. This unpaid activity, and the use of private cars, homes, offices, equipment, and other things not included in agency budgets, immensely magnifies the significance of voluntary welfare. To try to run the American National Red Cross, the Boy or Girl Scouts, or various denominationally operated welfare groups on the basis of hiring staffs to do on salary what volunteers do free would be financially devastating. To provide state automobiles, buildings, and equipment to replace the same items provided free of charge by responsible citizens as individuals, or through service with Kiwanis, Lions, Rotary, Elks, and ladies auxiliaries of every description would swell government budgets for social welfare to new highs. The impact and financial significance of the volunteer are sometimes overlooked by persons addicted to ridiculing the value of nongovernmental activities in social welfare.

The government and voluntary social welfare total, including all social insurance but excluding even an approximate figure for donated time and materials, may come to over twenty-four billion dollars. One cannot be more precise. Some may want to subtract from this either part or all of the $13,400,000,000 figure for social insurance benefits and costs. Others would not want to include various portions of the $2,800,000,000 in veterans benefits.

If the definition and delineation of social welfare which was made in Chapter II is accepted, certain data gathered in accordance with it will have special interest. At the close of my book *California Social Welfare* (Englewood Cliffs, N.J., Prentice Hall, 1956) is Table U, which attempts to determine the full extent of the financing of organized voluntary and public welfare in a single metropolitan area. Voluntary welfare budgets in the five counties bordering picturesque San Francisco Bay, an area with 2,700,000 people, came to $18,059,902 for the year 1954. Government social welfare expenditures—excluding those by social security and for veterans—came to $98,196,636. Voluntary welfare was 15.5 per cent of total social welfare financing in the area. Where did this money for voluntary welfare come from?

The united fund in the area, the United Bay Area Crusade, provided about 49 per cent of the funds obtained by voluntary agencies and causes from all sources. This made the united drive in the autumn the single most important source of voluntary welfare financing in the area. As far as community chest member agencies were concerned, this "give once" drive provided 63.5 per cent of the money that voluntary welfare needed to survive; the remainder came from independent campaigns and from gifts, fees, and memberships.

In 1959 such united-fund and community-chest drives raised in the United States in all probability, somewhat more than four hundred million dollars. It is not possible even to speculate on the total financing of voluntary agencies in the two thousand or more communities whose contributions to joint fund-raising drives form the basis for a four-hundred-million-dollar estimate. Some figures for certain large federated drives for the year 1956 may prove interesting:

	Number of Givers	Total Raised
Akron	118,408	$ 2,585,370
Cincinnati	248,501	5,189,739
Cleveland	488,718	8,870,804
Dallas	202,015	2,573,468
Denver	183,531	2,511,396

Houston	253,620	4,961,655
Milwaukee	314,312	4,522,099
Minneapolis	215,583	3,083,369
Philadelphia	636,135	12,623,503
Portland	152,913	3,063,303
St. Louis	322,856	8,015,757
San Francisco Bay Area	527,781	10,145,926
Seattle	208,212	3,975,926
Syracuse	124,421	2,535,156
Toronto	483,259	7,595,638

There is little point in giving the size of the population covered by these campaigns or in computing per capita gift by cities for comparative purposes. Such figures only have meaning when used after precise research on the number and types of causes included in the campaign. (Inclusion or exclusion of Heart, Cancer, or Red Cross, for example, makes a great difference in the gross amount raised in such campaigns.)

Everyone knows that government expenditures for social welfare have grown like Jack's beanstalk since the 1920's and that voluntary welfare financing has failed to keep pace. Strangely enough it is one thing to know this and quite another to back it up with statistics. These parallel developments can be seen fully at the county level where the grant-in-aid payments of the federal and state governments can be added to county, city, and district expenditures, allowing the combined total to be evaluated in relation to population and area.

I computed the total annual government expenditures for health, welfare, and recreation (that is, "social welfare") in two California counties for a period of three decades, taking every fifth year. In Alameda County (the home of industrial Oakland and Berkeley) government expenditures for social welfare increased sixteen and one-half times from 1924 to 1954. In San Francisco there was a tenfold increase.

To provide a comparison with a substantial portion of voluntary welfare, funds alloted to agencies by all community chests were carefully computed. The result was that the increases for voluntary welfare were not sixteen and one-half and ten, but a

57

mere two and four-tenths and one and one-half, respectively! Chest and federated-financing had not been able to expand community financing of the vitally important voluntary agencies sufficiently to permit them to keep up with multiplying government activity.

In these two large California counties the expansion of government social welfare was giant-sized, no matter how the figures were adjusted. Per capita expenditures by government in Alameda County, for example, rose, in terms of dollars of 1924 purchasing power from $4.29 to $26.03 over a thirty-year period. The gain in San Francisco was from $5.81 to $20.10. In unadjusted dollars the rise was even greater. The 1954 figure for government spending for social welfare was $34,500,000 in Alameda County and $37,-400,000 in San Francisco.

Interested researchers can compile similar figures for their own counties. Unless these two counties are proved atypical by subsequent research, it must be said that government-financed welfare has come to dwarf voluntary welfare in dollar expenditures. Only because voluntary welfare has other income and the help of innumerable unpaid volunteers (and thus stretches its dollars to cover much activity) is it possible to continue to treat voluntary welfare as a full-fledged partner of the ever growing government-services giant.

The ratio of government-financing to voluntary-financing in the social welfare activity of the Metropolitan San Francisco Bay Area, a ratio I have named the *Social Welfare Financing Ratio*, came to 5.44 to 1. This statistic may have some meaning for the nation as well. (Note that it excludes federal government social insurance and veterans benefit payments; nor are state mental hospital, educational, or any prison or court costs included. A far higher ratio would result from their inclusion.)

A division of government expenditures in the five counties surrounding San Francisco Bay showed that of the total $98,000,-000, fully $56,000,000 consisted of public assistance payments and overhead; $29,400,000 went for health purposes; and $12,000,000 was for recreation. The importance of studying a metropolitan area was very clear in these figures, for the corresponding three-

58

way division in each of the five component counties was much different from the 11-4-1 relationship of public aid-health-recreation in the total urban and suburban area.

The 58 counties of California are remarkably diverse in industrial and agricultural productivity, population density, and physical appearance. Studies of the state's economic life take on some of the aspects of a national survey in miniature. In this, the nation's second largest state according to population, payments of public aid to the needy have cost $30.72 per capita. Here is a minimum government-payments cost figure. What of voluntary welfare? Coming to only $3.34 per capita in the state were all the contributions to united funds and community chests, to Red Cross, and to the five largest national health organizations. Here is a measure of money—not total effort or significance; yet one cannot overlook this strictly financial relationship of over nine to one in favor of government.

From 1950 to 1957 in California, the cost of public assistance remained reasonably stable. Old-Age and Survivors Insurance kept expanding its coverage, however, and as recipients of Old Age Assistance (the public aid counterpart of four of OASI's six parts) died, they were only partially replaced by new persons. It seemed likely that public assistance for the aging would be whittled away, case by case, especially in urban areas. Much the same pattern was developing in other industrialized states. Here was something that had been predicted in the 1930's and 1940's, but which had been long in coming.

Faced with ever mounting totals for social-insurance payments, many observers have wondered for years if the point would ever come when public assistance could be abandoned. Surely, these critics have said, there will not always be the necessity for maintaining two benefit-payments systems adjoining each other: one with aid to dependent children, the other with benefits for children and mothers; one with old age assistance, the other with old-age, widow's, wife's, and parent's benefits: and both with programs for some disabled.

Public assistance in a state has been a major item, regardless of the existence of social security payments, veterans benefits, and

59

other programs of public and voluntary agencies. In Ohio, for example, the year 1956 saw $140,000,000 spent for public aid, 78 per cent of the amount going for the maintenance of recipients, and over 12 per cent for health care. The money came from federal, state, and local governments (forty-three cents, fifty-two cents, and five cents, respectively, a ratio variable among the states). The aging got fifty-five cents of each dollar, general relief twenty-four cents, dependent children fifteen cents, the disabled four cents, and the blind two cents. There has been much pressure in magazines of mass circulation and elsewhere to minimize direct-aid payments, for in a large state like California they total more than $30,000,000 monthly. The recession of 1958 saw temporary increases in public assistance in many states, although direct relief took most of the burden. Hard-pressed administrators sought supplementary appropriations from supervisors or legislators, tried to purge existing rolls, and in many cases, attempted to find loopholes that would permit the transfer of direct relief cases to "categorical aids" where federal grants might carry much of the load. In Cook County, Illinois, it seemed for a time in 1958 that the needy might go without their checks for one or more payment periods, but several of the expedients just mentioned saved the day.

Part of the pressure for the abandonment of old age assistance comes from those who know that this program is in many states the preserve of special interest groups. Some resentment stems from the sometimes loose local administration of the Aid to Dependent Children program—already vulnerable because easy to charge with being in some part a haven for unmarried mothers, and even in rare instances, perhaps, a subsidy to ease continuing production of illegitimate children. Such common charges, vying with overly flattering but vacuous press releases, have left the public confused and uncertain. Divorce or family desertion and unmarried motherhood at tragically young ages statistically swamp cases of orthodox widowhood on the ADC rolls.

In the Congress, a number of attacks have centered on the costs of administering the whole public assistance program in the states and counties of the nation, although the federal government has underwritten somewhat less than half the administrative costs of the categorical aid programs. Of the $211,300,000 in such costs anticipated for 1958, the federal share was $104,500,000. While social security has cost about 2 per cent to administer, public assistance salaries and overhead have run 16 per cent in New York but as little as 4.1 per cent in West Virginia and 3.6 per cent in Oklahoma. Such figures have invited acid attention. In 1957, the House of Representatives tried to put a ceiling on the amount of federal funds that could be used for the administrative expenses of state and local public welfare agencies; the Senate would not accede to this point of view. The House leaders wrote that they remained "still convinced that some action should be taken to curb the ever-increasing costs of administering this program." Assured by the Commissioner of Social Security that appropriate action would be taken to assure that no more funds than necessary would be expended for the efficient administration of the public aid programs, the House Committee on Appropriations insisted that a full report on the matter be made by the Commissioner.

The administrative problem is that public assistance has long been handled by the states and by such local authorities as the states may select, while social security is separately administered. This has meant that in thousands of buildings all over the nation there exists giant interviewing and need-ascertaining machinery, much of it adjunct to the paying of monthly amounts from federal, state, and county funds. Meanwhile, by the end of 1957, the U.S. Department of Health, Education, and Welfare's Social Security Administration had 21,037 employees of its own. Its 550 district offices maintained a regular service at a special time at 3,600 "contact points." Nevertheless, the Social Security Administration has had its central activities in Washington and Baltimore.

The Bureau of Old-Age, Survivors, and Disability Insurance operates an IBM type 705, a machine records system installed in 1956 in Baltimore. This amazing machinery performs the following tasks with its half-inch-wide magnetic tapes: It annually "associates" 240,000,000 quarterly earnings reports for covered individuals with their 120,000,000 summary earnings records, so that new summaries are produced. Condensed summary earnings records are then produced on punchcards. The machine catches nearly all of the nine million erroneous social security numbers that come to the Bureau each year. The 705 also prepares three million summary cards for claimants and produces statistical data regularly for a 1 per cent sample. While it is true that in larger counties around the nation card-sorting machinery has been installed and genuine efforts at efficiency have been made (I can testify to the size of the New York City IBM unit), in the long run the efficiency and economy of the centralized social security system was bound to make the high overhead of the uneconomical, county-by-county payment practices of public assistance look worse and worse.

Social workers have insisted that nothing can be a substitute for their interviews with claimants, and they are determined to extend this process. How else, they ask, can eligibility for a "categorical aid" program (payment to an aging or blind person or a broken family) be established except by interviewing and visiting? Increasingly, the intellectuals of social work have insisted that the public assistance programs ought to be turned into casework operations. Emphasis would then shift away from the machinery of issuing checks. New stress would be placed on psychiatric procedures, vocational guidance, rehabilitation, and job-finding. To some extent the agitation of the 1950's made headway. In many instances it helped people to get off public-aid rolls, but at the same time it helped to make permanent the current jobs in county public welfare departments and increased salary overhead. Optimistic social work experts remain confident that salaries for more and better caseworkers can, in the end, be made available by savings in payments of aid, for it seems obvious to them that the rolls will shrink in response to the efforts of social workers, and people will be pushed toward respectability.

What this debate boils down to is a question of faith. Do the social workers have what it takes to rehabilitate people? Are they trained for the task they have outlined? The public is not well informed on the education, talents, or nature of social workers, collectively or individually. Observers are in no position to know which side to take in the emerging dispute. Hence the emphasis on the duties of social workers in this book.

Public assistance and social insurance, particularly in their payments to aging citizens, have become real competitors. Marion B. Folsom, the second secretary of Health, Education and Welfare, in his regular appearance before the House Appropriations Subcommittee on February 11, 1957, stated, "I think everybody agrees that this contributory insurance program [OASDI, social security] is a better approach to the problem of income maintenance than Old Age Assistance." No doubt most of the public, to the extent that there is knowledge about the matter, would agree. Subsequent interviewing of the Secretary by members of the committee elicited additional opinions. Its chairman, John E. Fogarty of Rhode Island, asked, "Do you think social security insurance will ever supplant public assistance in this country?" The essence of the reply was that universal coverage at the outset of federal social insurance activity in the 1930's would have made a great difference:

> Those of us who worked on this twenty years ago thought that the Old Age Assistance would be a much smaller factor than it is now, and we assumed that we would get universal coverage which we did not get. It will gradually go down. . . .
> I wouldn't want to forecast when Old Age Assistance will be out of the picture.

Later, Congressman Winfield K. Denton of Indiana inquired, "You had a great deal to do with writing the original social security provisions, did you not?" The Secretary replied, "I was on the council." And, "At that time it was thought that the old-age assistance would be done away with?" Mr. Folsom replied, "Yes."

Later in the hearings the Secretary commented candidly on the possible fate of the officeholders administering public aid in the light of the great shift to social insurance and away from public assistance. "I don't see how they can exist if the people are drawing the money from social security," he said. Here arose a frightening ogre for the army of employees in public welfare departments all over the nation.

Later in those committee hearings Mr. Jay L. Roney, director of the Bureau of Public Assistance, was testifying. Chairman Fogarty noted the bureau's request for an increase of $104,-000,000 in public assistance appropriations by Congress at a time when Old-Age and Survivors Insurance was mushrooming, and he asked, "Social security insurance has not had quite the effect on this that was originally estimated, has it?" The director, certainly a recognized national expert on the subject, replied:

> It has definitely had its effect, I believe, Mr. Fogarty, but perhaps not to the extent that it was, shall we say, hoped. Several factors have been . . . operating. One is the increase in the total number of aged, and the other is an increase in the cost of living for assistance recipients, which has resulted in some supplemental assistance to the old-age and survivors insurance beneficiaries. I think one other factor is that the complete coverage of old-age and survivors insurance has been comparatively recent—especially the farm coverage.
>
> Secondly, a year or so ago a large number of [OAA] recipients, a large proportion of recipients, were in the rural areas, and also a quite large number were women who had not been able to get [OASI] coverage. In the next few years I believe these factors are going to be even more significant.

Finally, there was the questioning of Charles I. Schottland, then commissioner of Social Security, by Congressman Denton, an attorney and formerly a member of the Budget Committee in the Indiana Legislature. Mr. Denton asked, on February 21, when the nation would get to the point where the "stopgap" public assistance programs would end and give way to social security. Were the aid programs to be permanent? In reply, the Commissioner stated that Old Age Assistance was becoming primarily a rural, a very old age, and a women's program. He said that there was very little hope that the nation would come to the point where it would be free of persons without the work experience necessary to be eligible for social security. Speaking off the cuff, the Commissioner, formerly in charge of public assistance administration in California, said he did not think that those framing the Social Security Act had intended to get everything "under one program." Congressman Denton expressed surprise at this, saying, "I would like to put them all under one." Thus there were revealed distinct differences of opinion among experts in the government and some well-informed congressmen on the future of public aid. Its future role in the long-range pattern of government social-welfare activity remained shrouded in doubt, but by 1960 there were four and one-half times as many aged persons receiving OASDI as obtained Old Age Assistance payments.

There can be no question, in summary, that as the fate of public assistance is debated in Congress, in state legislatures, and in the chambers of county and city officials, the concern of leaders in social work will be a compound of theoretical arguments for aid payments versus the equally persuasive arguments for social insurance benefits (the kind of debate that intellectuals might find appealing). And in the background must lurk the more practical problem of job security for social workers who now investigate "need" but wish they had the time, training, and funds to rehabilitate families. Demands for the payment of federal and state funds to provide education for untrained social workers, so that they can enter the social-work job market on a competitive basis, if worse comes to worst, seem only logical when seen in this realistic framework. The social insurances, meanwhile, have virtually no trained social workers and are content to leave well enough alone. Are money payments enough? The social workers don't think so.

When the subject of appropriating perhaps three million dollars for training public assistance workers arose in the 1957 House hearings, opinions on the possible permanence of public aid programs became directly pertinent. Should such training be government financed, asked Congressman Denton, when social insurance might soon take over and leave "a great many unemployed welfare workers"? The director of the Bureau of Public Assistance said such training ought to be given in any case, but added, "I think there is going to be a need for many more trained [social work] personnel for a good many years to come." But the appropriation did not pass.

There have been statistical grounds for the belief that OASDI (known to the public as "social security") coverage ought to be able to reduce OAA public aid payments in the long run to a very minor figure. OASDI increased its beneficiaries from just under a million at the close of World War II to over six and one-half million a decade later. Old Age Assistance, meanwhile, grew from two million to slightly over two and one-half million recipients in five years, then entered on a gradual decline. Still, as states maintained liberal attitudes in the matter of eligibility, the drop in prosperous 1956–57 was only thirty-eight thousand out of the two and one-half million on the rolls. These received $146,-900,000 in the single month of June, 1957.

The trend in Aid to Dependent Children, moreover, was up in the nation as a whole, as fathers walked away from their responsibilities and got away with it. (In June, 1957, 647,208 families with 1,831,925 children obtained $62,500,000 from this program, 5 per cent more families and 14 per cent more money than the same month a year earlier.) Over-all, monthly payments for public assistance rose by over twenty million dollars during the year. And all this happened at a time when payments for social insurance for the month of June bloomed from $897,000,000 to $1,046,000,000 during the same annual period.

From the standpoint of national statistics in a time of prosperity, therefore, it looked as though public assistance and social insurance were apt to have a long parallel life in the nation, unless Congress should face squarely the problem posed by rival administrative machinery in the future. Yet the recession of 1958 blurred the whole issue as aid rolls climbed temporarily. And the old cry to bring federal grants-in-aid to the local county relief programs (with the states as intermediaries) was heard again in the land.

Before leaving the subject of public aid, consideration of the extent of programs in New York City alone may give pause to any who think that public assistance programs can easily be abandoned, out-of-hand, without strain or pain. The New York City Department of Welfare early in 1957 estimated its 1957–58 requirements at $203,729,240. The city's share would be $65,-

000,000. Aid to Dependent Children would require 45 per cent of all public assistance funds for its 161,766 recipients, while Old Age Assistance would get 26.6 per cent; Aid to the Permanently and Totally Disabled, 15.6 per cent; and Aid to the Blind 1.8 per cent. Home Relief and aid for veterans at the local level would account for 11.1 per cent. Total expenditures for calendar 1957, it turned out, came to $266,464,008.

The economic recession in 1958 brought inevitable increases in many programs of public assistance in the states. Yet lawmakers the year before had guaranteed not only the survival but the expansion of annual costs of public assistance programs for at least awhile by passing innumerable amendments to state laws "eliminating inequities" in administration, by increasing the amounts to be paid each person and family, and by adding half a billion dollar public-aid medical-benefits program.

If there is any answer to the question "Will public assistance programs fade away?" it is, in part, that men in public office will have to do their share to make them self-liquidating. Whether the best path lies in converting public-aid staffs to the casework procedures taught in the social work schools and close liaison with government departments of employment and vocational rehabilitation (and voluntary agencies) or in moving aid recipients over into the social security system en masse, is a question of public policy for the public to help decide. Certainly many believe that something will have to be substituted for the uninspiring and routine delivery of monthly public aid checks by the mailmen of the nation following little more than clerical "need" evaluations. The debate on this matter, as it evolves, ought to be given wide publicity in the mass communication media so that the public will have at least some idea of what the issues are.

Sometimes it seems that federal-government programs in the social-welfare field stand serenely above political parties, platforms, and winning candidates—far more so than even the technical area of foreign policy. From a broad view there seems to be little in the statistics of public assistance or social insurance from 1935 to date to lead one to draw the conclusion that parties or their leaders have had, when in or out of office, patterned influence on major social-welfare programs. There were minor tendencies, to be sure, and the language of leaders of factions within parties has often been patterned to include the "welfare state" concept and other vacuous generalities. But social insurance and public assistance both flourished under the Democratic supremacy of the Truman administration, and neither suffered vital blows under the Eisenhower administration—quite the contrary.

Why has government social welfare been so unresponsive on the whole to party change? Party platforms have been a bit hazy on particulars, for one thing. Yet in 1952 the platforms differed completely on the socialization of medicine and the people did have a clear-cut choice. The Ewing Plan as such was cast aside, but by 1958–59 parts of it had emerged again—like the seven-year locusts—to threaten vast increases in government intervention in the medical field. In Congress, most followers of states rights and men whose religious conviction strengthened their belief in the voluntary way could be counted on to oppose such changes in the American social welfare pattern. But there remained all too many political figures willing to equate "liberalism" with spending government funds and with expanding government bureaus, regardless of realistic needs.

Perhaps the attitude of several highly placed governmental leaders will be informative on the problems politicians face in the social-welfare area. President Eisenhower defended the domestic phases of his budget in 1957 with the comment, "As long as the American people demand—and in my opinion, deserve—the kind of services this budget provides, we have got to spend this kind of money." His secretary of Health, Education and Welfare at the time, Marion B. Folsom, stated to Congress a month later: "We say the federal government would fail to serve the people's interest if it stood idly by, indifferent to broad deficiencies in health, education, or economic security. . . . We believe the federal government . . . can and should act in these fields for the benefit of the people." The budget request of his department was for $2,632,033,762. Of the amount requested, 88.9 per cent consisted of grants-in-aid by the federal government to the states. The remainder was divided as follows: 9 per cent for federal hospitals,

Social Security Administration

These magnetic tape batteries in the Social Security Administration headquarters, Baltimore, Maryland, are one of three groups linked with an IBM 705 computer. The system operates constantly on some 80,000,000 active social security accounts.

H. Armstrong Roberts, Philadelphia

After about one month of intensified training on the premises of a reputable agency (like Seeing Eye, Inc., Morristown, New Jersey, or Guide Dogs for the Blind, Inc., San Rafael, California), a new world opens up for the blind.

health, and medical research operations; 0.3 per cent for federal administrative costs attending the various grant-in-aid programs; and 1.8 per cent for all other operating programs.

As Secretary Folsom defended his budget request before the Democratic-controlled Congress, he found himself in the position of satisfying senators and representatives—and particularly the head of the House Appropriations Subcommittee—that he was asking for enough money for welfare programs. Congressman Fogarty asked repeatedly if specific items were going to be large enough to meet human needs. This line of interrogation put the Secretary in a peculiar position. On the one hand, he felt obliged to establish that his party was conscious of human needs and, more particularly, that his own department was straining every muscle to serve them. On the other hand (conscious of economy-minded members of the Republican party), this cabinet member wanted it known in some quarters that the administration was not going overboard with welfare-statism. It was a trying verbal assignment.

Explaining that the population of the nation had been growing and that living expenses were up, Secretary Folsom said in his testimony of February 11, 1957, that "many of these services, many of these programs, are bound to increase in cost as the population increases and the economy expands. We just can't help it." An unfriendly observer might have added to this the thought that an expanding economy and the unexampled productivity of the nation, coupled with the high employment of those years, might seem to indicate less need than before for welfare programs. Asked by Mr. Fogarty, a Democrat, "Is there any place in your budget that you think we can cut?" the Secretary replied, "No. I would stick by the budget we have presented." Increases, he added, were normally based on legislation over which the department had little control. "We don't have a very big area in which we can operate when it comes to reducing costs, unless it is in cutting out programs," he stated, noting that only 2.1 per cent of his total budget went for administration. (States and counties carry most of the costs of salaries and buildings.)

Shifting the attack from the possibility of cutting the budget to the adequacy of services, Mr. Fogarty turned to various programs and asked repeatedly why apparent "needs" had not been met. What, he asked, about hospital construction under the Hill-Burton Act? Why had it lagged? The Secretary replied, "It simply takes time and you have to put pressure on the local communities to see the need for it [sic!]." Mr. Fogarty listened to the Secretary explain that his department was moving fast on most programs; then he said, "But we should be moving a little faster. I said the same thing to Mr. Ewing when he was in your position, and I said the same thing to Mrs. Hobby when she was in your position." The reply of Secretary Folsom to this was, "That is why we are increasing the staff."

Later in the day, Secretary Folsom was pressed by several congressmen to encourage the federal government to pass laws to force employers to hire persons aged forty to sixty-five. Asked if he was "satisfied" with progress being made, the Secretary replied, "We won't be satisfied until we have all the problems licked 100 per cent. It is a matter of judgment as to how fast you can move." In 1956 in the health field, he said on another occasion, the 1956 congressional appropriations had been "practically everything" his department sought. This gave congressmen a chance to inquire why additional funds asked for medical research had not been sought earlier.

In his own testimony on the matter of services versus dollar costs, Commissioner Schottland defended existing programs, urged new services, asked for increased personnel and funds for training, and put much of the blame for climbing public-aid expenditures on the states. "You have some states," he said, "that take the position that the primary responsibility is to see that the persons are eligible for public assistance and once they are eligible their responsibility more or less ceases." He did not suggest curtailing any grant-in-aid programs, however, nor did congressmen of either party make strenuous efforts in that direction.

The United States Chamber of Commerce, through a subcommittee on social legislation, studied the federal grant-in-aid programs in the 1950's and came up with many facts and suggestions in a 1954 pamphlet, "Federal Grant-in-Aid Programs." In

1920, it said, such grants were confined to ten functions and came to a little over $100,000,000 annually, 75 per cent of it for highways. But in 1953 these grants came to $2,600,000,000—a quarter of the tax revenues of the states. And more than forty programs were included. The chamber wanted an end to many of these federal grants, relinquishing, at the same time, certain taxes to the states—particularly in the excise-tax area.

In 1957 the chamber urged that $500,000,000 be taken from the $1,679,400,000 scheduled to go to the states for public assistance programs. Mr. Clarence R. Miles explained the chamber's reasoning in a letter to the House Appropriations Subcommittee. The grants, he said, had been started during the Depression to encourage and assist states in establishing adequate aid programs. At that time the states needed help. But passage of the years had brought local acceptance of programs and much liberality in aid payments. The economy had long been healthy. And social security had come to cover nine out of ten working people; it paid benefits to five out of ten aged persons.

> The time has now come when encouragement of the states is no longer needed. They have accepted and are performing well their responsibilities in the social-welfare field. With the expansion of social benefits, it is a propitious time to make sizeable and progressive reductions in the Federal grants program. . . . By reducing the federal burden upon the people of the states, this job could be assumed by the states and be done more efficiently and effectively.

The American Public Welfare Association, in the meantime, was bringing pressure to bear from another direction altogether. If the President's 1958 budget were only to be revised upward in line with association recommendations for new staff jobs and new programs, it would "make possible not only a continuation of basic welfare programs, but also an extension and improvement" in them, it felt. In Los Angeles, more than half of the 1,100 social caseworkers in the County Bureau of Public Assistance voted to "dig into their own pockets" to finance a long-range public relations program "to help the BPA become better known and accepted by the public" and to realize certain other objectives—like higher salaries. Many of the county government's social workers were taking public speaking courses. Social insurance will not triumph over public assistance without a fight from many modestly educated persons who have done little more than ascertain the legality of paying monthly checks to those who claim financial "need."

Yet some public welfare departments, as the 1960's began, sensed that the true "need" was for them to justify their own existence through doing vastly more than merely paying checks. These few public welfare departments did more than pay lip service to "problem solving" and "rehabilitation." This was especially true in Minnesota, and in San Francisco where a pilot effort of the Public Welfare Department, directed by Ronald Born, held promise of future accomplishment. Organized after research by and endorsement of Community Research Associates, Inc. of New York, and rooted in experiments conducted in St. Paul, in Maryland, and in San Mateo County, California, the concept seemed likely to catch fire nationally, as bankruptcy in alternative ideas among social-work intellectuals and leaders of taxpayers' associations alike revealed a deficiency in plans and creative action. Still, substantial change in welfare administration across the country would take years. Moreover, grave doubts were expressed whether the self-styled "hard-headed" would countenance increased administrative expenditures made necessary by the addition of new services. In the complete reorganization and retraining of existing staffs lay some hope of progress, especially in the effectiveness of the Aid to Dependent Children program.

Political figures have long found themselves caught between the advocates of expanded programs and those who hope to curtail or eliminate them. As can be seen in the competent testimony of the secretary of Health, Education and Welfare and the comments of top administrative heads in his department, there is a distinct feeling that those who direct welfare programs must, at all times, align themselves with "humanity" against all who merely call for "economy." Humanity feels! Equally important, as political figures know, humanity votes! Even though the modern trend has been for the public to insist on business-like approaches to government administration (with economy the touchstone), how can those who administer social-welfare programs ever come before the peoples' representatives with a request for less money? From that time forth, every unmet "need" that might be uncovered by those in political opposition could be blamed specifically on heartless administrators who were offered the money and had the opportunity to meet needs—but held back.

Who is to gain the credit—or bear the responsibility—for the ever-increasing social-welfare services of government? Listen to the people who advised officials of government how much Congress should appropriate for 1958. There are lessons to be learned.

As Congress considered expending $3,500,000 for a new building for the National Institute of Dental Research, letters urging the expenditures came from two of the highest officials of the American Dental Association and from various deans of university schools of dentistry. Three representatives of the association came in person to urge construction and to ask for a million-dollar increase in appropriations to the Institute.

The voluntary National Association for Retarded Children urged that an increase from $750,000 to $1,500,000 be made in one area of interest to it; that the Children's Bureau get an extra $2,500,000 for services and $80,566 for new staff; that the Office of Vocational Rehabilitation be provided $2,000,000 more "for programs in the field of mental retardation"; and that the office of Education get an extra $250,000.

The president of the Massachusetts Institute of Technology and other educators came before the Congress to urge higher grants to their institutions to cover administrative costs connected with research, for plain research grants were not considered to be enough. The president of M.I.T. said that, in connection with $142,000,000 in federal funds spent by universities in 1953-54, only 70 per cent of the indirect expense burden had been federally financed. "The schools and hospitals cannot continue indefinitely to channel an increasing part of their resources into the indirect expenses of research and still carry on effectively with their other obligations and responsibilities," he urged.

73

The president of the American Nurses Association supported $5,300,000 scheduled by the administration for appropriation in areas of interest to her group. Her reception from Congressman Fogarty, however, proved both disconcerting and most heartening. He thought the appropriation entirely inadequate.

> What will I tell some of these nurses in Rhode Island when they tell me we haven't appropriated sufficient funds and they could use more money? Shall I quote you as saying that you told the committee you were satisfied with the amounts suggested by the administration this year for these purposes? I want to be able to give them a good answer.

After more than a little evasion, the witness finally gave the indicated reply, "We would be delighted if you feel you could give us more money [than scheduled]."

The American Legion had four of its top lobbyists appear before the subcommittee to urge federal scholarships for nursing education and other expenditures. Noting that one-third of the labor market consisted of veterans, and that rehabilitation is best measured by one's ability to obtain a job, these veterans urged continuation of maximum appropriations for the Bureau of Veterans Re-employment Rights in the Department of Labor.

The lobbyist for the national Congress of Parents and Teachers appeared to support several budget items, her philosophy in this being that "Americans believe that all children have a right to grow up under the conditions most favorable to their development." Since "not all children have parents who can give them care, security, a happy home," she expressed the conviction that "we all have a responsibility to these children." And the federal government, she thought in summary, would fulfill "our corporate responsibility."

Here, in the persons of these representatives of legitimate pressure groups, was the voice of the people—or some of them. How many? The executive director of the Child Welfare League of America, Inc., said he was "representing the board of directors" before the committee as he asked Congress to appropriate a round $12,000,000 for grants to states for child-welfare services—a $3,-

74

400,000 increase. The position he felt he occupied in his group has enduring interest for all who have listened to less candid representatives of pressure groups.

> I wish to emphasize that I am here speaking for the board of directors of the league and not necessarily for every one of our members for the simple reason that in this type of organization we cannot poll each member and there may be some divergent views and therefore we do not want to represent ourselves as representing every member. . . .
>
> I am not pretending to have polled every one of our 250 members and speak in their name. . . . we are here today not as a pressure group speaking for our own personal interests but as a voluntary organization, one of whose responsibilities it is to speak for a group that cannot represent itself, namely, the several million disadvantaged children in the United States, and for whom these appropriations are primarily intended.

The speaker judged that "there is not a state in the United States that is adequately caring for its dependent and neglected children." The role for the federal government, therefore, was to pave the way within the various states by "demonstration projects." Then the states would finance the work permanently—and more heavily than before—he declared.

The concern at the outset of this chapter was said to be the detection of an "emerging welfare pattern." That such a pattern is in the long run likely to be compounded of the voices of whole choruses of pressure groups in Washington, D.C., the state capitals, and the counties and cities of the nation should now be quite plain. The extent of their influence on government should clearly have more than a little to do with the future of social welfare. But one further voice needs to be heard briefly. It comes from one of the many government councils or planning groups, composed of administrators as a rule and often to be found in Washington or in the states in a policy-making—or propaganda—role.

In January, 1957, the infant Federal Council on Aging made its first annual report to the President. Representing thirteen large departments in the federal government, the council's members reported, "It seems apparent that legislative activity in the

75

field of aging will continue to increase and the Federal Council should assist in the formulation of a co-ordinated Executive Branch position on legislation in the field of aging, as a supplement and aid to the normal channels for the formulation of decisions relating to legislation." It suggested no laws in its first report, but it did express its basic philosophy:

> The federal government should continue to strengthen its activities in the fields of encouraging job opportunities for older persons, assuring basic income in retirement, supporting health research and assisting in the provision of adequate health services, encouraging better housing for older persons, improving their educational opportunities, and encouraging increased participation in community activities by older persons. . . .

This view contains the seeds of giant action by government in the decades to come. If we substitute the words "all persons" for "older persons" at the outset of this rather mild sounding credo and modify the rest accordingly, the extent of government intervention felt to be inevitable and proper becomes clearer. That age 65 is to be made a chronological way station, passage of which will entitle one to many special privileges, seems inescapable in this policy statement by a Republican administration. Will the Democrats raise the bid? Those over sixty-five are to depart from the world of strife, competition, and independence. They will move back into the sheltered world they left at age seventeen or twenty-one. Protected and advised by their parents in formative years, the now aging Americans may expect the same care from a zealously paternal government during their so-called golden years.

But the Federal Council on Aging did issue three pertinent warnings which, if taken seriously through the years, could greatly affect at least the kind of governmental intervention envisaged for our personal lives. Measures taken, it said, should assist the individual to preserve his independence—that is, his freedom and responsibility—to a maximum extent. Government should also try to utilize the sources closest to the individual when providing services. Among these are the family, employer, trade union, voluntary and religious organizations, local government, and state government. There was a broad hint in these remarks of the council that the federal government ought to intervene in the plans of churches, unions, service clubs, and other groups close to the citizen in his own community—all for his own good, of course! This has an ominous ring, one that it is strongly to be hoped the council did not intend. Finally, the council aptly warned that all such activity should be "consistent with the welfare of the population as a whole, and the maintenance of a sound economy."

There was wisdom in this final plea to provide only the services that can be given within a special context: *the welfare of all society.* The personal and financial needs of people at all levels are important, and nowhere more so than in a state which proclaims the importance of every individual—not merely disadvantaged persons, and certainly not merely aging citizens. The president of the American Public Welfare Association very properly warned in December, 1956, that the aged, possessing the vote, can, and indeed have, put undue pressure on legislators. Make sure "our kiddies are not short-changed," he advised.

The pressure to preserve the Old Age Assistance program at all costs will be overwhelming. The director of the State Department of Social Welfare of California, in an official report to the governor in 1957, noted that in seven years the proportion of all the state's aged receiving Old Age Assistance had dropped from 30 to 23 per cent while the proportion getting social security benefits had climbed from 20 to more than 50 per cent. We are under no obligation to agree, however, with his conclusion that "there is good reason to believe that the need for Old Age Assistance will continue for many years, if not indefinitely." Should society maintain the giant administrative machinery of public assistance when its payment programs dwindle to minor cash totals? When that day comes, it may be wise to consider alternatives with great care. But must we sit back and wait, doing nothing to improve local welfare department staffs and programs in the meantime?

The problem of noting, on the one hand, a partially institutionalized welfare pattern and of indicating, on the other, that still another may be "emerging" is a great one. Effective pressure groups make forecasting difficult. Moreover, new financial realities in the voluntary welfare field may emerge at any time. These two eventualities often render future predictions unprofitable. Government has shown that it has the power to tax the individual to support the several aspects of government's share of the welfare pattern. It remains to be seen if voluntary welfare can meet its own financial needs. If it cannot, the welfare "table" may emerge in coming years with three, or even two, legs. A new financial dedication by the churches, as they taper off on church building programs in suburbs or cut back on activities overseas, would make a difference. But with poorly financed voluntary organizations supported by contributions, and perhaps with grudging personal charity, what would be left except public aid and social insurance—institutionalized and not deriving directly from the individual heart? Special veterans benefits will live on, it can easily be predicted. The pressure from beneficiaries is overwhelming. Care for the veteran, it may also be remembered, is related in several ways to recruiting and retainment programs on which the national defense depends.

The salvation of voluntary welfare lies with its friends. The future of public-aid programs lies in their continued acceptance by a public increasingly burdened by social-security taxes. By 1969, the year when social security taxes will reach 9 per cent from whatever base amount may then be established, the public may have come to think that the social welfare table need have only the one giant leg of social insurance; the charitable impulse may be crushed by taxation and government services, especially if another 3 per cent should be placed on the social-security tax to finance national health insurance in one form or another. Will individual charity, the financing of voluntary organizations, and even public-aid programs survive in the face of a social-insurance tax of 12 per cent? What will happen to the voluntary agencies which, in the 1950's, were already confronted with a hand-to-mouth existence as irresponsible critics begrudged them the small percentages of administrative overhead needed to solicit annual contributions?

Armed with statistics on the gross national product, some social-work experts will continue to say that the public can afford the costs of almost any conceivable government welfare program. Perhaps so. But only heavy borrowing made possible the financing of major war expenditures. The money did not come from placing the whole load on the taxpayers of the day, and it has not been paid back. If the public is to be forced by overseas threats to finance the total security of society, will it voluntarily and cheerfully continue to finance at the same time a multitude of voluntary welfare programs? Time will tell.

Until the "international situation" and the "economic situation" can be predicted with total assurance (and this is hardly likely), the nature of the future welfare pattern must remain in doubt. Meanwhile, it seems reasonable to assume that the American pattern in financing social welfare activities will remain to some extent an amalgam of the several major programs, government and voluntary, that the public has come to accept through the years of our national history.

CHAPTER IV

Sentimentality + Practicality = Motive?

Why do they give, of time, of money, of self?
Is it to guarantee perpetuation of person
Through time, and space, and eternity?

Some say (one hates to tell it, but)
Some say, "They give to gain reward
Immediately, if not sooner."

Surely one can find within the distant and
Subtle reaches of the human spirit better
Motives than this weak and selfish thing.

Service to God; service to man. Only then
Service to self. This is, above all,
The innermost heart of voluntary welfare.

VOLUNTARY WELFARE has a heart. Many an enthusiast has said so. Many persons have gone on to charge that government welfare, replete with what is scathingly called "bureaucracy," does not have a heart. Do these propositions have universal validity? Will they pass muster on all occasions and in all instances? They will not.

Voluntary welfare workers, either salaried or unpaid, can be chilly, businesslike, and or even frighteningly automatic on occasions. Government welfare agencies, moreover, are now staffed with thousands of persons who by no stretch of the imagination can be labeled by critics "bureaucrats of social welfare." Receipt of a county salary check need not indicate that a social worker may prove more impatient than she would be in a private agency, although high caseloads might enhance such a trait. To volunteer one's services to a retarded children's nursery school does not guarantee that the volunteer will be effective, much less self-effacing. Those who do social work for pay cannot be separated arbitrarily from those who choose to work without salary—much as one separates sheep and goats! The fact remains, however, that the halo of humanitarianism is often conceptualized over the head of the volunteer, something the salaried social worker has trouble obtaining from a materialistic world much too likely to say, "He gets paid for it, doesn't he?"

The motives of those who serve the voluntary welfare field in their spare time are seldom questioned, seldom analyzed. And only the fund-raiser normally shows much interest in the contributor's motives and point of view. Why do men and women give their time and money to benefit others? The citizen is not sure, but maybe he would like to give it a moment's thought.

Most thoughtful Christians know some of the famous words of Jesus which insist that human beings perform charitable acts. "It is more blessed to give than to receive," he said. "Sell all that thou hast, and distribute unto the poor, and thou shalt have treasure in heaven," he urged. A treasure laid up in heaven would not fail the giver, especially if he gave to those he despised, gave a high percentage of what he had while still alive, and took pains to avoid making the source of the gift known. To such forthright sentiments in the New Testament can be traced many of the notable philanthropic activities of good Christians. A Methodist church bulletin offers this anonymous quotation for the consideration of the charitable:

> Who would have guessed that my money is really another pair of feet to walk today where Christ would walk if he were still a man on earth? Or what is my money but another pair of hands to heal and feed and bless the desperate families of earth? What is my money but my prayer of intercession suddenly crossing time and space to help answer its own petition in one swift unselfish gesture? What is my money but my Other Self—either hard and cold and metallic, like cash in a cashbox, or warm and exciting and compassionate—tenderness in action! It is my Christian life.

Jews in the modern world, denying the divinity of Jesus, have generally accorded him the status of a prophet, and his teachings have had an effect on them. But Jewish philanthropy, of which there has been so much, has its own wellsprings. These are lofty in themselves. The idea of the tithe (tenth) is an Old Testament idea, and among the orthodox in the faith it has remained a potent reminder of charitable duties to be performed. "He that giveth unto the poor shall not lack; but he that hideth his eyes shall have many a curse."

Late in the twelfth century Rabbi Moses ben Maimon (1135–1204), generally known as Maimonides, aided the perplexed among his people by recording in *Mishneh Torah* his deepest thoughts on charitable giving. "There are eight degrees in the giving of charity, one higher than the other," he began. "The highest degree, than which there is nothing higher, is to take hold of a Jew who has been crushed and to give him a gift or a loan, or to enter into partnership with him, or to find work for him, and thus to put him on his feet so that he will not be dependent on his fellow-men." Seven other degrees in charitable giving follow in descending order:

> Lower in degree to this is the one who gives charity to the poor, but does not know to whom he gives it, nor does the poor man know from whom he receives it. . . .
> Lower in degree to this is when the giver knows to whom he gives, but the poor does not know from whom he receives. An example of this is the great scholars who used to go about in secret and leave their money at the door of the poor. This is proper practice, particularly meritorious when the officers in charge of charity are not administering properly.
> Lower in degree to this is when the poor knows from whom he receives but the giver does not know to whom he gives. An example of this is the great scholars who used to tie up their money in [a corner of] their cloaks and throw them back over their shoulders. The poor would then come and take it without being put to shame.
> Lower in degree to this is when one gives even before he is asked.
> Lower in degree to this is when one gives after he has been asked.
> Lower in degree to this is when one gives less than he should but graciously.
> Lower in degree to this is when one gives grudgingly.

The highly regarded propounder of these thoughtful words has had his name attached to Jewish hospitals, homes, and other philanthropic enterprises. It may be presumed that, in addition to the wisdom in the books of the Prophets, the spirit of selfless giving and service to one's fellow man which Maimonides proclaimed motivates the performance of the day's tasks in most of the Jewish welfare agencies of the world.

Each Protestant denomination has found in its own creed, early leadership, and history, special encouragement to engage in social welfare work. The social creed of the Methodist church is founded on the labors of John Wesley, ministering to the physical, intellectual, and social needs of the people of his day. Lutheran spokesmen believe that their welfare activity is "faith active in love, sensitive to the Holy Spirit, and responsive to human need." A commission of the Society of Friends, a religious organization widely known for its work among all suffering people regardless of national identity, says,

> Friends of the Five Years Meeting have not yet developed any striking testimony on the social and economic order. They have been inclined to accept the prevailing economic and political pattern in which they lived while endeavoring to promote justice, to ameliorate harsh conditions, to cultivate the middle class personal virtues, and to be sensitive to the requirements of Christian love in business and in the duties of citizenship.

The Congregational Christian Service Committee announced in 1955 in the name of the church that

> The love of Christ constrains us when we see children of the Most High hungry and naked, sick or in any kind of imprisonment. To make that love effective, ministries of compassion have been set up that enable those members of the Body of Christ who are relatively strong to bear some of the burdens of the weak.

Professor Victor Obenhaus of the Chicago Theological Seminary has pointed out that an important function undertaken by the Congregational church is helping servants of the state understand

83

"the meaning of their stewardship of God's order as entrusted to them." Other groups no doubt have felt similar responsibilities.

As Protestant churches looked at government social welfare in the 1950's, however, they found full unity hard to achieve. Judging from their orderly statements in *Churches and Social Welfare*, Vol. I, *The Activating Concern*, a small book edited by E. Theodore Bachman, they felt, for the most part, that they had to accept the fact of major programs of government in social welfare. Yet they wanted to make it clear to themselves as well as to others that religious organizations have something special to add. Differences of substance and degree separated many churchmen. Consider the following judgments on the matter of church, state, and social welfare. Each is the pronouncement of an official denominational commission that spoke out in 1955.

The Service Commission of the Church of the Brethren said that "the church must remain true to its own mission and heritage, and never allow itself to become the tool of government or of some secular purpose." The Presbyterian Church, U.S.A., took this stand: "First, not to accept any subsidies from public funds. Second, to stimulate and assist the development of public or private agencies to meet common health, educational, and welfare needs." Services that should be clearly recognized to be a public responsibility ought to be transferred to government or private support wherever possible, unless some "plus value" of religious service might be involved.

A Lutheran commission representing nearly three million church members decided, however, that

> Governmental agencies are looked upon by Lutherans as partners. . . . In a relationship of mutual respect and cooperation between church and state, Lutherans count on governmental agencies to carry out the responsibilities for the establishment of minimum standards for the protection and promotion of well-being among the people. . . . Lutheran agencies, for the most part, accept the theory that government has the responsibility to purchase services for persons otherwise unable to do so. . . .

84

The door, in short, was left ajar. Reverend Almon R. Pepper, director of the Department of Christian Social Relations of the Protestant Episcopal Church, wrote on behalf of that denomination:

> Today, as a matter of principle and practicality, an increasing number of churchmen accept the increased assumption of responsibility being taken by tax-supported agencies. They see less reason for the church as such to organize or support similar services for the general welfare, but do recognize that certain skills and insights are of value in all levels of social and economic circumstances.

Have the Protestant churches abandoned voluntary welfare? The apparent defeatism implicit in some of the words just quoted does not stem from convictions of long standing, in my opinion. It is a rationalization of the all too-evident failure of the Protestant churches to raise from their own membership the large sums of money needed to make government expansion in welfare—past, present, and future—unnecessary.

Since a great many charitable deeds have somewhere behind them a religious motivation deriving from lofty sentiments, the role of religion in the social-welfare field remains vitally important. Yet some church groups and leading individuals in them often seem perfectly content to "let the state do it." They find it all too easy to sit by and let the religiously oriented but nondenominational YMCA, YWCA, Salvation Army, Volunteers of America, and Goodwill Industries work in the general name of Protestantism. Not so the Jews, the Catholics, the Latter-day Saints (Mormons), and certain other denominations.

The Catholic Church acts through the National Conference of Catholic Charities (community organization work), the National Catholic Welfare Conference (National Council of Catholic Women, National Council of Catholic Men), the National Catholic Rural Life Conference, the Society of St. Vincent de Paul, and other groups. Six Catholic schools of social work train workers for Catholic welfare agencies. A city with a heavy Catholic population like San Francisco, Boston, or Philadelphia may have as many as two dozen or more Catholic welfare agencies.

Catholic charity has deep roots. St. Vincent de Paul (1576–1660) established in 1617 the "Ladies of Charity," women who visited the poor in their homes in compliance with his judgment that "to send money is good, but we have not really begun to serve the poor till we visit them." Men were similarly organized. In 1633 he organized the Sisters of Charity, recruited for the most part from country girls. Two hundred years later, in Paris, the Society of St. Vincent de Paul was founded in his honor, and it has been extraordinarily active ever since.

Protestants seem vaguely aware that some of this Catholic activity is being carried on, often directly parallel to tax-supported agencies created for somewhat the same purposes, but the leaders of many Protestant denominations nurture the illusion that they are doing much the same thing. This is very doubtful. Many non-church members help support Protestant church institutions through community chest donations and legacies. Fees, as will be seen, are the financial backbone of church-related hospitals and old-age homes.

After this chapter was in final form I came across the concurring judgment of two researchers whose work was sponsored by the National Council of Churches. They had just interviewed a number of executive directors of Protestant church-related welfare agencies. "There is a recurrent theme of complaint, even bitterness, running through the interviews," they wrote. "The complaint is that the churches which are so ready to claim credit for sponsoring and initiating welfare programs are notably reluctant to enlarge their direct financial support, or even to solicit such support energetically from lay church people." They concluded on an even less enthusiastic note:

> Roman Catholics and Jews are well organized for welfare work among their own groups, both in the definition of their clientele and the soliciting of support. Protestantism, in contrast, seems to be in a state of utter confusion. . . . there is a growing suspicion that large blocks of Protestants may be losing their habits of stewardship in relation to private phi-

lanthropy. . . . In some cities the weakness of organized Protestant work has become glaringly evident.

I concur fully, having examined scores of financial statements by Protestant church-related institutions and agencies. Often the percentage of financing by the parent church body through congregational giving was as low as 6 to 12 per cent of the whole. Still, the denominational name was on the door. In fifty-one cities with Protestant councils of churches in 1956, eleven councils had to obtain community chest assistance for their work, and in four cases this financial aid came to more than three-fourths of the council's operating budgets. Some might say that if churches cannot support their own councils without outside help, they have indeed reached bottom. Possibly an answer is that, as in the case of Hill-Burton funds, community chest money seemed easy to get. Catholic and Jewish federations of agencies were getting it, so the Protestants stepped forward. That, to gain eligibility for funds, they submitted to some outside control of their range of activities as councils is true, at least in some, and possibly all, cases.

The financing of Protestant welfare agencies was studied intensively in 1954. Of 2,783 Protestant church-related welfare agencies and institutions, 986 replied to this National Council of Churches survey. The results were published in Horace R. Cayton and S. M. Nishi, *Churches and Social Welfare*, Vol. II, *The Changing Scene* (1955). Strangely, only 66 per cent of the agencies replying received "significant financial support from religious sources." Of all 986 replying agencies, 22 per cent got more than half, 19 per cent obtained less than half, while the rest received virtually none.

Although the total operating income of all the 986 Protestant institutions and agencies reached $262,782,000 annually (a sizable total), this was only a little more than federal and state expenditures for the school lunch program that year. And it included $179,000,000 in hospital income, 96 per cent of which was fees, as well as the $20,000,000 merchandising budget of Christian but non-denominational Goodwill Industries.

The contributed funds of 934 of the Protestant agencies and

institutions came to $58,000,000, only $15,200,000 of which was from religious sources. (The rest: chests $5,100,000, government $1,200,000, individuals $14,400,000, other $25,000,000.) While these figures could be projected to cover all 2,783 Protestant church-related organizations engaged in social welfare by multiplying them by about three, no one knows whether the resulting figures would have any validity. The record of church support is not overly inspiring in any case. All who are concerned might note the sober reminder by the board of directors of the Methodist operated Fred Finch Children's Home (Oakland, California) in one of its annual reports:

> The significant business of the care of other people's disturbed children demands every resource of the best skill it is possible to secure and give. The consecrated Christian love which is the plus offering of the Church is no substitute for the understood and accepted standards of social welfare technique in child care. The day of untrained, underpaid, well-meaning services in child care is in the past—and should be. We are using and planning more extensive use of competent volunteer workers in those places of program where that is possible.
>
> Inadequate finances for operating program continue to seriously limit employment of social service and other needed staff for case work within the group and extension of foster boarding home program so seriously needed. A sense of responsible concern to make the Conference Children's Home a planned part of each church program is needed.

While 257 churches in that conference had given in one year an average of $81.12 each, 86 others had given nothing. Eighteen churches had given $5.00 each, an amount which the Home declared on another occasion would buy one bedspread for a contemplated new wing.

Formalized agency social welfare is not the whole picture of religious work in this field. Protestant ministers often act as part-time "social welfare workers" during the week days, engaging in counseling and guidance, strictly amateur psychiatric practices, and what amounts to religion-centered casework. Surveys of the extent of "social work" in the nation might well take account of this social-welfare work by the Protestant ministry. The confessional of the priests is one of the many places where the black-robed leaders of the Roman Catholic faith concern themselves with the spiritual and temporal well-being of individuals.

The ministry has long performed this vital role, which considerably antedates the casework and other procedures of the social workers. In recent years, it is said, theological schools have taken official notice that their graduates are being forced by the necessities of modern life to become practitioners of social work. A small amount of appropriate training material is being added to the school curriculum as a consequence. Members of the Latter-day Saints strongly stress mutual aid by one family for another, bearing in mind the urgings of Mormon on faith, hope, and charity. Activated by the tenets of the Law and the Prophets, Jews have for centuries been solicitous for the welfare of members of their faith. Every man his own social worker.

All of this may appear to be a plea for Protestants to check up on their own denominationally controlled social-agency work. They could do worse. Many a Baptist or Methodist orphanage is miserably financed by the denomination that founded it. Read the annual reports of these marginal activities! Presbyterian support for certain urban missions bearing the denominational name is not what it might be. The trouble is that religious denominations have been busy financing the construction of church buildings in newly settled suburban areas. This has been a heavy monetary drain. Welfare agencies in postwar years obtained only the crumbs. Neither the suburban ministries nor their flocks had the time, in many instances, nor the inclination to worry greatly about tired old institutions built years ago and now finally falling apart at the seams.

Another apparent truth is the passive or even antagonistic attitude some ministers and laymen have taken toward chests and united funds which dared to embrace agencies bearing the names of other faiths. "Why should Catholics support the Salvation Army?" some asked. "Why should Protestants give money for Catholic Social Service"? asked others. "We have our own charitable programs," say many. The result of all this?—financial sickness for all of voluntary social welfare.

Charity remains a poor place for religious prejudice. Where "Give Once, the United Way" has won a central financing position in urban areas and where community chests are well established, the luxury of such narrow attitudes as these cannot be indulged in. Years of research in social welfare tended to improve the present writer's knowledge of the virtues in the social-work programs of several religious groups. Coordinating groups would do well to strike back with facts when under attack by religious bigots; they should not ignore, but answer the fulminations of "letter to the editor" writers who try to use denominational antipathies to keep charity drives from reaching their goals.

The heart of voluntary welfare is giving and volunteering. Men and women have long given of both money and time to aid others. This is a fact. It is accepted as such by all Americans, whether they give or not. Yet why do people give? Their complex motives can scarcely be reduced to a few generalizations, but one may try, recognizing that the charitable impulse hardly lends itself to being reduced to a written formula. With these misgivings, then, what are the motives of givers?

Commendable, of course, are the feelings of Christian or Jewish compassion that sweep over men, women, youths, and even children when they sense that other human beings are in need. Altruism, born of a feeling of brotherhood, of oneness with all mankind, is clearly a genuine and persuasive impulse behind the giving of one's money and one's self for the benefit of another. Writing out checks for a charitable agency which is engaged in "good works" has for several generations become an accepted habit for many Americans. Even in foreign lands, Americans practice the generosity which the world has long associated with them. In the *London Times* for January 22, 1958, the British co-ordinator of Anglo-American Community Relations wrote as follows about American servicemen:

> I think it is only fair ... that their very generous actions at Christmas time, which are usually reported only in the local press, should be made known to the public generally.

These men and their families spend much energy, time, good will, and money in making Christmas happier for our aged, sick, and orphans. In the vicinity of every United States Air Force base, many people have good cause to thank them for their great kindness and generosity. American hospitality is a byword, but during Christmas season the effort made to brighten the lives of the orphans, the needy, and the old has been remarkable.

He then went on to quote from a few of the innumerable expressions of thanks received from institutions and individuals. Who can assess the motives of these American soldiers, thousands of miles from home, as they "do good" in a strange land?

Writing in *This Week*, Kathryn Holme, the author of *The Nun's Story*, conceded that charitable contributions often have to be identified for tax or other reasons. But she noted that this was not always the case, and she endorsed the motto, "Do good and disappear." Such selflessness is difficult, she admitted, for "it is as if one has a gaunt and rapacious wolf inside one, hungry for gratitude."

It may be, as some charge and as an avowed Hedonist might insist, that the cheerful giver who begins from nobility of motive, pitying those in distress, gets direct personal benefits from the gift. Nevertheless, the gift should be credited in his favor, even if he aids another for no other reason than his joy at being a secure and safe member of the human race on a planet beset with misery. To get pleasure from seeing happy, healthy children at play in a decent environment may well be a form of selfishness in an individual who helped make the condition possible; if so, the frailty is one widely shared.

Many men and women have contributed time and money regularly to bring wholesome recreation to slum areas and to further equal opportunity among all children. Perhaps such earnest givers may feel a sense of guilt at their own good fortune. But no matter. Society can also overlook the weakness exhibited by persons who give money expressly to avoid having to visit and sympathize directly with the underprivileged. But strange indeed are the scoffers who jest at those who work actively for charitable

91

causes with neither thought nor possibility of material reward. One busy merchant-philanthropist, George A. Scott of San Diego, a department store owner, throws such critics back on their heels with this vigorous remark: "We do not mind being called 'do-gooders' by those who do nothing."

Some charitable giving in the twentieth century has unquestionably come to rest upon motives less than noble. Limitation of giving to solicitors from "pet" charities, when the giver knows that the paid executives will see that public recognition results, is an example. A wise man once wrote that "the charity that hastens to proclaim its good deeds ceases to be charity and is only pride and ostentation." Should not charitable deeds be such as to be called "love in action"? Yet there are much worse ways of courting attention than by this method—which does good in spite of the motives of the giver. Charity may indeed begin at home, with tolerance towards the high climbers of society who do good on their way up, sometimes more interested in the society pages than in the virtue of giving as such. These people at least give of what they have on hand, of both time and money. An old Jewish proverb suggests that there are special virtues in timeliness: "What you give for the cause of charity in health is gold; what you give in sickness is silver; what you give after death is lead."

Must we admit that some Americans have long been giving solely to avoid taxes—or because they realize that the government will end up "paying" a very substantial part of their gift through its tax losses? We cannot be sure of the answer to such touchy questions. The only ones who know the answers are the opportunistic givers themselves—and they are not saying. Yet there are realists who would agree with Harry Graham Balter, a Los Angeles attorney, who, writing on "Taxes and Charity" in a recent issue of a law review, summarized the position thus: "Not only does giving to charity bespeak a generous heart, but for some fortunate taxpayers (in the higher tax brackets) their generosity may actually put money in their pockets. Even for the rest of us less fortunate taxpayers, it may honestly be said that 'it pays to be charitable—almost.'"

A similar estimate was made by Walter H. Wheeler, Jr., the

president of a corporation in Stamford, Connecticut, in *Nation's Business*: "The United States Government, through its income tax legislation, in effect says to corporations and others in the higher tax brackets, 'you take care of the charitable needs of your community and we'll pay half the cost (through income tax deductions) and you can run the show.' " Nevertheless, many givers remain aware that before a percentage of the gift can come out of income tax, the whole amount comes out of income.

Without any doubt some giving is intended to win power or influence for the giver. This may be especially true of some business and professional men who work for giant fund drives, with the presumption that much newspaper publicity will result from press releases prepared by public-relations personnel for the fund-raising group. The ability to attract public attention, after all, has never been evenly distributed among occupations. Those who are given the opportunity, fortuitously, at fund-raising time, can be forgiven for getting their pictures in the papers, cast in the roles of benevolent citizens.

There can be no question that some wealthy persons give large amounts of money with self-serving strings attached. A building must be named for them—or an agency's program must be changed or modified along certain lines. Such changes may not be undesirable. Indeed, the big giver may be quite right in the matter of program, and those nominally in control may have been quite wrong for years. Time has a way of taking care of names, however, even the names of buildings. They are simply names. But philanthropy motivated chiefly by desire to get one's own way is certainly a less nobly conceived kind than history ordinarily accords immortality.

Then there are those who give only when a solicitor "points a gun" at them—they give only under duress. I recall that a fund-raiser for a large research hospital told during an interview—with some relish—how in public meetings he would shame or humiliate wealthy men into giving large sums. One giver would be primed to come to the platform early in the proceedings and donate several thousand dollars. Others on the platform and in the audience would be named individually by the master of ceremonies and asked publicly to match or exceed the exorbitant first gift. Here is shameless fund-raising with a vengeance! Many gifts have been obtained by log-rolling techniques, moreover; that is, "You give to my charity and I'll give to yours." On the volunteering level this becomes "I raised money for your agency, now you work on my drive." This technique is so common in American society that it needs no elaboration. It is, however, a prime reason why old and moribund agencies neither die nor fade away.

There is little doubt that the reasons people give can be grossly oversimplified in such stereotypes. Consider these diverse and very human reasons for gifts made to the New York *Times* Neediest Cases Fund: ten dollars in memory of a second lieutenant in the Marine Corps who was killed in Korea three years earlier; fifteen dollars "in memory of Franklin D. Roosevelt"; one hundred dollars in memory of a wife and the same amount in memory of a mother; and a gift of two dollars was accompanied with this explanation: "To renew our faith in human brotherhood; to kindle new hope in heavy hearts; to participate humbly in this great fund for charity." A gift of ten dollars was "in memory of my friends who died in Bergen Belsen concentration camp while my wife and I have been lucky enough to be liberated."

One of the tendencies in the voluntary welfare field may be the centralization of fund-raising in the hands of too few volunteers. A woman who solicits successfully for one drive is promptly chosen for several others, as soon as the word gets around. By the next year she can hardly call her life her own. She quickly wears out her welcome among personal friends. In time she, too, is worn out. To live for others is a noble thing. But those whose home life is totally disrupted by too much volunteering have forgotten that members of their immediate families are among the "others" for whom they live.

The observers who contend that volunteering money or time, coupled with the desire to give and to serve, should begin at an early age are penetrating in their insights. Some grade schools and many high schools try to ingrain these characteristics in their students. The Junior Red Cross, long active in the schools, has enlisted support from the young people of the nation. Will the youngsters who engage in such social-welfare work be the civic leaders of tomorrow? It seems more than likely that they will be.

Many examples of community service activities by school students are available. In the senior high school of Butler, Pennsylvania, the student council was deeply stirred by an emotional letter received from a Butler alumnus in war-torn Korea. These young people determined on the spur of the moment to "do something" for suffering Korean children. Learning that the GI's in the soldier's own outfit had donated $3,544, the students felt sure they could uncover enough clothing in the town to round out the humanitarian task of the soldiers. Organizing into groups, arranging for publicity, and doing everything themselves, the students gathered $15,000 worth of good used clothing. An adult who watched them at work commented that the students were rewarded by "the satisfaction they received from an enthusiastic community, the personal warmth that came in knowing their contribution would do some real good for some real people, and a sense of elation over the way the student body had accepted the challenge to help others."

Since that first triumph, the young people on the Butler school council have helped a local family, taken part in the Heart, Red Cross, and March of Dimes drives, and collected one thousand toys. Overly enthusiastic on one occasion and beset by bad luck, the students had one major effort backfire on them but in defeat they learned much of value. The outsider can easily surmise that this town in the Keystone State may be able to keep voluntary welfare alive for another generation.

Some people who decline to give make a big issue of the fact that their dollars go to a big organization; they make this an excuse for giving grudgingly if at all. But in the twentieth century the trend towards organization has reached full flower. When Clara Barton built the American Red Cross in the nineteenth century, she sought the establishment of an organization where none had existed before. She knew that, single-handed, she could do little in time of disaster. Her permanent monument is an organization—an instrumentality which, in successive hands, will carry forward her objectives through many generations.

95

Thus realistic Americans have come to accept, though often reluctantly, the long trend towards the organization of welfare work, recognizing that even Andrew Carnegie and John D. Rockefeller, Sr., despite their vast personal resources, found organization essential to the giving of money. Carnegie gave notable expression to his program of organized philanthropy in the statement that "public sentiment will come to be, that the man who dies rich dies disgraced." But the pioneer organization in philanthropy remains the enlightened, well-run Rockefeller Foundation, which is dedicated to the promotion of "the welfare of mankind throughout the world." It has been followed by many others, perhaps chief among them the Ford Foundation, which is now operating in many fields. Similarly, organized effort, permitting millions of relatively small income-receivers to participate in welfare work, much as, singly, the men of great wealth have done, is characteristic of our times. Through a well-organized, well-run unit devoted to welfare programs, the average man may achieve goals scarcely dreamed of in the centuries before our own.

The obvious is not always accepted, however, and never sheerly on its merits. There will always be those who, on personal or other grounds, will dissociate themselves from organized effort. In our time, the number of people who are opposed to organized philanthropy, based upon a broad solicitation, is in a sense puzzling. The position they take is a familiar one: organization as such is an evil; individual good works, on the other hand, are unqualifiedly good. One is reminded of Immanuel Kant's statement that the only unqualifiedly good thing in the world is a good will. But the argument outlined above owes nothing to the systematic thinking of that philosopher. Those in opposition rarely miss an opportunity to criticize the YMCA, the Boy Scouts, and especially the Red Cross. Philanthropies of this magnitude can stand criticism, for they have been standing it for decades, but they cannot stand an expansion of the habit of withholding dollars. Any effort to rebut the arguments of those who oppose organizational work is met with the statement that they find few organizations worthy of their gifts. It is not enough to give to the church, deserving though that institution admittedly is. The simple fact is that well-organized voluntary organizations are now doing work of the utmost importance.

If the truth be known, many a solvent citizen is not really giving at all! A gift of one hundred dollars by all too many of these idle critics is far less than a donation of one dollar by a pensioner. If the critics will not give to a united fund, a chest, or a national health agency, to what organized charitable cause will they give? Perhaps they spend their days seeking out indigent men on street corners to hand them fifty dollars each—not even knowing if such direct charity, in the pattern of a few years ago, duplicates checks mailed out by the county welfare department. And what happens to the recipient when the fifty dollars is gone? Do the direct givers include their name and address? The organizations at least have continuity.

If voluntary welfare is to survive and flourish, the whisperers must be thwarted. The only way to do this is by facing false charges squarely and telling the truth. The Red Cross in particular needs to still the savage criticism by overseas veterans of recent wars, who have devoted themselves too much to yesterday's failings by this entirely human service organization. Yesterday's veteran is today's citizen. From the standpoint of the Red Cross, as the decades move on he is even more important as a parent. Are the sly digs and usually ill-founded rumors of World War II going to gain immortality, untouched by the organization most affected? Nearly bankrupt in cash reserves in the late 1950's, as the result of a succession of disasters occasioned by wind and rain, the Red Cross needed every friend it could get. Somehow it must tap the non-giver. Participation in 842 united funds in 1956 (compared with 641 a year earlier) is, interestingly enough, a symbol of the weakness of this venerable—but vulnerable—organization in the portwar world. The Red Cross of the 1930's would never have surrendered its basic fund-raising to an outside group; the organization of the 1950's had to, for many reasons; and one was that it had failed to disarm its covert critics. Yet widespread distribution of its 1957 booklet, "Since You Ask Me, Here Are the Facts," would do wonders—if the critics would read it.

Other organizations have their own detractors. Safe in the

97

fold of a united fund, these agencies, too, find it expedient to ignore the existence of critics. The detractors are having a field day because men of good will do not have the facts with which to offer rebuttal.

Sometimes one hears sour commentary on the conduct of volunteers. A point of origin is the formal charity banquet, an annual affair designed to memorialize an agency anniversary. On such an occasion, with dinner at five dollars a plate, often in the most lavish surroundings in town, female volunteers, bedecked in expensive new dresses and furs, comment happily on matters often far removed from the simple charity which brings them together. Fresh from an intimate pre-dinner party attended by a carefully chosen inner circle, a volunteer on the platform reassures fellow volunteers in the audience that by attending half a dozen board meetings a year they are participating in charity at its best. Lady Bountiful is dead? Not on these festive, self-congratulatory occasions. Agency business is not the exclusive purpose of these purely social gatherings, these "victory banquets" where nothing of significance to charity seems, on the surface, to be accomplished.

But here, we need to be reminded, is human nature at work. The small sin of self-congratulation is widespread amongst the race. It is difficult to deny even the most privileged of our fellow beings the right to expand on occasion in self-righteousness. That this sort of affair strengthens the organizational machinery of social welfare is undeniable, and that it will soon disappear is unlikely. The personal expenditures on such occasions might have made a real dent in the 10 per cent deficit of the last fund-raising drive. But diverting them to this purpose suggests a quality of self-denial which is difficult to reconcile with reality. Until man becomes ascetic by nature, the news of hospital auxiliaries will still make the society pages. Due credit will be laid up on earth in pleasant surroundings. I have had an excellent time at some of these charity banquets. As for the pictures and headlines, we may ask how, without newspaper publicity for voluntary welfare activities, could the outsider come to know the stature of those who lend their time and names to agencies and drives? Without these names, active or not, well- or badly-motivated, most large-scale voluntary welfare would simply collapse. The lower income receivers, as a class, are incapable of keeping voluntary social-work organizations alive.

To conclude the matter of volunteering one's time for others, the opinion of the famous Family Service Association of America should be quoted. Why do people step forward to serve?

> ... the wish to be needed, to *count*, to feel now and then not expendable; the human desire to be the determinant in a balanced or hung-fire situation—to tip the scales; the wish to be a part of an identified, purposeful group activity, and one that both takes and gives; the wish to be creative, to build, and to see completion; the wish to be a controlled and disciplined influence toward the well-being of numbers of people; the need of us all to *affirm* life and its meaning in the midst of much that is life-negating in our community life; the need to enlarge our own life to touch the lives of others and be touched by them.

Volunteers attend board meetings and do their share in fund-raising for still other reasons, however. Personal friendship with other board members can be a powerful stimulus. No doubt a few at the top of society have a sense of *noblesse oblige* that will not remain quiescent. Finally, some men and women simply cannot say "No!"

But this hardly explains the long hours put in year after year by the Gray Ladies of the Red Cross. What of the weekly problems of Camp Fire Girl and Girl Scout leaders as they try to instill knowledge and good traits into willful young minds?

Like others, I have often speculated on the matter at hand, for in the United States the idea of "service" is a deeply ingrained trait. Why do most men and women volunteer? The tentative conclusion is this: People give of themselves because, in the final analysis, even when unformulated and unexpressed, work for others makes the volunteer "feel good inside." Vaguely, there is the realization that if *I* do not do these things, they will not be done. And in the very act of their doing, not only man, but God and civilization as concept and stream of reality are being served.

CHAPTER V

Fee-charging as Destructive Force

"Why not make
A business of voluntary welfare,
Charging each and every customer
All the traffic will bear?

"Results! That is what
We want. Results, like
Better buildings, higher pay, and
Tests of the real worth of
Services to the served."

Tempting. Ah, so tempting;
But a force destructive to
The heritage of the centuries, and,
In the last analysis, to
Voluntary welfare.

IN 1957 I ATTENDED three conferences widely separated geographically. These meetings were called by three different groups, dealt with three different subjects, and had three different audiences. Yet there was one theme that arose at all three, stirring up debate and revealing sharply conflicting points of view. The problem— one of the thorny questions in American social welfare—was fee-charging by voluntary welfare agencies.

The pressure for expanding the practice of charging fees to clients for services rendered by voluntary agencies is coming from three groups. The first two are the highly placed businessmen and other persons of power, influence, and wealth in the community, and the salaried executives who guide the destinies of united funds. These articulate people tend to believe that a social-welfare agency should not serve any person who has an immediate relative able to pay for health, welfare, or recreational services. The third group advocating fee-charging is the family-service-agency executive group. These say that charging a troubled person a fee for casework services can help a "patient" or "client" by increasing his self-respect. Agency income will grow, furthermore, and there will result increases in staff, many of whose members will be better paid—and, therefore, more effective in their work. The argument has a ring of persuasiveness about it. Nevertheless, it is short-sighted.

Fee-charging as an idea is not new. One out of four Jewish family-service agencies has been charging fees. While only two member agencies of the Family Service Association of America charged fees in 1941, and only thirty by the close of World War II, the number reached 135 agencies by 1954. There has been no national uniformity on the fee scales or on exemptions. (Some of the family-agency people are unhappy over this partial conversion of their work into a private business—especially since, as social workers, they do not think in conventional business terms.) In 1955, in any case, only about 6 per cent of the income of family-service agencies came from fees.

Clinics have charged small fees on many occasions when it was felt that the person obtaining medical service had the ability to pay in whole or in part. This was particularly easy to do because the patients well understood the expense of medicines and of treatment by highly trained physicians. At the same time they were so much better off than if they had paid in full for their own medical expenses that they did not resent the cost. Adoption agencies have long had the practice of charging as much as several hundred dollars to adoptive parents, who have usually been delighted to pay anything within their financial ability to obtain a young child to enrich their lives. As Clyde Getz, an adoption-agency executive, put it in the *Social Work Yearbook*: "Such fees are in keeping with the principle that [adoption] services should be available to the general public and that, therefore, people who can afford to should and will want to help defray the cost of services rendered."

Other agencies have charged fees. YMCA and YWCA have long practiced the policy of charging locker fees for storing clothes adjacent to swimming pools and gymnasiums. Thirty-seven per cent of their annual income is derived from fees. They have charged solid sums to businessmen who use YMCA facilities during the noon hour (and have given some of these "friends of the Y" de luxe facilities not made available free to the run-of-the-mill kids from the streets). A membership fee has often been charged young men participating in boys' club activities and athletic programs. The national YMCA people have issued various publications supporting fee-charging (at the same time, perhaps by coincidence, noticeably cutting back on earlier religious aspects of the Y program to satisfy denominational critics).

Senior centers may ask token fees of several dollars of the old people who use their recreational facilities, although these charges have been waived readily out of consideration for the difficult economic circumstances of many aged persons. Homemaker service is so expensive by necessity that recipients have often paid substantial fees at the time or later—and no doubt this is the only way to finance such a major service, one that provides the comprehensive and trained "servant" to so few. The Scouts have sought small "membership" contributions from parents of Scouts; nearly 16 per cent of Scout income in urban areas has come from such fees. Camps serving city children in twenty-three cities studied have got 64 per cent of all their income from tuition fees. One expects this, somehow. Recreational community centers and settlement houses received 23 per cent, while clubs for boys and girls obtained only 7 per cent from fee charges in these surveyed cities.

Thus there are ample precedents for fee-charging. While the idea is not new, certain concepts are of recent origin: (1) The concept that fees should be substantial and that they should be universally applied to employed persons—even at low or moderate income jobs. Let the parent "make do" for his own child! But if the struggling parent is reluctant, his children will lose the opportunity to participate. (2) Apparently new also is the belief that a very large part of the over-all agency budget ought to be raised by this method. (3) What is new is forthright justification of fee-charging as democratic and desirable—a replacement for the apologetic approach that it was at best a necessary evil. (4) Very new is the belligerent advocacy of fee-charging by many lay and professional fund-raisers. (5) Especially new is the total disregard of the over-all social and philosophic problems which can, and in my view will, attend final victory in the fight for income being waged by the fee-schedule people. The clouds on the horizon are large and a hurricane is in the offing.

Especially affected will be the Scouting movements. In Kansas City in 1956, after several years of effort, those who controlled the federated fund were able to persuade many parents of Boy Scouts to pay an aggregate of 20 per cent of the total Scout budget. This was raised in the form of five- to ten-dollar payments in the form of outright "membership" donations for fees. The method was a compound of persuasive mailing and some pressure tactics, but it was not put over without considerable opposition. But no dent could be made on the Girl Scouts or Camp Fire Girls, probably because these organizations rested in the hands of women whose national organizations have abhorred collection of more than "token" fees.

The president of the Kansas City Community Chest told an audience in 1957 that with voluntary agencies' professing to have ever larger needs for funds, the federated fund-raisers were distinctly of the opinion that these higher amounts could not be raised from givers in the community. The dollar ceiling had been reached. To the speaker and his fellows this made fees the logical solution to the now insuperable problem of making annual increases in total voluntary social-welfare budgets. A businessman from San Diego who commented on the speech called the fee idea a "bright new frontier." The audience of professional fund-raisers and a few volunteers applauded all of this with some enthusiasm. (A handful of agency social workers shuddered quietly, possibly because they had heard of the National Social Welfare Assembly's opposition to the idea of high registration fees or membership dues in the Scouting movements.) A speaker from a Santa Clara County, California, family-service agency had related to an earlier meeting of some of these same fund-raisers how his agency had greatly increased fee scales for those able to pay; he had urged that this practice become universal. Thus the brainwashing of social workers on the whole matter has steadily increased.

There is no end to the mischief which expanded fee-charging would create if it should become general. It seems so easy to say, "All parents with the ability to pay are to give the Scouts ten dollars for each child registered." For a brief period the system could be made to work in such a way as to give the illusion that all was well. Perhaps a fifth or even a quarter of the parents would pay without noticeable protest the first year, and the percentage could no doubt be increased slightly the second year. Soon, however, the new system would begin to show structural weaknesses. The crux of the matter is "ability to pay."

It is the concept of "need" that has caused so much overhead for the administrators of public assistance. This concept necessitates setting up criteria so that there will be agreement on who is a needy person and what constitutes a needy family; this has already become necessary in public aid programs. It will be equally necessary in voluntary welfare. Nothing else would be fair to those who pay. The next step will be to determine whether or not there is in fact any ability to pay. This means investigations. These mean staffs. Result: more overhead.

If voluntary welfare is deliberately setting out to make enemies for itself (and trying to augment government programs at its own expense), no quicker way can be found than to have a new group of paid or unpaid persons investigating families in "our town" in order to determine "ability to pay." The sequence necessitating investigations is clear: (1) Not all can be made to pay. (2) Since only those able to pay will be expected to pay, the next step is (3) to determine which ones can pay and which ones cannot. Unless this determination is made there will be extremely bad feeling arising in some neighborhoods as the word spreads that certain reasonably well-to-do families in the community are not paying their ten dollars to the Scouts while others with far smaller financial resources pay regularly without audible protest. Inequalities cannot be kept secret.

What is implied in the new fee-charging trend goes considerably beyond anything contemplated in the 1940's, or even the 1950's. Some fund-raisers have in mind, as a preliminary goal, across-the-board membership fees of ten dollars per youth in the Scouting movements. The fee-chargers will next encourage, if they are consistent, the charging of fees by Travelers' Aid booths. The weary traveler will no doubt pay or tip ten cents for directions to the right bus, twenty-five cents for instructions on how to get to a distant part of town, and fifty cents for written information on where to get lodgings for the night; a dollar will possibly be paid when several telephone calls are required. This is the logical outgrowth of the fee-charging philosophy. How else can fee-charging be generalized and made fair between agencies? Soon the Red Cross will have to charge ten dollars to teach a boy to swim; ten dollars might also be deducted from a serviceman's pay when he uses the Red Cross to investigate his prospects of getting a leave to come home to be with his dying father. Catholic Social Service will be expected to have a cashier at the front door to pick up five or ten dollars from each father and mother who enter in an effort to avoid breaking up their home. Salvation Army will struggle mightily to get eventual reimbursement for costs of housing an unmarried mother. Will very large agencies hire their own bill-collectors or use the same facilities businesses do?

Once again, ability to pay is to be the criterion. First an agency will inquire pointedly and then make a more or less formal investigation to determine whether the family has any hidden resources. In some cases there will be close financial inquiries. Will the word of a family spokesman be good enough? Soon there will arise the concept of "need," and this will have to be formalized in the dollars and cents of real and personal property ownership. Before too long, there could exist *both* voluntary and public welfare investigating staffs. What punishment will be devised for untruths?

All this is no dream. Already the fee-chargers have a yardstick, a 1957 publication by the Community Council of Greater New York called *How to Measure Ability to Pay for Social and Health Services*. Here we find a neat scale:

If number of persons in family is:						
1	2	3	4	5	6–7	8

Then no fee payment is to be charged if weekly income is below:						
$50	$70	$80	$90	$95	$110	$130

But this does not end the task of the bureaucrats, for "Adjustments are to be made for certain family compositions and special needs, such as heavy medical debts, cost of child care, etc."

Will certain terms commonly heard in the public-welfare field soon have equivalents in the voluntary arena as fees take firm root? The fee-charging advocates will find it necessary to develop a "relative's responsibility" custom for voluntary welfare. Will a twenty-two-year-old son of a fairly rich person be given free casework just because the parent refuses to recognize any financial obligation? Probably. But is this fair to the parents who do pay?

At the very outset the fee-chargers have stated that ability to pay is to be the measuring stick. Soon they will (of necessity) be forced to convert from this stage to the next stage. This will have to be almost universal, nine-cases-out-of-ten payment of fees, for a loose and liberal application of the "ability to pay" measuring stick is not going to satisfy anybody. To obtain general payment from those who use voluntary agencies is likely to require a certain amount of duress. This suasion will be exerted directly on the recipient and [or] his parents and relatives by the agencies. They will be acting under instructions from the fund-raisers, who are saying, "Raise money by fees or else!" Where did voluntary welfare go?

Leaders among the fee-charging advocates, undoubtedly well-motivated and sincere in their evaluation of financial needs of voluntary agencies, still seem to me to be serious threats to the survival of voluntary welfare in the United States. Indeed, thinking of a standardized Scouting membership fee of substantial proportions as an example (ten dollars per boy, or more), this movement could be nicknamed "The Ten-dollar Sellout of Voluntary Welfare," unpleasant though this may sound. One hates to put it so bluntly, but the reality, if it comes, will be worse than the description.

An advocate of fee-charging, who laid his case on the line to a de luxe audience of united fund, chest, and council professionals in the West in 1957, rested his side of the story chiefly on the desires of the givers and on immediate solvency of the agencies. In a speech later included in the proceedings *(Proceedings, Com-*

munity Chests, United Funds & Councils, 1957 Western Conference, San Diego, California, 1957), Don R. Armacost, president of a manufacturing concern in Kansas City, said the question is: "What does the giver want us to do? It is his money and he ought to be allowed to write the ticket." What this able speaker and experienced volunteer overlooked, I think, is that very few of the thousands of small givers have been consulted in any way on the matter of fee-charging. Their opinions, as small givers, have not been asked. It is the big givers and the top executives who are writing the fee-charging ticket. And the persons punching and distributing it are the professionals who serve as paid directors of the important united funds and large chests. The Kansas City exponent of fee-charging told his audience:

> The agencies are generally resistant to change. The agency executives are better at being welfare workers than they are salesmen, and they enjoy giving things away more than they do charging for them. Those are the factors that make it a slow thing, but we are beginning to get there.
>
> It is a matter that requires constant attention. I would say that this fall our approach will begin to get a little tougher. We find that agencies who can get their money easier from the Community Chest don't care to get it the hard way. They have ignored our request—some of them—they have ignored our request for collection of fees from participants. All of them, as I said to a young lady this morning, all of them think it is a wonderful, wonderful idea for all of the other agencies. They see that it increases the pot, but "for our agency it just won't work."

Earlier in his talk Mr. Armacost quoted verbatim from the fee-policy statement of his chest, which referred to "relatively high family income," "increased demands for services," and "growing costs." Then he said, "it is imperative that each agency, insofar as possible, look to the people it serves as a basic source of income for their operating budgets." But, when questioned from the floor, Mr. Armacost had to admit that there had been no initial success in forcing this new policy on the larger voluntary-welfare organizations—the American National Red Cross, the Girl Scouts, and the big national health agencies. He expressed distinct optimism, nevertheless, that their day to give in to fee-charging would soon come. As he put it extemporaneously:

> [On the Boy Scouts:] They have been irritated with us, yes. For two years straight, they have been irritated with us but they have co-operated.
>
> [Asked from the audience if the Girl Scouts and other youth agencies were charging fees as yet, he replied:] The answer is no, they are not. Just as in the case of many of our agencies, there has been a reluctance to really get serious about collection of fees; but we have constantly reminded them that we expect it. And as I said toward the end of my talk, we think the only answer will be in removal of the [united drive] funds, then the fee will come along.
>
> [On the giant Red Cross:] As yet we have not, and neither has the Red Cross, found an area in which fee charges would apply other than those that they have traditionally had for years. We have not asked the Red Cross to pursue our fee policy in any unusual degree.

If words mean anything, this quotation indicates that the fee-chargers are first picking on the weaker agencies and those they control through dual-board memberships. Agencies that still have the power to raise their own money, if need be, are being left alone—for now.

A good case can be made for some fee-charging, particularly by clinics and thoroughgoing casework agencies. One director of a family-service agency feels that the role of a welfare agency is "to give service to people who cannot afford to pay. If they can afford it, we charge them." Another advocate of fee-charging in family casework agencies finds that "it enables people from a broader segment of society to utilize social services. Certain classes of counseling are of equal value to various groups within society. Furthermore, it is a source of income to agencies." He claims that fees assure the caseworker that the client is "well motivated." The client feels, moreover, that he is not beholden to anyone. (After all, shall we say in passing, he is a paying customer.) Finally, this official sympathizes with the view that a chest exists to help agencies get what they cannot raise themselves. "A lot of social workers disagree with this," he adds candidly, but he says in summary that "wherever a fee can be utilized, it should be."

One may be very doubtful if any generally acceptable case can be made for fee-charging in the Scouting movement or in any character building recreational agency. The Boy Scouts of America have made their grounds for opposition clear. The organization has said in an elaborate document:

> From time to time a question is raised relative to the advisability of having the Boy Scout registration fee increased under conditions where the amount of the increase would . . . [offset] money which is now required from the united fund. . . . The registration fee . . . is basically a nominal fee paid by the boy to the National Council for his membership in the Boy Scouts of America. It is not a contribution . . . . The fee is deliberately kept at a nominal amount so that no boy, by reason of the cost of registration, is denied the privilege and opportunity of being a Scout.

The Scouts have a persuasive case.

It is very easy to urge that persons who come to a family and children's agency for ten separate hour-long interviews regarding their personality adjustment or their marital problems ought to pay something for the privilege; that is, if they are perfectly solvent. To justify fees in this instance is one thing. But the advocates of fee-charging have moved much beyond this point. They seem oblivious to the over-all social implications of expanding the practice *throughout* the voluntary field. Society must take a serious look at these matters. Slight dollar increases in agency financing are by no means all, or even an important part, of the story.

The movement toward fee-charging is compounded of a desire for solvency and the certainty that welfare organizations, to be effective, must be fairly large and of a certain degree of elaboration. In the end, both mean money. The need for assuring it may, indeed, prompt a doctrine of solvency at any price, which is not the surest of all means of guaranteeing the salvation of voluntary welfare in America. The Section on Administering Church Agencies and Institutions of the 1955 Cleveland Conference of the Protestant Churches found itself face-to-face with this eventuality. It said of fee-charging:

"This is not only proper but should be developed as far as possible. It is considered wise to use even legal compulsion to require persons to pay fees if they are financially able to do so."

At first glance, the doctrine here propounded sounds dangerously un-Christian. Actually, it is rooted in two very large services, homes for the aging, which get well over half of their income from life-care contracts and government payments, and hospitals, which obtain 96 per cent of their income from fees. It is not these services, necessarily, which should abandon fee-charging, but others which have no such justification for it.

Behind the ideas propounded at the Cleveland Conference was also the thought, ultimately expressed there, that the Section on Church Services saw no objection to the "purchase of services" by government from church-related agencies, since this is "no violation of the church-state relationship."

What is "voluntary welfare" anyway? It is an organized extension of the private charity of yesteryear—when one person gave money to another person directly or rendered him a personal service. The interposition of agencies and trained staff members between the nobly motivated giver and the desperately needy receiver has not changed this basic concept of voluntary social welfare. But what shall we call this thing if these welfare agencies come to be financed far more than half by sales of their services (for this is what a fee really is) and much less than half by contributions? Will this not convert our voluntary welfare agencies into non-profit businesses which, on the side, still do some free and part-pay charitable work? Businesses! This will mark the end of the road for American charity as an individual impulse and as an organized movement.

What will be the long-range result of fee-charging? A board member of one Girl Scout council assured me that we could be headed for a period of extremely unpleasant personal incidents between the local volunteer Scout leaders and the parents of some girls. We could also be headed for a "first-class" and a "second-class" citizenship among the Scouts. Will they not be divided ever so slightly into those who paid their own freight and those who received the "charity"? This sort of thing cannot be kept secret, let it be repeated, for we are dealing with human nature. In the case of great movements like the Red Cross and others where volunteers predominate, the local records will be well known to housewives who have had very little training in social work; they will not always appreciate the virtue of keeping confidential matters quiet.

Consider the average contributor—or as we prefer to call him at this moment, the "charitable giver." He is, on the average, the person who has been giving five to fifteen dollars annually to the community chest or the united fund. Let us add up his bill. We are about to ask that he pay the Girl Scouts ten dollars for his eight-year-old Brownie and the Boy Scouts ten dollars for his nine-year-old Cub. Will he permit them to join? We will expect him to pay five dollars for each child to the Red Cross each year for several years to teach them both to swim, and there will be another fifteen dollars for the YMCA so that his twelve-year-old boy can play basketball or lift weights. This parent can logically be asked to pay one dollar for literature on the dangers of cancer, and another dollar, perhaps, for pamphlets on the symptoms of heart disease. His X-rays at the mobile unit for tuberculosis will no longer be free if the federated fund-raisers can force local Tuberculosis Associations into their fold. Will our citizen still go to be X-rayed? If none of this happens to our citizen, partly because he is childless and healthy, he may retell with much embellishment the fee-paying complaints of those who do pay. And this brings up another matter.

Autumn arrives. This is the time for the big voluntary welfare campaign—the one big give for charity, the time to give for the needy. Slogans are heard: "Give 'till it hurts." "Give the united way to help your fellow man." "Give them your hand, the one in your pocket." What is the attitude of our fee-charged giver now? His total bill from agencies, as presented in the previous paragraph, came to fifty dollars! Does he give? Nobody knows.

A questioner asked one fee-charging protagonist in 1957 whether a family paying up to fifty dollars in fees to the Scouts, a clinic, and other services would pay its usual six dollars to charity drives. His reply was (and it has been recorded in cold print), "Well, I wish I had a crystal ball." This is hardly a basis for making fundamental changes in American social welfare! Such candor reveals fully that what has been discussed in this chapter has not been tested fully or even studied very much.

One may suspect that the fee-charged citizen will not give and that he will be extremely unpleasant and vocal on the whole subject. He may be belligerent and even nasty. And many people will feel that he has a right to take this attitude. Yet any increase in non-givers will inevitably mean more and higher fees. A very vicious circle. As the Reverend Holly Jarvis of Richland, Washington, put it after discussing the issue with a handful of other small-town residents, " . . . we are embarking on philosophy here that could very well snowball into mass resistance. . . . " How will one be able to talk about voluntary welfare, or charity, when its practitioners come to the point of selling their product on every corner?

Social welfare is not a business, but some well-motivated businessmen are trying to turn it into one. Their thinking, entirely apt in their own field, lacks both insight and applicable logic in welfare. Here is an example of non-profit analogy: "I would say this, that the fee payments that they have made are not contributions to charity. The fee payments that they have made have been exactly the same as if they had a grocery store where they could go and buy groceries at cost. They have gone to our agencies and obtained services at cost, at agency cost, and we have asked them to pay only those costs, no profit."

To the unthinking businessman, it will be enough if voluntary welfare is nonprofit. He is apparently not much concerned over whether or not it is financed by contributions made from the heart. To make voluntary welfare agencies efficient and solvent is one thing. To make them into nonprofit hardware or clothing stores is something else again.

It is my considered judgment that the advocates of heavy

and universal fee-charging of those with the ability to pay are turning out the lights on voluntary social welfare as it has been known in the United States. And charity in action has been one of the greatest glories of the American way of life.

The ardent fee-chargers are unwittingly guaranteeing that the voting public will insist that government take over most of the voluntary welfare field within our own lifetime. This concept is hard to believe? Consider for a moment.

Will a middle-class family with an income of $4,500 be eager to preserve the free voluntary nature of the Camp Fire Girls if it is costing them ten dollars a year (or perhaps even more, depending on the number of children in the family)? What price tag does the freedom and independence of an organization wear? The first thing that many families are likely to say is, "Why not let the government finance the Scouts? Then they will be paid for by taxes that we all pay. And my share will be very small, maybe only twenty-five cents on my property tax bill!" Renters may feel that having the county do it guarantees them something for nothing. Some will want the costs neatly scaled through financing from income or sales tax receipts more or less in accordance with ability to pay. The fee-charged parent will know perfectly well that if the government runs the Boy Scouts it will not cost him ten dollars for his family. (He does not yet see the new army of recreation department employees over the horizon.) Corporation taxes will do it! The argument is all too plausible.

Another example. Why should anyone contribute to the Christmas Seal drive if it is going to cost him two dollars for an X-ray? The X-ray has long been the one direct contact between the Tuberculosis Association and a public which knows little of the Tuberculosis group's other activities. Why not turn the whole program over to the county and have several cents a year added to the property tax in the community? After all, it will be reasoned, is this not a small and simple service which government could do as well as a voluntary agency? More and more we will hear the argument that "After all, government in a democracy is representative of all citizens." To this will be added a cry increasingly to be heard: that the private welfare field has come to represent only the desires of a few astute and aggressive leaders at the top level of the local united fund drive. How strange, a fee-charged public will say; these persons do not seem to be selected by the public at large—the way we choose councilmen and supervisors.

Professional social workers in the voluntary field have a social duty to perform if they really believe that voluntary welfare ought to be preserved as a counterweight to government welfare. If they allow voluntary welfare gradually to become just another business, selling its products, they will be more than derelict in their duty; they will betray some of the most important traditions in the history of the nation.

Already, one social work educator, Frances Lomas Feldman, has noted that frequently in health agencies the task of deciding the amount of fees to be paid falls, not on a caseworker, but on "a non-professional admissions worker who is not equipped by training and experience to take into account individual differences." Here is one more unpredictable and unprofessional aspect of contemporary social-work trends for experts to ponder.

Social workers devoted to government welfare, moreover, should remember one thing: aside from the churches, it is voluntary welfare organizations, secular or sectarian, that keep the idea of "giving" alive as a desirable trait in American life. Certainly the public-welfare people spend little or no time writing publicity releases on charitable instincts and persuading people to give of their time and money for others. If the existing organized agitation on this matter dies out for ten or twenty years, as voluntary agencies turn increasingly to pay-as-you-go and curb most fund-raising, there will be a threat of monumental proportions to the survival of at least some government welfare programs. People vote their beliefs, and only a belief in the importance of helping others keeps the tax money coming into the public assistance programs.

The new style fee-setting idea, not yet much debated or well publicized, had not run into much opposition from organized labor by 1960. Labor's first tentative reaction seems to have been, in essence, "Of course, heavy fees for the scouting programs should be charged all those with ability to pay." By this the labor leaders thought they meant that typical union members would not have the defined ability to pay. The "common man" would be ruled exempt, but "the man on the hill" would at last pay his fair share. This was precisely the reaction of one labor leader I interviewed after the close of a speech advocating fee-charging. If labor leaders believe this they are in for a considerable awakening, for without relatively universal fee-charging the idea will not be tolerated—and it will not raise important money. Labor should speak up, for the fee advocates have enlarged their goals. In the late 1950's a drive began to hike tuition charges in public universities to what some regarded as unrealistic levels. While "pay as you go" is a motto of society with the force of habit behind it, there are areas of activity where all society, not just the nearest individual, should pay. The problem, of course, is to determine which area is which.

The fee-chargers came to feel in the 1950's that they had "the givers" behind them—people allegedly determined that recipients should first strip themselves of their worldly goods. By "the givers" was meant the big givers. This seems reasonably clear. Now, the slogan that "what the givers want is what ought to be done" can be an extremely dangerous one. No doubt it evokes applause from large groups in the creamed-chicken luncheon circuit, and one quickly agrees that the idea sounds at first both equalitarian and democratic, but it may have dire consequences. This can be true for the reason that the average giver, generous or not, is poorly informed on modern social welfare. We have professional social workers and highly trained laymen who work in the voluntary field, both of whom are perfectly competent to defend before the general public the vital need for preserving voluntary welfare. Speak up, ladies and gentlemen!

In the coming debate on fee-charging, minor arguments should not be relied upon. Here are my reactions to three of these: (1) It is unlikely, for instance, that the time will ever come when there will be in clinics and family agencies one level of service for those who pay heavily and a lower level for the "charity" cases. Or is it so unlikely? (2) And it seems doubtful that there will ever be delays in giving badly needed service while one's ability to pay is being researched. But this evil could happen. (3) Differences in fee schedules from town to town and from agency to agency might or might not lead to bad feeling. Fee scales can be tricky, and uniformity may be demanded of agencies, so that fees could be forced much lower or much higher than particular agencies may desire.

With courage and determination, all persons who understand the real basis for American charity, who know the importance of keeping the impulse to give well exercised for generations to come, and who understand the true meaning of the religious motives possessed by the founders of many voluntary agencies, ought to fight for their convictions. They ought to say that the pay-your-own-way idea is dynamite. They should state that an extra 10 or 20 per cent of annual gross agency income is not needed badly enough to justify a blind date with the future of both voluntary and government welfare activity. They will say in succinct summary that there is no good reason for preserving voluntary welfare separate from government welfare unless voluntary welfare remains predominantly voluntary.

CHAPTER VI

Bone of Contention

I

There was a man who said, "I'll give
Just once—no more." He's dead now; killed
They say, from giving once—a day,
That is, all the livelong year.

II

There was a man who said, "I'll try
To bring a certain unity to giving
For noble purposes. Surely there must be
Some common meeting ground on which
Fund-raisers can unite." Alas
He found a resting place, poor soul,
Where slings and arrows of outraged
Humanitarians come no more.

III

There was a man who said, "There are
Many benefits in diversity. Why should
We give our independent souls to any of
Totalitarian bent? We'll fight it out
All summer—and all autumn, too." He's gone;
Dead of quota fever and pocketbook starvation.

IV

There was a child who said, "I thought
That people liked to give. And that we need but
Ask, and they would give of what they have."
He's grown, now, and he knows that
Childhood is a time for dreaming dreams.

VOLUNTARY WELFARE, to survive, must be adequately financed.
How shall it be done? The idea of the community chest in an
earlier day was to unify the fund-raising of local agencies—for
that was about all there was at the time, although Red Cross,
YMCA, the Scouts, and Salvation Army, among others, were national in organization and coverage. Yet their fund-raising was
local for the most part, and most were quickly enfolded in the
chest movement. But times changed.

The national health agencies which solicited in competition with the local chests after World War II had special causes, some of them involving the transfer of large sums out of the local community. They strove to get their messages across to the public. The polio group in particular became a recognized fund-raising force, riding high on its identification with a four-term president of the United States and winning favor with its useful goal and astute management. The cancer and heart groups, dedicated to eradication of major diseases and backed by physicians opposed, for the most part, to expansion of government activities in the medical field, sometimes joined the united funds which were born in the 1950's. Yet often they held back. Convinced at length that more dollars could be raised outside federation than in, these groups finally sought to go their own fund-raising ways. This led to heated exchanges of words, and old friendships were shaken by the ensuing battle of the Titans in cities across the nation. Yet the united way ("federation") continued to grow for a time. By the end of the decade, however, unity between local agencies and giant health agencies in fund-raising seemed to be anything but a lifetime marriage. And nothing had been done to solve, "the united way," the problem of capital fund campaigns for building construction. "Give Once" was still a bone of contention.

Consolidation and expansion in twentieth century fund-raising took time. At first a few local agencies banded together to raise funds jointly under the community chest label. Then certain national agencies were brought into these drives, and united funds seemed to be born. The next step was for communities to be banded together into ever larger united fund crusades—an example being the United Bay Area Crusade which covered five California counties with many separate communities. A further step was being considered as the 1960's dawned and had already arrived in some areas, for several states developed state-wide community chests; it was proposed in other states, moreover, that united funds and community chests band together to form even larger drives. For a time it seemed that such super funds might, indeed, be the "wave of the future." Some said that such giant drives could come to rest squarely on the backs of in-plant solicitation and payroll deductions. Others seemed to think that the idea was "nonsense" or "premature." Few if any raised the cry—really quite proper under the circumstances—of "monopoly." The united fund advocates were almost ready to wage the battle for the erasure of city boundaries when a sudden stiffening of resistance by the American Cancer Society, and, to a lesser degree, by the American Heart Association turned the united fund expansion plans into a struggle for mere survival. So it was that at the close of the 1950's, as at their beginning, arguments over "Give Once" were heard across the land. How did the charges and countercharges take shape, and what is the observer to think about it all?

It was argued initially that one drive a year would not be enough to take care of the publicity and advertising that were thought essential to arousing the public to give the dollars needed to keep voluntary welfare alive. Predictions were made that big givers would give a far smaller sum when they were approached only once every twelve months (by large charitable and health groups) rather than more often by the largest causes separately. Experience on this turned out to be variable. Most prepared statistics have been partisan or downright deceptive.

Alarmed opponents of the united funds predicted direly at the outset that these funds could never collect enough money to take care of all the needs of member agencies. The validity of this argument must be tested against each community's experience. In weighing the matter, attention must be given the figure which the agencies felt to be essential, in their initial communications with the fund-raisers—as well as the figure which was ultimately raised in actual fact. Quota figures can seldom be used as a point of departure, since they are set by a strange outer-space method which, at its worst, amounts to conspiracy and, at its best, to guesswork. The Boy Scouts of America said in this connection in 1956, "There are times when [united fund] goals are based on what the community leaders think can be raised, rather than on agency needs. Basic fund philosophy is 'preached' better than it is 'practiced' in these communities."

When the united funds decided to rely heavily on pledges

which would be collected by payroll deductions, complaints were heard that contributing to charity by the installment plan method would fail dismally. Here the record may be variable from area to area and even from plant to plant, but articulate, printed complaints turned out to be few. Readers may want to give some thought to the "Give Your Time" alternative described in the chapter on labor and welfare. Payroll deductions did serve a need, but it must be said that no one really knows the long-range effect of payroll deductions on the charitable instinct. They worked well in some plants.

The unfairness of allocating quotas to national agencies in accordance with their success in community fund-raising up to the time of admission to the united fund has always been stressed heavily by health agencies and the Red Cross. It was one reason why some of these groups held out until the last moment and why others remained aloof. "Perhaps this year our position will be stronger," they said, hopefully. Waiting would get them off on the right financial foot in the united fund, they felt, and there have been real gains achieved at the budget bargaining table through such delays.

Before continuing further with this discussion, I must enter a disclaimer in one respect. In the effort to generalize across the national fund-raising spectrum, it is inevitable that many comments made on united funds, their problems, and the conduct of those who control them will not fit the local pattern in a particular city or town. How could it be otherwise? But I must also say that this is the way the total picture has seemed, in this debate over the organization, operation, and survival of united funds in America.

A persistent charge was the idea that a single agency (an adoption service, for example) might muster more of an emotional appeal for itself in independent fund-raising than any united abstraction could ever do. The united fund people struggled mightily to overcome this emotional handicap, however, and they made real headway in some communities. Their public relations personnel, fresh from the breakfast-food-advertising circuit, explain calmly that it is all a matter of selling words and phrases and of the association of ideas. Many of the united funds came to have the large public relations firms of the nation advising them on a free or part-pay basis, so that the same men who knew how to persuade the public to use shampoo were soon hard at work choosing a picture with the "right" emotional impact and a slogan with "guts" to accompany each annual drive. Tremendous effort went into all this. But some remained skeptical. George V. Christie of the Bank of Arizona, Phoenix, wrote his feelings in a letter to the editor of *Nation's Business* in October, 1955: "A united drive, there is no doubt, is convenient, time saving, and I will even concede that it might produce larger totals but, unless those dollars are accompanied by the milk of human kindness, the relief of unfortunate people becomes a business employing people and ultimately attains the status of a bureaucracy." Here is something to be avoided at all costs if voluntary welfare is to survive over the long term.

The big national agencies have long raised sharply varying amounts of their income from certain of the most highly organized metropolitan, urban, and suburban areas. Rural citizens have contributed little or nothing to certain drives (a fact apparently substantiated for the first time in the tables and maps of the book, *California Social Welfare*). When certain of the health agencies depended heavily on television audiences for their money, did the technique tap the rich or the poor? Downtown or suburbs? Does anyone know? Appraising the united fund method, the national health agencies have looked with alarm on the establishment of semipermanent arithmetical quota systems which would force them into a rigidly prorated fund-raising pattern. With new health agencies being born, however, some of the more timid national groups already in united funds began to see at least some virtue in stabilizing budget patterns and existing levels.

One of the more effective arguments used by opponents of united funds at the outset, as well as in later years, was the certainly valid observation that innumerable local groups continue to raise money despite the existence of a "give once" campaign. High school and college organizations, ladies' auxiliaries, church groups, the town band or orchestra, educational institutions and hospitals, and fraternal bodies go right on raising money from the public as though the united funds had never been born. The Tuberculosis Association, Boys' Town, crippled children's groups, and polio organizations plough the field unscathed by the battle over federation that rages around them. So extensive is fund-raising for worthy (and some unworthy) causes that few communities can arrive at even a close approximation of the total raised. More than 3,000 non-religious affiliated organizations registered in 1957 to raise funds in New York State, for example, even though many major cities there boasted community chests or united funds. The existence of all these groups with hands outstretched certainly wounded the basic argument for the unified drive idea. In other states the same situation obtained, with variations. No doubt the glaring distinction between overstated claims of unity and the plain fact of multiplicity confuses and annoys the contributing public, downtown merchants in particular. Again, multiple appeals greatly reduce the effectiveness of the slogan "Give Once," even though the unified drive relieves very considerably the problem that otherwise could exist.

Probably unjustified is the charge that the united funds would inevitably have heavier fund-raising overhead percentages than any of the other agencies had borne. It was asserted that whole armies of expensive fund-raising specialists would be needed to persuade the public to make one big gift. Ironclad rebuttal of this charge is difficult. To check minutely the fund-raising overhead of the large number of agencies soliciting individually before creation of a united fund is a difficult research job. The overall percentage of the New York State miscellaneous fund-seeking groups was 12.8 per cent. United funds and chests almost invariably beat this, although the addition of certain administrative and fund-raising costs of individual agencies, costs that continue to exist despite the one drive, would raise cost figures somewhat.

United fund partisans have long claimed that to solicit once means less strain on the volunteers who have to go out to the grass roots and ask for the money. Perennial volunteers are in agreement with them, but many volunteers certainly solicit no more than once annually. This matter is discussed elsewhere.

Some of the united fund opponents who have thought in terms of the American competitive system have argued that in competition itself there is strength. They say that it is a positive good for Heart to compete with Cancer in raising funds. And does not Red Cross competition with the Community Chest and the health agencies keep all on their toes? While this argument sounds plausible and may have something to be said for it, one remains skeptical. How can their solicitation appeals be compared? These causes are not one in their emotional appeal. As campaigns they do not operate alike. No doubt any fund-raising organization can profit from watching another. Where the argument breaks down, however, is the fact that united funds study each other. Since their beginnings, the top executives of these funds have examined each other's methods closely. To some extent the powerful men who control the united funds enter into friendly competition, treating the annual drive as if it were a good old American game. The paid professionals recognize that there are better jobs with other funds awaiting the man who can make quotas. Competition in fund-raising does exist, but it is at the intercommunity level. Perhaps this new competition is in some ways more significant and valid than the previous struggle among multitudes of agencies.

A national co-ordinating body (and pressure group) for the united funds musters partisan figures from time to time in an effort to refute all arguments against the principle of federation. Some of the large national health agencies, on the other hand, have issued leaflets and even brief books designed to further anti-united fund arguments. The tone of brochures like "Boy Scouts of America and United Community Funds" (1956) was far more restrained than the small 1948 book *Common Sense About Fund-Raising*, which hinted that united drives were rooted in Fascist philosophy. But bitterness has marked this area of controversy more recently. Meanwhile, few fair-minded or relatively unbiased researchers went into these matters, so that the united-fund spokesmen and the national-health-agency spokesmen obtained the field for themselves. The venerable Commonwealth Club of California spent thousands of dollars to "get the facts" about social welfare in California without fear or favor however, and cities like Indianapolis were thoroughly researched.

To guarantee a united front in the nation, the executive directors of the ten largest united federations have made it a practice to meet annually for a week to plan ways and means of reaching common objectives. Similar national and regional meetings of executives and subordinates became common. Always the publicity releases announced cheerfully that federation was spreading like wildfire and was an irresistible force: Last year federation raised 68 per cent of the chest-united funds joint total; this year it raised 80 per cent; next year it would raise 90! Fifty-eight per cent of Red Cross funds were raised the united way in 1958, it was asserted. As "the word" filtered down to laymen in community fund-raising, local resistance often faded for a time. Here was the bandwagon effect in the hands of masters. The polio people nevertheless stood foursquare for independence. Crippled Children and Tuberculosis were also obstinate in the matter, while Heart and Cancer developed a strong yearning for complete independence matched by that of the National Foundation. Local Cancer chapters, indeed, faced an ultimatum from the national body to leave United Funds by 1960—or else. Nearly all complied.

As a citizen looking over the field of fund-raising in the United States in recent years, I must agree that the trend toward consolidation seemed for a time to be inexorable. Behind unity as an idea have been major economic interests in the greater community—corporations, businesses, and especially manufacturing plants which stood to gain financially by cutting down substantially on time lost by foremen and employees because of multiple in-plant solicitations of funds. The mass communication media were also determined to have unified drives, thinking of valuable donated space and radio and TV time to be salvaged if at least some of the wistful pleas of the virtuous (and not very newsworthy) charitable and health groups could be sidetracked. Men who in large advertising firms devote their lives to swaying the minds of the masses through psychological means helped the unified drives to success. A national organization called the Advertising Council, able to assure or withhold a low-cost, concentrated and co-ordinated campaign in the mass media, was strongly united-fund conscious (but unwilling to freeze out the large and more popular health agencies). A spokesman for the Advertising Council pointed out with pride that the mass media (TV, radio, billboards, magazines, and newspapers) "are enormously effective in moving people to do the things that in turn induce other people to give money or do the other things that need doing."

Modern office machinery became the *sine qua non* of organized fund-raising, and the united funds adopted the card-sorting, filing, and accounting machinery of IBM, Remington-Rand, Burroughs, and the others. As skilled united-fund subordinates became more adept in the use of this machinery, and as the files on individuals and companies grew in size and recorded detail, the undertaking of greater and greater fund-raising programs became possible. The efficient organizers who guided the destinies of the united funds finally reached the point where they believed it would be entirely feasible for a single organization to keep permanent file cards on all of the adult citizens or families of a major industrialized city or even state. Some prepared to do just that.

I was privileged to make a close examination of the files and electronic equipment of the United Foundation of (Detroit). Anyone would be impressed by the smooth efficiency exhibited by the staff headed by a former investment banker who has served as director of finance for this marvel of twentieth-century automation. In an instant, a clerk can produce a card showing what a given physician, banker, attorney, or man of affairs has contributed to the united drive annually. Armed with such data (which the contributor himself has probably forgotten), the solicitor has a considerable advantage over the uninformed position he occupied years ago. It is a simple matter to account for each dollar contributed and to arrive at precise breakdowns of contributions by economic groups. This is one fundamental reason for the outward confidence exhibited by the united-fund professional executives—who seldom seemed deeply ruffled by their remaining opponents—at least, until the Cancer and Heart withdrawal crisis of 1958–60. Machine record-keeping is, after all, twentieth-century institutional practice.

While there had been fewer than two dozen community chests raising money for charitable agencies during World War I, there were several hundred by World War II. While there were no united funds before 1949, there were 1,263 ten years later. These federations raised about two-thirds of the total money contributed to chests and funds in recent years.

The united funds had powerful allies in their struggle towards dominance. One state governor, for example, went so far as to side openly with the united funds against their rivals. Ohio's Senator Frank Lausche, while still governor, urged citizens of his state "not to undertake any appeal or drive which would conflict with or detract from the paramount importance of a successful Community Chest or United Fund drive." The radio broadcast of President Eisenhower on behalf of the united campaigns in 1956 stressed the word *united*, saying that it meant that "many good and useful voluntary health and welfare agencies have teamed up to ask you just once a year for funds, instead of going out on separate and competing campaigns." The President remarked further that such unity "makes a great deal of sense, for man is a united human being." The White House thought the issue to be, in brief, "Are we interested in our fellow man?" To many partisans of firm views the issue is, rather, "Are we raising money by a method that will guarantee during our lives and those of our children's children the survival of a healthy, vigorous, and effective voluntary welfare system?"

One charge particularly disturbs sensitive administrators of united funds. The average citizen, perhaps represented by a spokesman, often asserts that the united fund in the community is putting unwarranted pressure on the small man to give more than he should—or, in any event, more than he cares to. The idea of giving "one day's wages" really bothers a good many sincere working men of good heart, who think that five dollars is not a bad charitable gift for welfare agencies. A certain proportion of these average people already give from twenty-five to one hundred dollars annually to the church of their choice, and some even tithe a full 10 per cent of their annual income for religious purposes. To these persons, the idea of contributing twenty-five dollars to the united fund is financially abhorrent—especially so, if they also contribute ten dollars to the Elks for cerebral-palsied children or fifteen dollars to some special cause. Parents who send their children to a young people's camp operated by their own religious denomination are of mixed loyalties when told that the united fund helps the scouting organizations—even though their own children may be scouts.

While "Give Where You Work" is an admirable slogan for the efficiency minded united fund enthusiasts, the average laboring man often thinks of the place where he works as just that—and no more. It is not his "community." It is a place where he receives salary for services rendered, and it is not a place where giving to take care of the welfare needs of children, youth, and the aged comes naturally. He has trouble thinking of the factory, the mill, or the department store as his community. His immediate neighborhood is much more likely to qualify for that label.

In recent years, the "Give Where You Work" program and the pledging program have been able to raise most of the funds needed for the minimum operation of agencies. Pledging in particular has proved popular and financially rewarding. But the Achilles' heel of federated fund-raising in America—the method whose advocates point to it as "an easier way to a better tomorrow" and claim it as a permanent feature of the landscape—is whether these joint-solicitation methods will survive shifting human loyalty to organized causes.

As fund drives grew larger there was an increasing trend toward leadership by executives representing the largest corporate enterprises in the community. The United States Chamber of Commerce claimed in its magazine *Nation's Business* (September, 1955) that "the Chamber has been primarily responsible for getting United Fund drives under way in Stamford, Connecticut; Seattle; Springfield, Ohio; Winston-Salem; Oklahoma City; Providence, R. I.; Montreal; New Haven; and Waterbury, as well as many other cities." According to an article in *Fortune* magazine, the Pittsburgh United Fund was born in the private office of the president of United States Steel. Large corporations with thousands of employees clearly dictated the creation of that fund, management being intent on internal plant efficiency at the expense of all other factors. Corporate management triumphed.

This development has meant that old families long identified with children's agencies and chests have lost the power which was based on status derived from pioneer residence. One leader holding high national office, Ray R. Eppert of Detroit, has justified the shift in power which has come with federation by saying that "the top attention of top people is required to solve the multiple campaign problem, and the creation of a united fund usually puts the first team into the ball game. Often it enlists the active performance of strong leaders who had not previously participated in federation."

Another leader from the corporation world is Albert J. Nesbitt, president of the national chests, funds, and councils group in 1954 and chairman of the board of the United Fund of Philadelphia. Management knows, he has said, that "if it fails to contribute its full share to the solution of the problems of social welfare, that does not mean that these problems remain unsolved, it simply means that they will be solved by others, possibly in a way management will not like." Management, he thought, "must avail itself of every opportunity to fulfill its responsibility in this field. . . ." Competent management from the business world has been taking over stewardship of the united funds in many instances in which it was not fully responsible for founding them. How has that stewardship been discharged?

In the Philadelphia fund the gross amount raised from 1950 (the year before its formation) to 1954 increased by 20 per cent. It was aided, of course, by the addition of new causes, inflation, and a growing city and economy. Yet corporate management's sense of dedicated responsibility was shown in some peculiar ways. In the first four campaigns, from 1951 to 1954, participating firms dropped from 7,142 to 6,816, while the number and amount of corporate gifts did not increase. The gift of corporations per employee declined from $8.98 to $7.54, and, worst of all, the corporation percentage of the total amount raised by the Philadelphia group dropped by 4.6 per cent. Such figures are not reassuring to the observer.

In many cities, there is a substantial group of citizens who lack full confidence in big finance and big management. The elimination of "chaos and waste," an objective of the new masters, has not won enough new friends to replace the ones who were either lost or became apathetic. This has weakened the very foundation of voluntary-welfare financing "The united fund should be a true community undertaking with people from all walks of life enthusiastically working for it," advocate the Boy Scouts. "Participation should be broad enough to include health and welfare programs, as well as character-building and citizenship-training programs of the community."

If management of large corporations seeks to acquire a virtual monopoly of power in voluntary-welfare agencies via financial control, this will, in the long run, have a profound effect on agency programs. Soon the leaders of big united drives may reach out to abolish old chests and councils, suburban planning bodies, and so-called "useless" agencies and programs. This is the factual present, not just the possible future, in many united fund cities. Big businessmen tend also to supplant old-line agency board members as delegates to budget-setting bodies. The Boy Scouts of America has written that it believes that "federated financing will grow and prosper in proportion to its encouragement of aggressive, strong, and responsible management of agencies by their own boards." Thus "initiative and autonomy" will not be destroyed.

Men like Albert J. Nesbitt of Philadelphia see in united funds a combination of enlightened community service and corporate self-interest. "Even to management that has no rudder other than selfishness," he once said in a speech (later printed as a booklet), "one can make a case that active and intelligent participation in the social welfare problems of the community is an opportunity no smart management should pass up." Corporations, he believes, can realize good employer and public relations with their increased participation in social welfare programs. In fact, "dollars and time spent here may very well build sales faster than the same dollars spent in product advertising." Nevertheless, corporate participation is justified on a spiritual level by this important leader, whose promise is, "Show me a corporation whose leadership is comprised of men with a religious background, and I will show you a management striving to meet its responsibilities in this field."

Internal efficiency has already resulted wherever the organization-minded men have taken over. Salaried fund-raisers have learned much from them. But will there be a piper to be paid? Social work degree holders with long community experience peer into the future and frown with a concern as yet not very well defined. The Community Chest of San Francisco, powerful and venerated in the years since its founding in 1922, is only one of the older groups which have served long, but whose independence was terminated in the name of efficiency. Such shifts of power are normally kept gradual, however, by interlocking directorships between the old chests and the new united funds. A committee composed very largely of oil-company efficiency experts has already urged formally in the San Francisco Bay Area that functions which were once the exclusive prerogative of chests and councils ought properly to be the function of the fund-raising organization. Reaction to this among informed social workers was adverse, of course.

There are grounds for believing that metropolitan united funds are only a way station. The railroad runs on to super funds, organized by whole states. Oregon and Rhode Island have state-wide chests. Other states are thinking about the idea. Writing in *Community*, the chairman of the National Advisory Committee on United Funds, Ray R. Eppert, once noted that state-wide funds had enjoyed what he called "excellent results." And he continued: "I look at a state organization as an instrument which gathers up what would otherwise be 'loose ends' in a voluntary system of giving. It permits the maximum practical federation and stops the included agencies from engaging in a trade war in our communities for the contributor's dollar. The implementation of a state organization requires leadership interest from the large cities." He "strongly" urged his readers to investigate this idea in their communities and states. Whether a state fund could ever provide the "unification without suffocation" called for in 1957 by Benson Ford is a question for those who worry about such large-scale consolidations. Do we need an anti-trust policy in fund-raising?

Sooner or later, agencies located deep in the heart of our

older cities reach the point where they can no longer ignore the poignant reality that the buildings of the past are not adequate for the needs of a new generation. The YMCA buildings erected at the turn of the century scarcely can meet the minimum needs of the 1960's. I have stayed in a dozen tired old YMCA structures in as many cities, with their old steam pipes, battered furniture, damp locker rooms, and bleak lobbies. Badly needing replacement also are many missions and settlement houses, headquarters buildings of youth groups, and a host of similar structures. Most chests and united funds occupy second- or third-rate offices, and these often have nothing to be said in their favor except apparent economy. *Voluntary welfare has the face of a sick man.*

One optimistic enthusiast has written that "all over the country communities are facing up to this problem," but I have strong reservations about the truth of the assertion. It is a fact, however, that during the five years ending in 1956, there were 239 cities that reported on capital fund drives. Of these only 39 were analogous to united funds in that they were "federated capital campaigns." The rest of these cities had individual agency campaigns totaling 1,118. Some of the united drives, like the major one in Indianapolis, were on behalf of hospital construction needs, not those of welfare agencies.

Authorities are by no means agreed on whether or not a united and federated campaign is the best way to raise capital funds. All agree, however, that replacement of major structures cannot be accomplished from funds normally used for maintenance and operation. This necessitates capital-fund drives. But should the agencies band together and seek to meet their needs by joint action? Opinions expressed by executives who bore capital fund-raising responsibilities in the 1950's were sharply variable on whether or not the unified campaigns were worth while. Neither was there full agreement on whether drives for construction money should be handled as part of the regular annual campaign for maintenance and operations contributions. Should small givers in a community be solicited or ignored? Here the authorities on capital drives disagreed in 1956 at 104 to 99.

The paid welfare executives and volunteer leaders in the

nation see eye to eye on one thing: it is necessary to maintain, improve, or replace worn-out voluntary welfare buildings. The public ought to agree with them. As has so often been the case, leadership in facing up to this major problem has come from Detroit, the industrial home of mass production.

Beginning in 1953 and ending in 1956, a Metropolitan Detroit Building Fund campaigned for capital funds for local agencies. These agencies agreed not to campaign separately for five years thereafter. Professional fund-raisers were hired to do the job, which lasted from June, 1955, to May, 1956. Eventually the new group managed to raise about 90 per cent of its $16,500,000 goal. While this figure seems very impressive, it must be realized that the agencies reluctantly scaled down $112,000,000 in original requests to $35,000,000 as a result of detailed probing by an allocations committee, consisting of twenty-two businessmen in seventy meetings. Because of this readjustment, some agencies were criticized as being apathetic toward subsequent campaigning, which seems to have succeeded as well as it did because of the support of corporation and foundation leaders. Since full capital needs were not met, part of the problem of capital funds needs in Detroit was passed on to the United Foundation, Detroit's united fund. As Ernest C. Kanzler of Universal C.I.T. Credit Corporation, chairman of the Fund, put it originally, "We know that the capital fund needs of highly-valued agencies have been neglected for years, and this is seriously hampering their efforts to serve a community that has grown to 2,500,000 persons in the last fifteen years."

The experience of the Metropolitan Detroit Building Fund should be detailed for the benefit of leaders worrying about capital-fund needs in other cities. Here was pioneering. Its allocations committee reported:

> The early months of the corporation's work were devoted to organization and to finding out from other communities about experiments and experiences that might be helpful. It became evident that although there had been some fragmentary efforts, no major metropolitan area had undertaken boldly to study building needs and, in a united effort, to se-

cure funds for this program. The new fund thus found itself
in an uncharted area with a pressing need to lay a course.

The predominantly corporation - management executives
who worked with the building fund drive took a broad view of
their responsibilities. It was their committee, after all. Of the
eighty-seven-member board of directors of the fund, 63 per cent
were officials of corporations, 5 per cent union leaders, 10 per
cent bankers, and 22 per cent were unidentified and miscellaneous (but probably industrially oriented). Only six of the eighty-
seven were women. Leaders of such enterprises were warned in
1956 by Charles Fleetwood of Houston, Texas, then chairman of
the Campaign Leaders Conference (a national body), that laymen who lead fund-raising campaigns must be concerned with
more than money. "We must be first—and always—concerned
with what that money is doing in terms of service and benefits
to our fellow human beings," he declared.

The Detroit leaders announced at the outset of their comprehensive study of capital-fund needs that the projects they were
going to recommend would have "not only a direct effect but also
an indirect effect upon the quality of community services in Detroit." They felt that agencies receiving grants would be better
equipped to provide service in the future. They pointed out that
many agencies had already made "definite commitments about
upgrading their services in accord with the allocations committee's principles." (The outsider must add the thought that the
power to deny can be the power to modify.)

The Detroit leaders decided early in their work that careful
study should precede any fund-raising action. They framed "general principles" to guide their work in deciding which capital-
fund requests would be honored and which would be denied. The
first of those principles rested on two key words: *minimum* and
essential. They approved of and quoted the remark made by John
D. Rockefeller, Sr. to the effect that "there is not enough money
in the world to do welfare work." Still, they were determined to
make their minimum quota high enough to provide the essential
services needed in the community. Applications were accepted

from voluntary (private) agencies, but not government organizations. All agencies had to be located within the area covered by the local united-fund drive. "The total amount approved should represent the minimum required to enable them to operate on an economical and efficient basis." It would be undesirable, they felt, to provide any new buildings which would inevitably add an impractical burden to the community's annual fundraising effort. Furthermore, no funds would be allocated for the construction of facilities which might very well become obsolete or uneconomical in the near future.

The allocations committee was not going to allocate money for buildings where services would be rendered in competition with government, "even though government services might be considered inadequate." Agencies would have to agree to put all of their unrestricted free funds into the fund-pot in order to be eligible. Assets of parent organizations were considered as well as those of local bodies, resulting in difficult judgments in some cases. Finally, the committee courageously agreed that its recommendations should be based on objective consideration of community needs and sound community planning "without reference to the pressures of individual groups or individual organizations."

As laymen have found so often in working on a voluntary basis in the welfare field, the capital-funds allocations committee in Detroit quickly discovered that "a basic problem in the various areas of service is that there has been no clear delineation of responsibility between the governmental agencies and the private agencies, and that citizens understandably are confused about what the governments' jobs are and what the private agencies should be doing." Nevertheless, they struggled forward. The members of the committee had been chosen originally, according to an official document, "because they were corporation and community leaders," and few of them had ever had any connection with specific agencies.

A thoroughgoing discussion of how specific agencies made out in their requests to the Metropolitan Detroit Building Fund would serve no useful purpose here. The total amount finally requested of the new group, as has been stated, was $112,433,148.

This amount was scaled down by the committee to $15,665,950. Study of the figures reveals, however, that the Boy Scouts, Camp Fire Girls, Catholic Youth Organization, and Girl Scouts were put down for amounts reasonably close to what they requested. Hospitals, in general, had to accede to substantial cuts in their requests, or their complete elimination, although this was not always true. Some community centers did very well while others did not. Rehabilitation seems to have interested the committee. So did certain religiously sponsored youth centers, as well as the Salvation Army—which was scheduled for somewhat more than one-third of its nearly $2,000,000 request. The visiting nurses organization was felt to need capital improvements quite badly, but the YMCA was scaled down from its request of $18,600,000 to $1,300,000. The YWCA was reduced from $7,500,000 to less than $1,000,000. Yet these two organizations were permitted some funds to expand into the suburbs.

From this résumé it is easy to see that the power to allocate funds raised from a capital fund-raising drive could be a very heady wine. When the welfare agencies of a community delegate the power to decide on improvement and expansion, they surrender the freedom of action which has been theirs for decades. Granted that an allocations committee made up of businessmen, corporation executives, and other well-meaning amateurs is likely to have some trained social workers available to them for guidance purposes, an unpleasant reality must be recorded: Complete power over the purse strings is being exerted by persons who have never studied social work, been social workers, or even given any concentrated thought to the social-welfare field until their appointment to an allocations committee, an appointment derived from the size of their respective corporations in the economic life of the city. Unless social workers and experienced citizen-volunteers in the community can come up with a better method of financing capital improvements for voluntary agencies, "the Detroit way," with its assets and liabilities, is likely to be the method by which the task is going to be done.

Who is there to say that the lethargy and apathy which have characterized many American cities and towns in this matter is better than the vigorous initiative of the industrial leaders who have made Detroit one of the greatest cities in the United States?

Why are some cities able to raise very large sums of money for charity per capita, while others raise far smaller amounts? Why do campaigns by chests or united funds in one city do remarkably well year after year, while they fail dismally in a near-by city? These are knotty questions. Is it the proportion of educated persons in the city—transitory economic conditions—or such intangibles as "civic pride"? Leadership by volunteers—or creative organizing by the fund-raising staff? Even authorities in the field wish fervently that they knew the answers.

To try to narrow the range for guesswork, one pioneering researcher examined figures from 181 cities which had community-chest campaigns in 1952. Using official figures, which he correlated with census and economic data, Professor C. Arnold Anderson could find no correlation between median levels of schooling, or even of individuals with a high school education, on the one hand, and chest fund-raising performance on the other. Neither the proportion of homes owned nor the proportion of women who were employed showed any association with the success of the chest campaign. "Even expenditure per school pupil (in cities over 25,000) was only slightly correlated with fund collections," he found. Pondering vast differences between chest-campaign successes from city to city, as measured in contributions per family, this scholar observed that "success" in a campaign rests on two things in particular: pledges from every citizen and persuading new families to give. Physical and economic differences between cities he thought to be not particularly important. In summary, he said:

> Organization of the campaign itself by chest executives and lay directors may be the strategic factor. Perhaps . . . the critical condition is the general level of civic pride, community integration, or whatever quality is implied by these widely used terms. Presumably the more "integrated" cities will obtain the more efficient chest executives and will select more capable directors of the annual drive.

He could not forbear pointing out that no fund-raising executive could "whistle out of a void" civic spirit or civic-mindedness where none had previously existed.

These observations are not welcomed by some lay leaders in fund drives, who prefer to think that failure is the fault of the paid executive director of the fund or chest. As has been wisely observed, however, leaders need followers. In a nation not yet free of the distrust of "special interests" and "big business," the forceful and civic-minded corporation-management executives who control our largest united funds ought to be bending over backward to elicit and retain grass-root support. Far too often they make all the key decisions themselves, after which they ask community groups and lesser lights to come to the aid of the cause. Too many "non-producing campaigners" (as G. R. Durham, executive director, Oregon State Chest, calls them) sit happily but inactively in key jobs. Mr. Durham, a highly capable and outspoken veteran of the Salvation Army, has some advice on the disposal of well placed volunteers in chests and funds who notoriously fail to pull their share:

> If at first you don't succeed, fire the guy and try again! . . . Now what happens to a man who does not carry out his responsibility to his employer? He gets fired, pure and simple. No business can long afford a non-producer on the payroll and I say that no Fund or Chest can afford non-producers among the corps, either, and that we should not hesitate to fire a volunteer that fails to produce, that the community expects us to fire him rather than letting him stand there in our way and eventually perhaps reward him even though he hasn't done anything. The man who takes a volunteer job because he wants the prestige should not be surprised when his failure to produce leads the community to fire him and replace him with someone else.

When the money does not appear in a united-fund drive it may be due to faulty daily technique; but it can also be the fault of paid or unpaid personnel handling the appeal. Still it may be the local economy, or something may be wrong with the people in the community. Finally, it can be the general method being used. When goals are not reached, how can one be sure that it is the fault of the "give once" method? Who can say? Few things are more complex than the financing of voluntary welfare.

CHAPTER VII

Voluntary Welfare:
Its New Methods and Masters

Power is a test
Of every man's
True character.

Flowing to the man
Who knows his way
Around, power does not
Rest alone on character.

So it is that those
Who seize and use
Great power may be
Giants or gnats
In the community.

How did they get
Their power? Was it
By consent of all of us
Who give or take or watch?

Able to make the
Dollars rain, and even
Able to make them flow
This way and that, here are
True Masters of the
Voluntary welfare of our day.

Shall we beg that they
Restrain themselves? Or
With our ballots and
Our experts shall we try,
Perhaps in vain, to tame them?

THE GREAT CHANGES in voluntary welfare in the twentieth century, beyond any doubt, have been its centralization, mechanization, and ever increasing subordination to those who are masters of its financing. No longer is the small agency serenely independent as it works for humanitarian causes entirely of its own choosing, financed by its friends. More than most Americans would care to admit, the former motivating spirit of charity and mercy has been replaced by competitive spirit, desire for progress, and obsession with efficiency—all bearing the aspect of being ends in themselves. Economic aid to individuals has been almost entirely depersonalized; the person being helped cannot even be sure that the giver intended that a person with his problem be helped. Such impersonality was increased by the rise of the united funds. These groups came to raise money for scores of agencies. They effectively stepped between the giver and the organization designed to put his gift to work for humanity.

The act of individual charity was increasingly dehydrated by the united fund-raising technique. So much seems clear, regardless of various positive aspects. The contributor often feels little or no thrill as he gives to "the one big cause." On the whole, he has little sense of accomplishment as he signs a pledge form to permit monthly payroll deductions for the united fund. To him it is likely to be almost like a tax—"just another tax"—to be paid to avoid argument with a supervisor, foreman, union representative, or forceful acquaintance. This is a soft spot in "Give Once."

This is not at all the way the united fund people want contributors to feel. Quite the contrary. Strenuous efforts at publicity for agencies, widespread use of photographs and TV, and formal tours of agencies are the substitutes recently worked out for the natural impulses rooted in religion. On the whole, these public-relations devices have not made an emotional impression upon the average person. Whether the instruments of modern public relations could be developed into a substitute for the once close contact between people and their direct satisfaction in knowing they had helped a needy neighbor remained, in the last decade, a puzzle with no solution.

Fund-raisers, in any event, are becoming more expert all the time. They are also developing "businesslike" characteristics to an alarming degree. In Champaign, Illinois, for example, they had the effrontery to set up a "yardstick" for rural giving based on the type of soil in the twenty-eight townships covered by the united fund. Gifts were supposed to vary from three cents per acre under cultivation (for tenant operators) to six cents for owner operators. Charitable attitudes have changed since Illinois was a frontier state producing humanitarians like Abraham Lincoln! Stirring up the charitable impulse has now become a game, complete with rules. Perhaps, say the publicity managers, the citizen can be subconsciously sold a feeling of obligation to give (much as he demonstrably can be sold the habit of purchasing a new brand of soap). The methods being used are nearly identical: radio and TV "spots," billboards and posters, and clever stunts.

A new hope of sophisticated money-raisers is "MR," that is, motivational research. The giver will be sold the idea that by his gift he gains emotional security, reassurance of his own value as an individual, "ego-gratification," a sense of creating something, and a feeling of immortality. Will MR work over the long pull? The fund-raisers wish they knew; meanwhile, they barge ahead. It may be that some motives which impel people to give will prove grossly unwholesome, selfish, and unpleasant—compared with old-fashioned *love*.

One has a right to be skeptical about such "progress." But is this a call to return to the days before the organization of community chests? Not at all. America is already an urbanized and metropolitan nation, organized and patterned, arranged and planned, counted and directed. Employment is typically in factories and businesses of great size. Clearly, Americans are not living the kind of life in their sanitary suburbs that facilitates much contact with the world of pain and strain. We may not be enthusiastic about depersonalized giving, but few of us would have the slightest idea where to begin a new personal routine of person-to-person direct charity. Nor could most people select intelligently from among the hundreds of existing welfare agencies when they happen to feel in the mood to give.

Americans began to seek the Holy Grail of "Give Once" because they felt unable to give more than a very few times. Enthusiastic over a new idea, they went overboard. Some were annoyed by multiple solicitations. To those who use the annoyance argument as a reason for pouring all charitable and health groups into one bottle, Basil O'Connor, a veteran manager of large independent organizations, had this to say to united-fund protagonists in 1959:

> I think today that we need not less of these organizations, as I know you feel, but more of them, because I have little patience with the argument about annoyance. I have been annoyed for years, with all due respect to my good friends in the insurance business, by insurance agents. I have been annoyed for years by my good friends in the magazine business and I still am. I have been annoyed by all those things and a multitude of others. But I don't think we should let annoyance influence our judgment with respect to something that is of fundamental value.

Surely most people, reasonably intelligent or not, are perfectly capable of deciding whether they want to support Heart, Cancer, Red Cross, local chest agencies as a bloc, CARE, or other heavily publicized groups. Many people have clear preferences; and, cumulatively, these have meaning. They want to scale their giving among these groups, and this is important in over-all results. To arrange things so that people delegate the entire allocations problem to others—friends or well meaning strangers—is to destroy an important part of the philanthropic process. But there would be no alternative in cities where the united fund might sweep all before it, clasping all the large charitable and health causes to its bosom. There were such cities at the beginning of the 1960's, and they posed a problem for all who were concerned primarily with preserving individual freedom.

In united-fund cities, is it possible to determine how the public really wants to divide (that is, to budget) the contributed dollar among member agencies? Could this be done by modern public-opinion-sampling techniques? If so, would such a democratic approach be desirable? These questions are not easily resolved.

To date, the vital decision in percentage allocation has been made for the public by persons who have been almost self-appointed in some instances. Members of the budget allocations committee are highly motivated, as a rule; but nearly all of them either are associated with a particular agency or are classed as management executives from the corporation world. Rarely would the political scientist or sociologist judge the budgeting groups as being clearly representative of classes, groups, and areas in a multi-structured community. Welfare budgeting in many cities has become essentially a process of logrolling, based on the power of existing agencies and the whims of powerful interests. There can be little room for doubt that the public, if it were armed with the power to vote on the matter, would come up with a different division of the pie. Is it possible in such instance to ascertain the views of the man in the street?

While public-opinion polls cannot always come within the three or four percentage points vital to picking a president, they can easily tell a corporation how safe it will be to launch a new product. Polling the layman to determine his agency preferences is entirely possible. But is it desirable? Do we really want wholly democratic determination of the disposal of "torch-drive" dollars? That is not the way we run our foreign relations or the federal reserve system. We must remember that "democratic" does not mean "fair" or "good public policy." It only means, in this instance, that the public gets what it wants. And there is grave doubt that the many organizations in the social-welfare field could ever be very well understood by the average person without a lengthy (and a most unlikely) program of intensive education.

Social workers know that some useful and worthwhile social-service activities cannot be sold to the typical layman. He does not "get it." Casework remains a poorly understood service, even though it is the core item of training for social workers. To the typical American, it is "talk"—not "doing good." For the average man who gives to a chest or fund visualizes his money being paid to a deserving person in need; it makes him mad to hear that his dollars may go for salaries or building maintenance. He hates to think, furthermore, that the day could come when a social worker might probe into his own personal life. It is an invasion of privacy. Seldom does he think that many of those who sit before the social worker are talking with the first friendly person they have seen in days—or even months. It is not privacy but understanding which they seek. Truly democratic determination of budget allocations would obviously lead to the quick death of some—and perhaps a good many—charitable and health agencies. And it might set social-service work back many decades. As for the programs of the national health agencies, it might be that the lay citizen would prefer to insist on the payment of patients' bills first—medical research second. However, through public education, the importance of long-range goals might be made understandable.

If direct democracy, or the "town hall" method, is impractical as a way of determining budget-allocation percentages in chests and united funds, perhaps the populace should be given the privilege of voting for candidates or slates of candidates for high office in these bodies. This idea is appealing, for the very process of voting would focus public attention on the field of voluntary welfare. At the same time it might be wise to have candidates for membership in the community council offer themselves to the electorate. And it may be remarked that the idea, however novel today, is no more unrealistic than the self-government which once was treated with undeniable skepticism. Americans are accustomed to choosing representatives to establish policy and conduct affairs. Here is a community activity of the utmost importance, nongovernmental to be sure, but vital in the realm of public policy. There is precedent in the selection of party committeemen, who hold no governmental office but still appear on the ballot in many states. We may be suggesting a way to make voluntary welfare more representative of popular desires, to instill confidence in what is being done, and to raise more money for charitable and health purposes from persons whose confidence in the whole voluntary system can be strengthened. Little can be said, after all, for the *status quo* in many cities.

Under the present system, prominent citizens get together with agency representatives and announce in the name of the contributing public that a united fund (or community chest) is being formed—or even that it has just been formed. Officials of banks, railroads, oil companies, department stores (in short, big employers) customarily hold key offices in these bodies, although the names of their organizations may or may not appear. Old families in the community may be represented, and the very rich, understandably, will not be ignored. Together, these persons will profess to speak in the name of "the people." Well motivated on the whole, well educated, and usually friendly to voluntary welfare, these volunteers make decisions on policy in the name of the community. Having agreed on what will be done, they tell the trained administrative executive to carry out their desires. He tells the social workers—the people who, supposedly, are qualified to use social services for the welfare of the individual. Clearly, the people who control the purse strings are the bosses.

The mid-century masters of metropolitan voluntary welfare cannot understand why the average factory worker, clerk, and housewife remain so apathetic to the cause on which they have decided. And why do social workers seem so often to have a chip on their shoulders? To those who have attained power, decisions made seem right and somehow inevitable. They *know* they are doing "what is best for the community!" This work, they and their families recognize, takes time they can ill afford to spare. Moreover, because of their deep concern with the united fund-raising drives, they are quite likely to give more of their own money than they would normally. Small wonder that the masters do not take kindly to criticism from citizens.

One trouble with united fund-raising is typified by the individual who gives less than twenty-five dollars. Despite the vast numbers represented by his kind, he has been left out of policy-making. It has been suggested that fully democratic determination of the course of voluntary welfare might be destructive. But its complete absence (except when group representation has been contrived with unusual artfulness) is also to be deplored. Consider the statistical importance of the small giver—the under twenty-five-dollar person. In 1956, he was 89 per cent of the givers in Santa Barbara, California; 99 per cent in Seattle; 94 per cent in Alexandria, Louisiana, and Petersburg, Virginia; and 92 per cent in Ashtabula, Ohio, and Atlantic City, New Jersey. Not to give him more than his due, the total gifts of his kind seldom, if

145

ever, came to more than half of the funds contributed. In the cities named, his group gave the following percentages of the total: 25, 58, 41, 47, 44, and 14, respectively. Even so, consulting the small giver on policy could be rewarding in increased good will. As a volunteer solicitor at the grass roots, he does most of the unpaid work in the campaign. In one year, the United Fund of Allegheny County (Pittsburgh) had 33,709 men and women who served as "in-plant solicitors" or "solicitors," but only 4,736 leaders with the title of "chairman" or "captain"—to say nothing of the very small number of leaders from steel, plate glass, and finance who exerted the real power over policy. So it is that decisions are being made in the name of the public and the "average giver" but not by him, and by no means always by his leave. When he is paid for his time, as in factories, some may say he has less claim in this respect. But the masters of the united funds themselves often use office time freely in pursuit of their objectives, and they feel free to charge luncheon checks to the company's stockholders, or, in part (through tax deductions), to government.

The relations of the average man with government are not the same as those he has with the united-fund organization. Angry at the school board, he votes its members out of office. Distressed over policies in the city government, he speaks his piece at the city-council meeting. But when he is out of sympathy with the community's sole united fund, he can only write an angry "letter to the editor" or complain to anyone who will listen. Meanwhile, the united fund speaks in the name of "the community."

No doubt, voluntary welfare can continue for some years to get along without worrying very much about what the average man thinks of the way united funds are controlled or the way contributed dollars are divided. But it is well to remember that from two-thirds to three-fourths of such dollars will continue to come from individuals, one by one, in big and (more often) little gifts.

It is contended here, therefore, that community chests, united funds, and community councils must find a way to guarantee a democratic character to their proceedings. It is not enough to pick and choose leaders from powerful organizations, influential pressure groups, and the top ten or thirty families measured by wealth or social standing. Putting a single union man on a board is no solution either, for reasons too obvious to be labored here. Adding a physician, an attorney, and a clergyman is commendable, of course, but isn't the result simply a makeshift? The addition of "housewives" from the realm of intelligent clubwomen (whose views are often carbon copies of those of their corporation-employed husbands) is also a useful device. But I remain convinced that any fair study of the control hierarchy of most united funds will show, in the last analysis, gross over-representation of big business and finance—in essence, what may be called "the skyscraper viewpoint in social welfare." A solution to this problem must be found if voluntary welfare is to survive in the United States.

Big united-fund organizations are not evil because they are big. Americans are accustomed to and accept bigness in many things. "Efficiency counts." "Results count." "Look at the product." All of these phrases are familiar, and the national health agencies have not, in their own gigantic size, found the argument of bigness a difficult one to use. On the whole, the public seems inclined to accept the idea of increasing size: in business, in government, and in organizations. This national orientation results in acquiescence in fund-raising on a grand scale—provided certain conditions are met.

The job of the "one big drive" is to raise money—big money. It does not do welfare work. It is not an agency. It should, therefore, be judged by both its immediate and its ultimate products. The immediate product is money; the ultimate product is the maintenance and the increase of good will toward voluntary welfare. They go hand in hand.

A united fund is raising enough money if three conditions are met: (1) If it is meeting more than the minimum dollar needs of agencies, as realistically agreed upon after budget hearings. (2) If it raises enough additional money each year to take care of the reduced annual purchasing power of the dollar. (3) If its funds increase concomitantly with the increase in member agencies, the increased population, and the augmented area solicited.

It is altogether probable that, judged by these criteria, many united funds of the last decade did not really experience the total success they proclaimed. They kidded the public and, in too many instances, they fooled even themselves. Let the slide-rule and calculating-machine experts test their own united funds with these yardsticks. The habit of including dollars that later prove uncollectible is only one of several devices by which the funds find it possible annually to proclaim that goals have been reached and annual expansion achieved. Far more important than this is the failure to allow for recent united-fund expansion into new territories, or to account for new population, new factories, and new member agencies.

The long-range product of the united fund has been identified here as good will toward voluntary welfare. The community chest and the united fund became, in the twentieth century, the main contact the public had with voluntary welfare. The public knows little or nothing about the county public welfare department. By law, all is confidential; and by habit and indifference in some cases much is complicated and confusing. There is little public contact with casework agencies, free and part-pay clinics, or other services, except by those who use them. The scouting programs are well known, and some aspects of the Red Cross program are understood. Increasingly, it has been the fund-raisers who have invited public attention. Between campaigns, they quite properly do all that they can to remain in the public eye. "Repetition is reputation." They front for the agencies and they encourage the agencies to mention the central fund in press releases and all booklets. This promotion may, indeed, be insisted upon. The red feather symbol or the torch is easily spotted in our cities.

Its central position makes the public relations of the united fund of prime importance. Fund-raisers are forever conducting seminars and clinics on this subject. Note carefully that emphasis has rested on selling the public on the worth of what exists. Stress is not being placed on changing the basic structure, programs, and approaches of the united funds to meet the unpublicized criticism of the man in the street.

The man in the factory, the white-collar man in the office,

and their wives are often unhappy about the "give a day's pay" and the other scientifically or arithmetically scaled approaches of eager community philanthropists. The giving-at-work approach has proved a simple way to get a captive contributing audience, but the wife of the captive giver is no longer being solicited directly by her own friends and neighbors in the old way. This could cut unnaturally across the giving population, particularly because in earlier decades it was the male wage earner who was ignored by solicitors. Yesterday's "momism" is being replaced by a new and "business-like" solicitation method—"man to man."

It is conceivable that no satisfactory way of appealing jointly to wage earner and spouse can be devised. Televised and printed messages may reach both, although modern posters aim at arousing emotions rather than conveying solid information. A family gift for charitable purposes, by rights, should come from the hearts of two people and, if possible, from their older children as well. A rigid "give where you work" solicitation does not usually accomplish this end. Voluntary welfare may be losing huge areas of future support as a result. Certainly it is making the financing of metropolitan voluntary welfare a man's world, except in instances where working women are reached in this way. Social welfare needs the unremitting interest and support of mothers in the home. Clearly, home solicitation has value, even if a high proportion of those solicited end up by giving the actual gift at work through payroll deductions.

In justice to the leaders of federated drives, it must be said that they are doing all they can to plug another of their public-relations loopholes. They are anxious for the public to understand the work of individual agencies. Nothing would please them more. The better federated funds continually indoctrinate staffs of member agencies in public relations techniques, and they call on them for newsworthy stories for the local press. While experience will vary from community to community, it can be said that the press relations of the clever and well-rounded public-relations people with the funds are at least as good as the agency people could command on their own. It is naïve to think that abolishing the centralized funds would, in itself, end blurring of the publicity image achieved by voluntary welfare. No significant gain is to be made by bringing back multiple campaigns to "our town."

United Community Funds and Councils of America, Inc., the aggressive New York City-based co-ordinating group for the united funds and chests (and councils) across the nation, claims that, once a united drive is attempted, the new method has come to stay. The truth of this claim was demonstrated for a time in the 1950's in big cities, although it was not necessarily true in small towns, where it was not unusual for the united drive to be abandoned after one or two campaigns—often because it included too few agencies. The small-town united drive that does not include Salvation Army, Catholic agencies, Red Cross, Heart, and perhaps Cancer at a minimum, plus many other local agencies with continuing administrative machinery, can expect rough sledding. But pioneering metropolitan united-fund organizations hung on consistently in their first decade, although the Polio group universally refused participation, and only 7 per cent of the Cancer chapters joined, most only temporarily.

Critics seemed to be wasting their breath, for the single funds had the backing of chambers of commerce, banks, merchandizing establishments, factories—in short, the major powers in the local economy. The local newspaper was often as happy as any other business to get out of giving to a dozen or more causes separately. Those who sought to kill a major united fund, from whatever motives, had a difficult time. Good men, united in huge health organizations, tried mightily. Yet, with the departure of Cancer, and sometimes Heart, from various united groups toward the close of the decade, many a leader of a collective crusade trembled.

But the metropolitan machinery of the united way lives on in the 1960's. The idea of a single campaign had caught the imaginations of many leaders; and, in some cities, it has become almost institutionalized in the space of a single decade. A trustee of the Mile-High United Fund of Denver was not quite whistling in the dark when he observed, "The growth of these voluntary organizations has been a phenomenon of our American way of life, corollary to the social, political, economic, and industrial development of our nation." Still the proclamation was, in certain ways, premature; for the decade 1949 to 1959 may well have been the climactic decade of the united funds.

Looking back a decade hence, it might be proper to speak of the "rise and fall of the united funds." With Polio, Crippled Children, and Tuberculosis still independent, with Heart normally aloof, and with Cancer standing with drawn sword at the close of the decade, the only true unity achieved, after all, was the return of Red Cross and the organization of new fund-raising machinery outside the chest structure. Even in 1958, however, the Red Cross obtained about 40 per cent of its funds outside the united fold. Moreover, Red Cross chapters time and again entered unified drives only on terms which made the marriage one of convenience, with substantial freedoms reserved to the Congressionally chartered body. That certain of the small national health agencies and miscellaneous groups joined the united funds scarcely changes this realistic picture.

These pages have much to say about united funds. This is quite necessary; for as machinery, as organizations, and as bureaucratic structures with paid employees and governing boards—and as bodies that raised approximately four hundred million dollars in the year marking the end of their first decade—they existed. But in truth the expression "united funds" remained, at the beginning of the 1960's, an absurdity. The vast bulk of the national health agencies remained independent; Red Cross remained free, in the last analysis, to campaign independently if it should so decide; and capital drives were seldom considered a responsibility of the united machinery. But of all this—little was said by united-fund sponsors.

Sooner or later these and other unpleasant facts will have to be faced by the otherwise realistic men of intelligence, experience, personality, talent, and character who serve, without salary, as leaders of the united funds in urban America. The organization does not exist that cannot be improved. Somehow these leaders will have to keep from identifying their personal prestige and careers with the untouchability of a voluntary organization which, in truth, belongs to the public. It is not theirs. It does not belong to the agencies. No stockholders sit in privileged positions—unless the contributors can be said to occupy such positions. Even so, the annual meeting of some funds is analogous to a stockholders' meeting—regardless of the fact that a large gift to the fund means no more, legally or morally, than a small one, either to God or to the united fund, so far as rights conveyed to the donor are concerned. Why should any non-profit, tax-exempt, fund-raising organization be above criticism? Why should a united fund or a community chest be a "sacred cow"?

William G. Hollister, in an article on "The Risks of Freedom-Giving Leadership," put his finger on the problem of informed support.

> Oddly enough, it is possible to lead and never become aware of any counter-action to one's leadership. First, people usually "take apart" a leader when he is not around so that often he never hears the diatribes against himself. Second, the majority of groups in our culture are run in a controlled way that keeps "leader hostility" bottled up or carefully redirected.

Letters-to-the-editor columns of newspapers are one of the very few places where overly persuasive "give once" solicitors can be raked over the coals. In the San Francisco *Chronicle*, July 26, 1957, a letter appeared from "a widow, the sole support of several children" who was quite unhappy about the local united drive. She wrote, in part:

> I have no objection to people who can afford to do so volunteering to support these agencies for the worthwhile work that they do for young people. However, I do think that "charity contributions" deducted from my low wages as an employee of a large corporation, under moral and social pressure, on a sort of "soak-the-poor" basis . . . should not be given to . . . [mentioning several agencies].

The local fund, the United Bay Area Crusade, had the good sense not to ignore this critical letter, and an answer over the signature of its president quickly appeared. He began, "Mrs. [. . . 's] thoughtful letter of July 28 merits a thoughtful reply." After answering her specific complaints about agencies, he concluded as follows:

> The Crusade is merely a convenient and more economical device for collecting most of their funds in a single campaign. The alternative would be repeated appeals at far greater cost, and with less time for each appealing agency to devote to service. . . . The Crusade only asks that every person give in accordance with his ability. The Crusade policy, frequently and emphatically expressed to all its representatives, and printed in its literature, reiterates this position. The United Crusade is locally established and locally directed, an enterprise of and for our own community.

The gains from this interchange are incontestable.

In making decisions on matters of such character the volunteer president of a united fund must remember his multiple constituencies. First, there are the people and organizations who give the money. Second, there are the individuals who will get the money in cash or services because they are thought to be in need. Standing between these groups are, third, the united-fund machinery which collects money from the givers and turns it over to the agencies, and, fourth, the agencies themselves who spend it on services and give a small amount of it away. The wise volunteer leader will keep these four groups and their needs constantly before him as he performs his hundreds of thankless tasks. Which group should have priority control of policy—the givers, the fund, the agencies, or the recipients? Decision is not easy.

The givers must be considered carefully, because the whole process will dry up unless they are contented. The fund must be stressed, because it is the vehicle which makes modern fund-raising possible. The agencies are highly important, because their financing and decisions are the core of voluntary welfare today. Moreover, their executives are true experts. The needs of the recipients are vital, because they are the original justification of organized voluntary welfare. How can one choose among these four? Must it be done? Of course not. It is obvious that all four are important. Each must be satisfied and infused with spirit, and a balance must be maintained among them.

The future of the large funds hangs not only upon these considerations but upon the early formulation of what may best be called a charter for givers. Some features of such a charter have already been discussed, but to bring them together and give them form, it may be said that givers need:

1. A chance to vote for candidates for high office in a given fund, so that normally at voting time they would have a choice between alternative slates or individuals.

2. An opportunity to advance criticism in either or both vehicles of a public forum on fund-raising and fund-administration: that is, in open meetings free of those calculated parliamentary procedures which stifle dissent; and, second, a house organ of the fund, fairly impartially edited, and widely distributed.

3. Press releases prepared by united-fund researchers with due consideration for the rights and needs of each of the four interested groups described earlier. The intent is to provide contributors with facts. The further intent is to encourage newspapermen to employ, in reporting united-fund activities, genuine reporting and interviewing techniques. The fact that fund-raising is worthy in itself should not mean that news media are obligated to handle united-fund and community-chest matters with kid gloves. The public badly needs editorials on the united funds, national health agencies, and local charitable organizations which are something more than puffs.

4. Givers need, finally, audited annual reports and frequent statistical releases which give the full, unvarnished facts about the progress (or lack of it) in the financing of voluntary welfare. There have been too many goals set and not attained, too many statements which gloss over an earlier stated objective by reference to collections "larger than ever before in the history of the community," which were in fact well under predetermined levels.

From the events and experiences of the last dozen years in united-fund and community-chest history, it would seem clear that a code for community leaders is almost equally necessary. The truth is that these powerful new recruits to philanthropy do not know what they want. Actually, they have hardly had time to find out. In practice, the novelty wears off and new faces come to represent the corporation on the fund committees. A certain degree of generalization may be permissible when we speculate about what goes on in the minds of the new masters of voluntary welfare.

Full-time social workers irritate them more than a little. Some of the programs for which they raise money just do not seem to make much sense to them. The fund-raisers pay constant lip service to "co-ordination" and "consolidation" of agencies. They call for "retrenchment" and "economy" and "business management," but they are at a loss to know how to implement these high-sounding but general terms in the strange, social-work world. They want research; they want "the facts"; but they do not always want them widely distributed to the public when the figures do not show what they hoped and predicted they would. They cannot always make head or tail of the social surveys which exist, and they are bored with them and do not trust them anyway. Community council professionals worry them; and, "How radical are those people, anyway"? Neither the textbooks nor the journal articles which appear in standard social-work journals reach the desks of these leaders, and if they did they would bring no sense of comfort. The jargon of social-work intellectuals bothers the ulcers of the businessmen-volunteers. "Why can't social agencies be run like businesses?" they inquire, forgetting that charitable agencies exist for what they pay out, not for what they take in.

No less a leader than James A. Linen of *Time* magazine, then president of the national co-ordinating organization of the united funds, warned in 1957: "I believe that the only real danger inherent in federation is that of becoming too much a 'big business' and thereby losing its human and spiritual side. A business like ours [*sic*] needs constantly to keep close to people. . . . Federation demands not only discipline from others but discipline of ourselves."

The new masters of voluntary welfare have had the power to lead and in many instances they have converted it into the power to rule. Because these top lay fund-raisers did not know what they wanted (in an ultimate sense), the executive directors of the funds, the council people, and the agency personnel still retained what seemed to many of them real power. That it was only a shell of the old absolute independence these officials had yet to learn. The day of their enlightenment seems likely to come early in some cities but not in others. As long as many large national or local fund-raising organizations continue to exist independent of the united-fund machines, total centralization of power and its exercise will prove difficult.

The character of welfare responsibility is easily modified, changed, or diverted. To paraphrase the table talk of one magnate, "We are not really trying to raise as much money as the agencies say they need. After all, the public welfare departments are spending more money every year and the need for voluntary welfare must be shrinking. We are facing facts." Again, in the exact words of a leading businessman, spoken in a banquet hall:

> I think we are going to have to remove the Community Chest funds before we will really begin to get action from agencies on . . . [a matter]. Now I realize that all of these things don't set well with agency people. I mean those of you who are connected with individual agencies don't like to hear the kind of thing that we're talking about. It's too much realism for you, if you don't mind my saying so. . . . [You] have the subconscious feeling that this federation was brought about by a voluntary joining together of agencies for the purpose of mutual fund raising. I don't know how it is in your community, but I can assure you in the Heart of America [Kansas City] nothing could be further from the truth than that assumption. The agencies have banded together, yes, but our contributors . . . wrapped their arms around the whole bunch of them and slammed them together.

The president of the National Association for Retarded Children declared late in 1959 that experience gained by 200 of her 682 member units in the united-fund fold might be summarized by saying "there are times when the wolf of coercion has stalked in the sheep's clothing of co-operation."

A convention luncheon companion of mine, a public-utility

executive from a major industrial state in the Midwest, pounded the table as he formulated this thought: "We told them [a famous national health agency] that they could join our united fund or they would never raise another nickel in our state." The same sentiment, expressed with even more force, was uttered two years later by a steel executive from the East. Plants in his town, he said, had signed a written pledge to let no organization but the united fund raise money in their factories. Again, in one Western city a team of experts on administration undertook to "streamline" the operations of the community chest. Seeing no need for a fact-finding research study which had been in progress for six months, this team of business experts canceled it out and put the researcher back on routine tasks. Three years later similar lay leaders remarked on what they called a lack of chest research along the same lines.

The Girl Scouts, Camp Fire Girls, YWCA, and other women's and girls' organizations are beginning to be aware of the new masculine domination of the purse strings, especially as "juvenile delinquency" is being equated in some men's minds with a need for fund allocations to organizations dealing with teen-age boys. Women, it is to be hoped, will prove less tractable than men when they are faced with overeager management-executive aggressiveness outside the factory gates. To women may go the responsibility for manning the guns.

The code for lay fund-raisers should embrace—in addition to a knowledge of what is needed, a cautious regard for power, and an understanding of the dangers of diverting social purpose—a willingness to learn at least the basic concepts of professional workers in social welfare. The latter have begun, somewhat hesitantly, the enormous task of educating leading male volunteers in the objectives and virtues of casework, counseling, guidance, homemaker service, alcoholic rehabilitation, and home-nursing service. This is obviously a problem in adult education, but neither educational techniques nor journalism have been part of the social-work graduate curriculum. Social-work executives try mightily to educate (or, perhaps, indoctrinate) their most influential lay leaders in the community, but it is an uphill task. Nor, in all candor, does the tendency to oversell the existing social-work product help much in gaining the confidence of businessmen.

Top lay leaders often control the salary strings in united funds, chests, and agencies. Here is a potent source of power. Salaries in the social-work field have never been equivalent to those in the business world. They even prove a shock at first to corporation executives, accustomed to private secretaries who make as much as many agency directors. When the layman steps forward to raise agency salaries, he wins very quickly what passes for personal popularity, and he gains in power. This is only natural. The executive director who runs the agency daily naturally tends to withhold all but absolutely essential criticisms of the conduct and plans of lay volunteers—especially those from big corporations who give (or are responsible for) three- to five-figure amounts. And leadership in criticism can scarcely be expected from agency executives, for few persons have less job security.

Nevertheless, if education and experience gained on the firing line in contact with young people, the aged, and the troubled are assets when we think about community social welfare, then the paid executives in the agencies have an obligation to speak their piece. Ideally, they should speak it in private to leading volunteers; when ignored, they may have to speak it to the press— if they are to save their souls. They are losing control of the voluntary part of the social-welfare field (to whatever degree they ever held it) to untrained men who, strictly speaking, know little or nothing about social work at all. If the general public remains unenlightened about the power struggle within the field of voluntary welfare, the fault lies in large part with the social-work executives. Simply stated, the spectre of unemployment hovers over many who would, under other circumstances, speak out.

During the decade just closed, the new masters of metropolitan voluntary health, welfare, and recreation began their careers by raising funds. They remained, in many instances, for the purpose of raising hob. In the process, as it continues, they will do both good and harm in unpredictable mixture. If they are fair with the public, the experts, and the people in need, they will be entitled to that measure of praise which benevolent despots have always enjoyed. But if they use their positions to remake their communities according to patterns which only they, their business associates, and their friends could possibly approve, they may maim, at best, or kill, at worst, voluntary welfare in metropolitan America. The men whose business is business must come to realize their limitations.

Society has not failed to express its gratitude to the men from the skyscrapers for their time, their thought, and their money. But society will do well to see that the churches, welfare-agency leaders, professional men, and the women of America have something to say about the content and organization of voluntary welfare. The success of the latter will take far more than expertness in bookkeeping and card-sorting equipment, advertising campaigns, personnel relations, and production—now and in the decades ahead.

CHAPTER VIII

United Fund-raising
in the Grand Manner: Detroit

How, then, shall we raise the dollars that we need?
By asking every housewife? Surely that is not the
Way to do the job. Perhaps by entering the plant
And asking every worker, using methods modern,
Doing it just once—but right—the dollar flow will come.

Deep in paneled offices where suits are always dark,
We'll find big wheels with power to contribute
Dollars that once went to those who clip their
Solitary coupons. In the name of all that's good
In corporation management, we'll light our Torch.

What we cannot understand is why it took so long
For urban man to learn the mysteries of modern
Charity. Persuade the workers and the plants to give
Unanimously and scientifically. Stopwatch the man
Who solicits! IBM will tell us all we need to know.

As ANY FUND-RAISER worthy of his calling is fully aware, the United
Foundation of the metropolitan Detroit area was, in the years
following 1949, the number-one federated solicitation organization in the voluntary welfare field. Much word-of-mouth publicity
was gained by this group as it conquered almost every obstacle in
its drive to consolidate agency fund-raising in the automobile capital of the world. The "Give Once" drives in Philadelphia and the
San Francisco Bay Area (the United Crusade), the next largest,
could not match its totals. When the United Foundation was being founded in 1948, the separate campaigns carried on in Detroit
raised $7,200,000. The first of the Torch Drives raised the figure
to $9,247,045 in 1949. Corporations contributed an initial 40.4
per cent of the total as the United Foundation got off to a flying
start. Never would it exceed or even match that percentage again.

Rising by roughly one million dollars a year in the days of
general prosperity, the Detroit united fund raised, in 1955, the
sum of $15,933,000. Thereafter, the total leveled off somewhat

with the 1957 campaign raising $16,651,000, a figure representative of solicitation of more townships and additional member agencies. A dramatic increase in contributions from the city's working population, given through payroll deductions, played a major role in these rising totals. Other factors were growth in Detroit's population and economy (until the recession of 1958) and inflation. There had been efficiency in operation and the best leadership, paid and unpaid, that any united fund could hope for. The United Foundation did not lack for volunteer, or salaried, talent. There were ample vice-presidents of big automobile companies, steel plants, and major labor unions. The wives of business executives were another source of help. Yet much of the organizational skill displayed in the nation's largest united drive stemmed from its talented paid staff (with scarcely a person trained in social work on the payroll). Its finance chairman was a trained and experienced investment banker. Its director was a man clearly at home with large figures and complex monetary ideas, but he was not a social worker either by training or inclination. A day spent with the executives of the fund was an illuminating experience for me.

At the top of the Torch Fund organization stood a man around whom the wheels revolved twelve months a year. Executive Vice-President Walter C. Laidlaw was a man federated-fund organizations all over the nation would have been happy to hire away from the Detroit people. His United Foundation raised more than $120,000,000 in nine campaigns for the support of between one hundred and two hundred local agencies and various national groups. I was immensely pleased to have the opportunity to probe, in 1957, the mind of this powerful and capable figure.

Tanned and well-built, in the manner of a chunky football hero and perfectly at ease, Walter Laidlaw had made himself into one of the most important men in American philanthropy. A recording device bothered him not at all. What follows was our conversation in his fourth-floor office in downtown Detroit about the responsibilities that accompany the directing of a powerful fund-raising organization:

Mr. Laidlaw, I would first like to ask a few simple things. How did you happen to get into fund-raising?

Well, quite honestly I needed a job. I was in investment banking at that time and we were having "scotch weeks," that is, you worked a full month but you were only paid for two weeks. Several of the board members of the old Community Fund were interested in reorganizing it. They asked if I would consider affiliating with the Community Fund, and I did as assistant to the county director and tried to bail it out, but it was practically impossible. Prior to that I was in the marketing side of banking, that is, the advertising side of it. I was in all facets of it—marketing, trade, and underwriting. So I'm a finance man, primarily, with marketing experience.

Do you find in retrospect that this work is perhaps a little harder on your nerves or your health than other work you have done?

Oh, very definitely! These are very high-pressure jobs, especially when you hit the top as we have. I don't know of a more difficult job to be in, than I am in now. Once you get on top you've got to stay on top.

Have you had any experience like one man in this type of operation who told me that he had not been able to have a single evening at home with his family in thirty days?

Oh, I've had that happen to me. I do every campaign. In fact, say from October 15 to November 10, I live at the hotel where we are headquartered. I go home week ends to recharge the battery.

That must make it a very demanding job. Then it drops off, perhaps in February and March?

It hasn't dropped off at all. As we grow there are more and more relationships with agencies, especially when we have been expanding into some of the unorganized areas and the adjoining counties—what we call the "fringe area." Also there are the delicate relationships with national agencies that require quite a bit of time. You get through with the campaign and you think you are going to have a breather and then you get involved in national situations. I don't believe in living in a shell here. I make my contributions of time nationally. I serve as a member of the board and am a former vice-president and chairman of the finance committee for a small health agency, the American Hearing Society. And I am also on the advisory and executive committee of the [national] United Funds Advisory Committee. There are great demands for your time. Then again you have the problem of other communities throughout the country who are considering the united-fund idea, and they ask if you won't come and visit with them and talk to them and perhaps get them on the right track so that they can go forward. In fact I have a request from [. . .] right now. I'm not going.

What is the official name of your organization?

The United Foundation. There's no "Metropolitan Detroit," and not even a "Detroit" in it.

You are aware that there is great variety in these united-fund names. Do you think there is anything in a name?

There's quite a bit in a name. In fact, when we set up the United Foundation (and we were the first one in America) we wanted to give it a completely new twist. We knew that the "community chest" was symbolic of purely local agencies. Too, many of the national agencies mistrusted many chests because of treatment given them when they were in community chests. That's very true of Red Cross. We also felt that we had a completely independent organization. If we were going out and consolidate drives and organize the givers we needed a name that we knew all agencies would have respect for.

Some of these organizations use the word "crusade." Or they use the word "fund"; or they don't use the word "united" at all. What do you think about these?

I think the best name is whatever best fits a single community. We have some cities that have Associated Charities, the Single Appeal Plan, the Heart of America Campaign— whatever best fits the locality.

Would you think it desirable that the names all be alike so that when people move from community to community— and they do—they would find the same name?

I do think if they could incorporate the word "united" in their name it would be helpful for the transients.

I have speculated on this point a little, Mr. Laidlaw: You work through the day every day and all year around; do you ever sit and think to yourself, "Now, what social purpose is all this serving?" Do you say to yourself, "This must mean something"? What does it all mean?

Well, we're not just in the business of raising money. That's one thing that has happened in this town. We've not only been successful in providing money for the agencies, but we have united the people of this town: labor and management—all classes, all religions, in one common endeavor. To us this is a great thing in our town, because often it will split into more factions "Detroit-wise" than any other city in America.

Then there is the money—and then this other thing?

Sure. That's a by-product that we have. Of course, I feel that our principle is to provide enough money to give minimum needed services to the people in our community.

Do you think that the people generally appreciate this and give you a good vocal "press" on the street corner? Do they talk kindly of your organization?

Oh sure. In fact, I was pointing out to a few people yesterday that under the old Community Chest during a campaign I had forty or fifty complaints. I always asked my operator to have a complaining contributor talk with me personally. Or if they wanted to see me I always have an open door. Today, after eight years in the united fund, I doubt if I receive fifty complaints in a year! People like the idea because we have done a job of consolidating drives, and they are not constantly annoyed.

Do you find that the interest in your cost of operating is decreasing—that people are no longer much interested in the per cent of overhead you run in raising your money?

Oh, I think they are! Very definitely! In fact, one of our salient facts in making a sale is that we have a low cost operation here.

I understand that your percentage is quite low. What is the figure?

It is 4.6 per cent.

And that is 4.6 per cent of the money actually raised?

That's both campaign and administrative costs.

This is a percentage of money that you actually got—it does not include pledges that you might or might not get— I mean uncollected pledges.

It is 4.6 per cent of the total pledge. We also incorporate in our campaign a reserve for "shrinkage." It was $850,000 in 1957. In 1955 we provided a shrinkage item of $850,000 and we only had a loss of $400,000. So those funds are surplus funds and we will put them to work. At the present time we are studying how we should spend these funds, or at least set them aside in reserve. We're considering setting up a Disaster Relief Fund so that we can act quickly during the time of a tornado or flood disaster or anything like that.

We are also considering providing funds for the maintenance of equipment and buildings. Our normal job is to provide operating funds. Now we feel that you have to take care of your capital investment as well as your personnel.

You have had capital fund drives here, haven't you?

Yes.

Were these under your management, or was each a separate organization?

Well, I set up two organizations prior to the United Foundation. I organized the Detroit Hospital Fund that incorporated about ten hospitals. Prior to that two hospitals had tremendous failures. Then we made a survey as to what the contemplated plans were as to new hospitals, and we found at that time that plans in people's minds or on drawing boards amounted to about $60,000,000 and would provide about 4,000 more beds. We established a survey committee under the leadership of the late Dr. Bruce Douglas, who was our Health Commissioner, bringing in outside consultants, and we found out that what we needed were only 1,500 beds. The hospitals had about $10 million, and so we went and campaigned for $20 million. I brought in Will Folsom Smith from New York to manage the campaign, and it was a very successful venture. It should have taken hospital beds until 1960, but with this tremendous shift of population into the suburbs we have to step up and face the problem today, more from the "fringe areas" and the suburban areas, than from the central part of town. We also established a Metropolitan Detroit Building Fund.

Do you find that your agencies are gradually finding that they are located in the wrong place—that this means new buildings, or moving out of favorable rental areas into areas where they have to pay twice as much rent, and this perhaps necessitates a new building?

You will find that most agencies want a new building if they have an old one. They are "expansionists." And with the Metropolitan Detroit Building Fund, which we organized (and I am secretary of the laymen and serve on it), we heard about all these campaigns. In fact, when I got into it the problem was $35,000,000 worth of new buildings! We knew that we had to do something about it. We couldn't let them all go out individually, and we knew that some of the thoughts and ideas that some of the organizations had were completely out of line. We also knew that the contributor market would not stand it. So we set up the Metropolitan Detroit Building Fund, and when they got through the requests for financing totaled over a hundred million dollars! Then we established an allocations committee and brought in some outside consultants (we just cannot do this alone on our day-to-day jobs) to measure what the minimum basic needs were. When we got through we found that they were about sixteen million dollars. We went and raised the sixteen million dollars about two years ago.

Has there been any great demand since for additional buildings or money? Or are the agencies satisfied?

Not entirely satisfied. We used fourteen agencies and the YMCA and YWCA are still talking about it and further expansion. They didn't get what they wanted, and I might add that there is a different philosophy about contributing to dormitories, or hostelries, than there was twenty years ago. You've had a re-distribution of income in this country—nobody is underpaid today. It used to be that when these kids came from out in the country and worked in the stores they had to have some place to live in a wholesome environment. Today they all are paid enough so that they can pay their own way.

I was talking to a young professor on a college campus the other day, and he said that in his opinion the only reason that laymen or citizens in the community worked for community chest drives was to advance themselves politically, gaining contacts thereby. I wonder if you feel that this is an extremely sour sort of statement?

I do think it is a sour statement.

Why do they work on these drives?

Well, for one thing they are interested in helping their neighbor. Two, they're interested in the health and social welfare problem in this country. Three, they are interested in building their communities—their firms are interested in taking on civic and community responsibilities, and they encourage the participants.

Do firms lend you young executives for a period of weeks and still pay their salaries?

We don't have a lend-lease program as such, although some funds do. We have about eighteen men, however, that we obtain through the companies to supplement our staff for maybe a four- or five-week period. Certainly they pay their salaries. But we haven't gone into that like other cities have. We've found that you can get nice young fellows, but what we want are people of influence in our drive to go out and make the actual solicitation.

Do you ever get a chance to talk with some of these young laymen that solicit for you—informally, I mean, to learn of their pleasant and unpleasant experiences?

I'd say they have very few unpleasant ones. I find that among our young executive group they all want to get back in the second year. They really enjoy it.

Is this good personality training for a young man?

I think so—definitely. I think it is the best there is. We've seen what has happened with some of these young men. They've been stepped right on up in their companies and jumped right out of the regular status.

Does it help them in public speaking and in meeting people?

Certainly it helps in meeting people. I was a young fellow who went into the banking business shortly out of college. I probably was a little shy and I worked for the president of the bank. He said, "I'm going to put you in the New Business end; now you go and make as many calls as you can make." I started out right here in downtown Detroit and went from the top of the building down to the bottom asking people to do business with our bank. That was the best training I ever had.

That's extremely interesting. Is it possible that these young men do get advancement, and even the older men get advancement after they get associated with the drives and get their pictures in the paper? This fund-raising does help them personally? Or is this their primary motive?

It's not their motive. If they come in with that motive then they don't get too far. But if they come in just as a citizen or their company encourages them to come in, you'll find that it's a great training ground for any of them. And they do advance. I've heard in the past some people say even top men, the presidents of companies, do advance because of their participation in the Community Chest or the United Fund or Foundation. These men have reached the top. It adds to their stature; in fact, we never have trouble in finding leaders because we are a popular organization. They are willing to associate their names with us, and they are willing to go out and work. And they are proud of what they have done.

I wonder if you think, Mr. Laidlaw, that the time has come for the business schools of the nation (that is, the graduate business schools like Harvard Business School or Stanford University, wherever they have a two-year degree) to offer a course or to give a little instruction in community matters of this character?

I would say "civic and community participation." They should acquaint the student with the beneficial activities within their home community. And they should stress the necessity of participation. Certainly labor is doing it more and more. The schools should advocate more participation on boards and agencies and more participation in the campaigns. Certainly! I feel that if the schools prepared men for what service problems they will run into and how to handle them they would build up better citizenship.

Do you suppose that the words United Foundation are ever mentioned in a high school program today?

They are in Detroit.

Is this partly on your initiative?

Partly, because the schools have a program of acquainting the students with the United Foundation.

How did this happen? It wasn't an accident, was it?

No, but they have civics classes and it is part of their discussion during our campaign period. They discuss in class what our United Foundation is. We're not too concerned with how much money we get from the students—we never look at that. They do in some cities—they measure very, very carefully and try to make gains.

Do you solicit in the schools?

Oh yes, we do solicit in the schools but it is a case of no pressure and the kids giving what they have. We encourage them to give as much as they can, but not anything that will interfere with the family budget.

I have a question on entirely a different tack. That is in relation to public welfare programs. Do you find that the subject of public welfare comes up sometimes in connection with your drives? Do people tell you when you ask for money, in effect, "After all we have this giant public welfare system going on and isn't this handling needs?" Do they say that "this should have something to do with how much I give"?

We have had very little of that. What they do ask is this

(and it was asked of me only yesterday), "Why do you keep increasing your goals during times of great prosperity?" The answer is, of course, that we have as many split homes. It costs more with the increased living costs. You have just as many kids who are delinquent—if not more; their parents are out more in the beer gardens; there are just as many desertions; and just as many are sick.

Do you think that taking into consideration the increase in population in your area and the decreased value in the dollar, you have really increased substantially the amount given for voluntary welfare?

Oh, certainly we have! Considerably. And also when you consider what the federal, county, and state governments take from us, the total dollar expended (except for direct relief, and that is down at the moment because we have fairly high employment) is far greater than before. When you examine this you have to look at the total dollar and not just the voluntary agencies or the public agencies. The trouble with so many of the people in the business is that they talk about "per capita giving" from city to city when each one of their packages is different. Why in this town our public dollar supports three hospital beds. In Cleveland it doesn't. That service is supported through their community chest. It's just like comparing apples and oranges—you can't do it.

Mr. Laidlaw, shall we look into the future for just a few minutes? I'm curious as to whether you feel that ten years from now your organization will be raising money more for youth, or more for children, or more for the aging. What is the shift likely to be in voluntary welfare, would you say?

The tremendous growth in the country makes me think that it will definitely be children in the next ten years. There will be greater and greater demands. It will affect your school systems, hospitals, everything else.

You mean children up to what age?

All the way through—that is, up through high school.

Children and youths then.

Yes. Then as people live longer with these wonder drugs, and because they just seem to be living longer this day and age, you are going to have more problems with the aged. Just look at the problems that have developed since you and I were kids. In the old days you had large houses, and the old grandfather and grandmother could live with the family. Today with the cost of homes, people have two or three bedrooms at the most. That is what the average person has today. And there's no place for grandparents, so perhaps you are going to have more homes for the aged. Of course, they can become self-supporting because of social security and old age assistance. And it won't be such a drain on the tax dollar except as maybe in rehabilitation programs. We have had several agencies, such as the "Drop In" agencies for the aged or retired workers sponsored by the CIO. Another is the Clinic Center which is sponsored by the Catholic church and several other settlement houses which have been long-time members of our Foundation. Now there is talk of expanding expenditures along that line, but I don't know how it will turn out.

What kind of people do you hire for your organization?

Actually, I operate considerably differently from other people in the united funds around the country. Surprisingly, three-quarters of my staff come out of business and industry rather than schools of social work. I daresay 80 or rather 90 per cent of my staff, because we look on ourselves as primarily a finance and marketing organization. I think that is one of the reasons that we are truly successful, because we hire people who have a background of marketing and organization.

Do you have a social work background yourself?

Oh no, except that I served six years as a member of the State Welfare Commission. This is one of the largest commissions in America. And I believe that was probably the greatest training that I could ever receive.

Is this considered an appropriate term—are you a "fund-raiser" by category? If the census came in and asked, "What do you do?" what would you answer?

I would say that I'm in the business of financing. Because it's not just fund-raising. It's administering and it is also concerning yourself with the finance problems of the whole health and social welfare field. Our job is quite different from the professional fund-raiser. If you have a problem that has to be financed—he'll come and raise the funds for a fee. In other words, he earns his living entirely this way. Three-quarters of my time is spent on financing—it used to be that three-quarters of my time was spent on the campaign, but not any more. This time was not entirely in the United Foundation—I spent a number of days last year in reorganizing our Hospital Council, which is quite unique. It's a hospital council of administrators—it's a nice club for the administrators! Nothing ever happened, but they did meet and talk about mutual problems. We have reorganized it with 50 per cent of the people representing the community, primarily the "gimme community" that has to put up the money for the new hospitals. We do have some labor leaders sprinkled in there, too, and various other citizens such as doctors, et cetera.

You mentioned labor—do you find in your community that labor has any trouble producing leaders for your drives?

I would say "yes." The trouble with labor is that every one of the labor leaders is so involved—they really lead a hell of a life, I would say, for the demands on their time, morning, noon, and night, are terrific. Consequently they have very few hours available. We have been able to free some of their staff members for work in our organization, such committees as our Goal and Allocations Committee, and they have really made a tremendous contribution. They are men with their "feet on the ground." Maybe they didn't have a college education, but they are practical and realistic, and I have a great admiration for those fellows. They don't like too many frills in health and social work. They want real service for people.

Mr. Laidlaw, I heard you say to the National Solicitations Conference something I would like you to repeat if you would. It was approximately that "the corporations that are located here in Detroit are very eager that corporations that do not have headquarters here, but have a branch plant here, do their share in contributing funds."

Absolutely!

How do they reason this out? What argument do they use to persuade these absentee corporations to do their share?

Well, we preach to our own corporations that every corporation should be a good citizen in the communities where they do business. In other words, if the company has a plant here, and has employees here, and stockholders here, they should all give consideration to our appeal for finances. It is difficult, because I realize that they should help their own home community. But they should not overweight it, either, to the point where other communities throughout America where they have plants doing business suffer.

That brings up my second point, which is—do these Detroit-based and controlled corporations follow in their plant branches this same advice that they give?

Absolutely. We're proud of our motor industry. Sure, may-

171

be there are a few weak spots in the whole deal, but we're awfully proud of the kind of a job that they are doing in other communities. It used to be a problem some years ago, but today they accept the corporate responsibility. In fact, yesterday I was talking about an hour on the phone with a Ford Motor Company official about a hospital drive going on in Cincinnati at the present time. They have about 7,000 employees, and when they were called upon to give in Cincinnati to the hospital drive they gave $250,000, which I am told is a little bit above the average, down there.

A friend of mine with an investment house says that he thinks corporations have no obligation to give anything to anybody because this "cuts the pie" before the stockholders get it. Do you agree with this?

No!

Why don't you agree with it?

In the first place, a corporation has to take into consideration its position in a community. They have an obligation for services provided to their own employees. For instance, if you have a visiting nurse that serves the employees of any one company (and maybe they are laid off at that time) they should be making a contribution toward that visiting nurse. The payment of her wages, that is.

How valuable is it to a corporation to have its employees properly cared for by social and health agencies in emergencies? Is it a "cash value" to a corporation to have a place where young people can go and play (as in the case of the YMCA) and to have a place where the wife and the husband can go to talk over their marital problems? Are these community services valuable to a corporation in any way?

Why certainly! If a fellow takes his problems to the office or the factory he's not going to be as good an employee as he would be if he were freed of his problems. This is definite and has been proven.

There's a real cash value then?

Yes. Also, in a good, wholesome community not involved with vice and corruption it has been proven that the tax load for a corporation is less.

Mr. Laidlaw, would you agree or not with the director of a public welfare department who told me a year ago in contempt (he was an old codger and very sour), "As far as I'm concerned, the whole field of voluntary welfare in my county could disappear and I'd never miss it!"

172

I would say that he was purely a "welfare bureaucrat," or a public agency bureaucrat. Maybe he wouldn't miss it, but the people sure would.

He felt that he was paying out millions, and he compared this with the smaller amounts that the voluntary field had available.

He was usually paying out direct relief. Feeding and housing.

You're not?

We're not. We do take care of some emergency situations.

Do you have the figures for your community of cash aid actually paid out by your agencies? How much cash is paid out?

Out of $16,000,000 it would be about $200,000 at the most. Primarily the biggest spender of that will be the Salvation Army. That will vary according to various employment conditions.

I calculated the voluntary agencies' cash payment figure for San Francisco at 1.7 per cent. Do you have any religious problems among your various member agencies?

Do you mean clashes? None whatever.

Do they have any in other communities?

They had one down in Lorain, Ohio, of major consequence. They have had some trouble in the South in some communities; they have had some with the Urban Leagues [Negro]. But in Lorain they were conducting a Capital Fund drive. Lorain is about 50 to 60 per cent Catholic, and several priests and a bishop objected to the financing of a Salvation Army building. There was quite a stir about it and later on they decided that the best thing to do was for the Salvation Army to be financed separately—if it was going to break up the community. In fact, many started to point their finger at the United Fund of Lorain on account of this problem. We wouldn't have that kind of a situation in Detroit. I'm satisfied that we have a very liberal-minded cardinal who is outstanding in the field of health and social welfare.

Is Planned Parenthood a member agency?

It is not—they tried to get in and we rejected them.

This had no religious overtone?

Well, this is what happened—they were refused admittance, and then they attempted to put on a designation campaign. (That is where they wrote letters to individuals and asked them to designate 10 per cent of their contribution to

Planned Parenthood.) We had up to that time honored designations, so I could see that it was a growing problem. So I reviewed the whole matter with my officers and made a recommendation that we no longer permit designations to outside agencies.

What do you mean by a "designation"?

Well, that's when you say 10 per cent or so of my pledge must go to Infantile Paralysis.

Even though it is not a member?

We would have sent that check to the Infantile Paralysis Association [a local body; not the National Foundation].

Do you believe in public regulation of voluntary agencies? Do you think that this is desirable philosophically?

On a limited basis entirely; very much limited. Yet licensing is very important—reporting to either a solicitations committee or the public welfare department or something like that.

Why should they report?

I think a report prevents fraud more than anything else. There have been proved rackets, and the only way you can keep them out is by licensing and reporting.

And this includes regulation of fund-raising; you would approve of such regulation by a public agency?

If it just doesn't have too many teeth in it. Some of these people just go completely overboard! They fail to take into consideration that in the long run public opinion takes care of things.

You feel to some extent that it's better to have a very small number of rackets than to have the government control too much voluntary activity?

That's a toughie! I would say that perhaps we have to put up with a few rackets, but I don't believe that to get rid of a few you should so bind your private agencies that it makes it difficult and costly for them to go out and do a soliciting job.

You are the largest voluntary fund-raising organization in the nation?

That's right—also in the world.

Yet you are publicly regulated, I suppose, and file a report?

Yes, we file a report with the Solicitations Committee.

In your opinion and perhaps in the opinion of the corporation men, professional men, etc., who are among those behind you, would you say that public regulation does not constitute government interference?

No, it doesn't, any more than when any corporation files
with the Securities and Exchange Commission.
Thank you very much, Mr. Laidlaw.

Here was the voice of a man dedicated to financing the
preservation of American voluntary welfare activity. At the time
of the interview it seemed inevitable that his way—the united
way—would sweep all before it in the cities and towns of the
nation. Boston, in 1957, had for the first time a united fund, including Red Cross; Chicago's Joint Appeal (not a true united
fund by any means) took in Red Cross; Cleveland did so, in 1958.
The battle of Pittsburgh was in the offing, but federated campaigns had annually increased the amount and the percentage
figures which were so hopefully totaled by protagonists-for-unity
in metropolitan board rooms. But clouds were on the horizon as
the American Cancer Society prepared to order its member groups
out of unified funds by a 1960 deadline and other health agencies
girded their loins. The cost of multiple solicitations in factories
had disturbed corporation management, and in the *Harvard Business Review* and elsewhere management men were being urged
to give "community service" work all they had.

Thirty years earlier, in 1928, a strong plea had been made
for corporations to assume their rightful share of financing community-chest agencies. The acting governor of the Federal Reserve Bank of New York, J. H. Case, warned at the time, "Unless
corporations generally can be induced to assume their fair share
of the cost of welfare work in their localities, welfare activities
in many communities will stagnate." Wealth in corporate form,
he noted on the eve of the Depression, was displacing individual
wealth. Local business was being matched in size and even replaced by chain corporations. So it was that this official found that
"many nationally organized, centrally officered corporations carry
no proportionate share of this local cost in the great majority of
places." Passage of three decades would change this picture substantially, but there were many to dispute the propriety of management's giving away the stockholders' profits. If Detroit is any
criterion, the peak in corporation giving to federated funds in
large cities may have passed. Consider some facts:

During the years from 1949 to 1957 in Detroit a substantial shift in giving among the three basic giving groups took place. The corporations increased their giving totals from $3,700,000 to $4,-800,000 as the community grew, population increased, sales multiplied, and new agencies joined the Torch Drive (and as federal defense expenditures soared), but the corporation share of the total raised fell sharply from 40.4 per cent to 29.3 per cent. Here was a drastic decline. At the same time, the "executive and salaried" employees of Detroit increased their proportion of the whole from 26.3 per cent to 37.5 per cent (from $2,400,000 to $6,200,000). And hourly employees increased the total of their small, individual gifts from nearly $2,000,000 to nearly $3,600,000. The amounts given by residential foundations and retired wealthy people changed very little.

The significance of these figures was not lost on the Detroit fund-raisers. The elaborate 11- by 14-inch brochure prepared for corporate attention in 1957 italicized three phrases which tell the story: One said the "corporations' part of total funds raised was reduced from 40.5 per cent to 31.4 per cent [1957]." On another page a second sentence said, "Consider the savings effected by the fact that during 1955 *no major health or charitable organization conducted a campaign directed at corporations or their personnel in this area.*" A third sentence urged that *"no corporation's gift should be less than it was in 1955."* But to keep over-all totals in line it would have had to exceed that of 1955.

In the year 1955, corporate giving as a percentage of the total given the United Foundation in Detroit (i.e., 31.5 per cent) was lower than any number of other cities in the nation, examples at random from cities raising over a million dollars being: Atlanta 39 per cent; Dayton, 38; Hartford, 43; Nashville, 34; Richmond, 36; San Diego, 38; and Worcester, 38. Of course, the corporate-giving percentage in Detroit was higher than in other cities that could be named. In the following thirteen cities, in 1956, the range in the percentage of the whole given by corporations and other businesses was from 26 to 47 per cent. Five were in the thirties; seven were in the forties. There may also be seen the many thousands of persons and firms who gave less than one hundred dollars each, and the small numbers who gave more than five thousand dollars each. These figures are not particularly surprising, but they do form a potent reminder that the small giver exists and that there are many of him. This is something for the big givers to remember.

BIG AND LITTLE GIVERS

	Per Cent of Total Given by Business Firms and Corporations	More Than $5,000	Number of Gifts of:		Ratio
			Less Than $100		
St. Louis	42	142	194,930	1 : 1,370	
Cincinnati	41	97	243,969	1 : 2,510	
Philadelphia	41	203	617,325	1 : 3,040	
United Bay Area Crusade	37	158	519,996	1 : 3,170	
Syracuse	33	37	122,063	1 : 3,300	
Cleveland	36	145	480,194	1 : 3,310	
Portland	34	37	150,122	1 : 4,060	
Toronto	44	116	475,080	1 : 4,100	
Milwaukee	47	72	311,565	1 : 4,330	
Seattle	42	44	206,244	1 : 4,690	
Minneapolis	42	42	212,930	1 : 5,070	
Denver	26	28	181,854	1 : 6,490	
Akron	36	15	116,982	1 : 7,790	

Corporation officials who can read the plain statistics on the United Foundation for a decade, figures which show a steady unloading of the contributions burden from corporations to individuals, must feel somewhat guiltily that "Give Once the United Way" was invented for the benefit of the stockholders in Detroit corporations. Unless the indicated trend should be arrested, the time will come when the burden of giving will fall overwhelmingly on individuals again—as in the early years of this century. After all, Detroit's individuals shouldered 47.5 per cent back in 1949. By 1957, they carried 59.2 per cent. Here was nearly a 25 per cent increase in their direct load.

177

In vain, one must presume, the United Foundation has pointed out to corporations and businesses in printed statements that "under today's tax laws, a corporation can give up to 5 per cent of its taxable income at an actual cost of approximately 50 per cent of its gifts (in some cases, even less)." Tax laws allow a corporation to deduct charitable contributions made during the year, provided they do not exceed 5 per cent of taxable income. It can even carry over into two succeeding years amounts in excess of 5 per cent which are contributed. The United States government (i.e., the corpus of taxpayers) loses taxes and therefore "pays" 30 per cent of gifts from a taxable income of less than $25,000. When income is more than that amount the government "gift" is a full 52 per cent. Even under these favorable conditions top management has dragged its feet in giving to the voluntary welfare field, and there is a feeling in some quarters that giving should come from stockholders—not from managerial largesse with their money.

Gifts of securities which have increased substantially in value have been very favorable donations for a corporation to make to a united fund. For example, Detroit firms are advised, and management should bear in mind, that: "A gift of securities having a market value of $10,000 and an original cost of $2,500 would result in a net cost to the corporation of $2,925 if the securities were held for more than six months. The net cost to the corporation would be only $900 if the securities had been held for less than six months. On the other hand, a similar gift of cash would cost the corporation $4,800."

In order to equalize their giving somewhat in both good years and bad (and to avoid giving in haste at the close of a tax year), some corporations are organizing charitable foundations or trusts and accumulating funds in these. Executive management of corporations, with such funds available to them, have been looking over the whole field of possible philanthropic giving; and much experimental giving has resulted, particularly to educational institutions and especially to those that train the engineers and scientists on whom corporations have come to lean so heavily. The United Foundation organized a Trust Division in an effort to act as trustee for a maximum number of such funds and to prevent the diversion of this money to other philanthropic purposes. Management seemed to be more sympathetic toward higher education in the 1950's than to voluntary welfare, and it may be suspected that antagonism toward the "recalcitrant" national health agencies for their independence of united drives had an effect on at least some corporation gifts to them. Ample publicity attended corporate gifts to education, on the whole, while similar publicity for gifts to united drives or other charitable causes could have been considered to border on bad taste.

In any case, the return in future engineers and scientists comprised a "safe" reason for making contributions to educational institutions, in the eyes of hardheaded executives who live with the problem of preparing an annual report and facing subsequent stockholders' meetings. Indeed, in the privacy of discussions on the subject, those charged with giving corporate dollars came to note wryly the wisdom of steering one's educational giving to institutions from which key stockholders or members of the board of directors had been graduated.

Is the increased corporation giving to education which followed Russia's successful launching of the Sputnik satellite coming in part from money that would otherwise have gone to community health, welfare, and recreation? Here is a most difficult question, one probably impossible to answer. Inasmuch as stockholders in large corporations are most unlikely to reside in the towns where the plants are located, it may be that management has come to regard "community" gifts as harder to explain to stockholders than scholarship grants to student engineers and gifts for practical research. It may be noted, moreover, that almost no women occupied the top public-relations' posts or vice presidencies where preliminary screening of requests for funds took place in the corporate world of the 1950's. The National Solicitations Conference of 1959, for example, had no woman delegate among its several hundred corporation representatives, so far as I could observe. The lone woman visible at this annual meeting of executives who give away the stockholders' money was an observer from the local League of Women Voters.

The Laidlaws of the nation are laboring mightily to keep the dollars coming to their united funds. Local agencies obviously need these dollars—and more. Red Cross has often joined forces with the united way and it expects results. Hopefully, United Community Funds and Councils instituted in April, 1958, a new measurement technique for ascertaining the "fund-raising potential" of corporations, using corporate new-income-after-taxes as a key ingredient. How many united funds would make the necessary computations was problematical, since *research*, as social scientists know the word, is almost unknown to even the largest of them. Getting the facts is a luxury item.

The burden on men like the executive head of the Torch Fund is heavy. But these executives bear the burden cheerfully. "We are living in an exciting period," says Raymond Baarts of United Bay Area Crusade, third largest in the nation. "We must forget our doubts, make the machinery work, and remember that united fund-raising is a union of three partners—agencies, volunteers, and the contributing public."

In Detroit, San Francisco, and elsewhere the "Give Once" protagonists are going to have to be dedicated to keeping the dollars coming if they are to avoid being swamped by a total welfare state. By keeping the dollars coming—and always remembering the over-all public interest—they can justify themselves in the eyes of contributors. They can also help guarantee the survival of the form of American society in which they so clearly believe.

CHAPTER IX

AFL-CIO Can Invigorate Voluntary Welfare

"Give your fair share!" What is
My share, when every dollar
That I make is used for food and
Clothes and cars and now and then
A beer?

"Give your time, then!" "Maybe
That would work, for work
Is what my Father did, full
Fifty hours—so he said more times
Than not.

"Our industry works forty hours now;
Perhaps some Saturday, or afternoons
We'd work. And then the Scouts
Would get the dough they need. Say,
Why not?

"But think of all the problems! And
We might get cheated. Still, there's
Joe—and Al—and Bill; they serve on
All those boards and things. Let's
Try it!"

LOCAL TRADE UNIONS, like other organizations in the United
States, have long tried to assume a certain amount of responsibility for the welfare of underprivileged persons. Akin to the
Masons, Elks, Lions, or American Association of University
Women in this respect, union locals have bought Christmas bas-
kets, sold benefit tickets, solicited funds, and made it their business to act constructively when a member's family might find itself in dire distress. International union organizations, on the
other hand, have continued to think of themselves as inherently
public-service organizations. By helping union members to get
higher wages, they feel they serve the greater community. Nevertheless, and perhaps for this very reason, labor leaders have been
slow to assume the policy-making and governing roles over the

destinies of welfare agencies which could be theirs. (Yet they have acted on occasion, as witness the dispute between the Red Cross and union leaders during World War II, when some spokesmen for the workers thought, for a time, that the best interests of the common man were not being served. Fortunately, that wartime controversy quickly faded and is now long dead.)

Only in the 1950's did organized labor, in the form of the newly united AFL-CIO, establish a Community Services Committee. According to the AFL-CIO constitution, the new committee was to "stimulate the active participation by members and affiliated unions in the affairs of their communities and the development of sound relationships with social agencies in such communities." Big unions, and both state federations and city centrals, were to form community services departments, complete with full-time staffs, wherever possible. The first chairman of the committee was Joseph A. Beirne, president of the Communications Workers. The national director was Leo Perlis. Great opportunities for service awaited the new group.

One of the first objectives of the new Community Services Committee was to see that union leaders participated fully in policy formation and fund-raising activities of the united funds and community chests of the nation. The United Community Funds and Councils organization, with headquarters in New York City, had for a decade tried to carry on a "working partnership" with the unions by employing labor-staff representatives. It finally stated, "Together we have developed a many-sided program; both have benefited by this partnership." But the limited degree of trade-union participation was satisfactory to neither the fund-raisers nor the unions. Approximately one hundred thousand union members volunteered for some sort of service in the 1955 campaigns, and this figure increased in subsequent years.

Having looked longingly at the big union organizations and wished somehow that their full machinery could be mustered behind the annual community-fund, the united funds and community chests have taken heart as union interest has increased. For their part, the unions are considering the course they should pursue. The direction of their thinking may be seen clearly in the resolution passed by the delegates to one of the national AFL-CIO conventions.

It was agreed that what is good for the community is good for labor. Therefore, the AFL-CIO would have, as a major objective, increased labor representation on welfare-agency boards and committees until their participation reached what was termed "an equitable basis." Labor would try to take a more active part in the formulation of welfare-agency policies and programs. Further, an effort would be made to acquaint union members with the welfare, health, and recreation services available to them in the community. (Civil defense and disaster-relief programs and operations were also slanted for full labor participation.) Labor's goal would be the "development of health and welfare services." Thus labor would participate in "genuine efforts designed to improve social-work standards and practices." Finally, and very important indeed, labor thought fund drives should be co-ordinated "through voluntary federation whenever possible." Here was labor's credo for the future; and, to the extent that words would be matched by deeds, it was a highly significant resolution. Opportunities for their work remain great.

There is much that an aroused and aggressive trade-union movement can do to strengthen and enlarge voluntary welfare. The time has come for AFL-CIO to step forward and save voluntary welfare: that is, the independent, nongovernmental welfare agencies. Labor's own official resolutions on participation and fund-raising indicate that the preservation and strengthening of voluntary welfare are policy objectives of the trade-union movement in America. In the light of these objectives, two things can be done: (1) Union leaders can play their rightful roles in fund-raising and agency policy-making only by complete participation as members of the boards of directors of the major agencies in voluntary welfare. (2) By consenting to try new departures in the field of fund-raising, the unions can greatly increase the total financing of the voluntary welfare field. The results of these two undertakings would be a profound change in the social-welfare structure in America.

There can be no question that, at the local level, a real impact could be made by even a single volunteer from labor's ranks—a man deeply stirred, intelligent, and willing to work with a committee, a man who would accept a leadership role when the opportunity presented itself. But under what circumstances does such a man step forward to serve? What happens when he does?

One of the many new community servants to be found in America is Alfred Clarence Offenstein of Salem, Oregon. As secretary of the Salem Printing Pressmen and Assistant's Union, local 247, he negotiated in the 1950's the contracts of three unions with the *Statesman Journal*. A pressman by trade, Mr. Offenstein came to Oregon by way of Wichita, Kansas, and Grand Rapids, Michigan. In his fifties, this orthodox trade union man began to take an active part as a volunteer in the financing of voluntary welfare in his adopted city. How did this happen, and what did this role mean for him, for labor, and for his community? Join us in a convention hotel room, over one thousand miles from his home city, where he sits, tired from listening to three days of speeches but entirely relaxed.

Tell us, Mr. Offenstein, how did you get started in social welfare activities?

It has been my task to negotiate the contracts for the Typographical Union, the Stereotyping Union, and the Pressman's Union. We have joint negotiations, and I have been the chairman for the past five years. At the end of a session five years ago, Mr. Bernard Mainwaring (who was at that time the publisher of the evening paper, the *Capitol Journal*) asked me why I didn't use some of my talents and get interested in the community chest which was in operation in Salem. Mr. Mainwaring at that time had always held an influential part in both city, county, and state government. At the time of his death he was a member of the higher Board of Education in Oregon. He held numerous high offices in civic organizations such as Kiwanis, and he had taken an active part in the formation of the Salem United Fund. He was a dedicated man who not only gave of his time and his talents, but he also gave very liberally of his money. When he asked me to become interested in the Salem United Fund, I told him that I didn't think I had the time to put into that sort of thing. "Well," he said, "you are taking the wrong viewpoint."

184

During the succeeding six months at various times when he had the chance he would call me into his office and start "telling me and selling me" on united fund work. Well, naturally I got to the point where I was either going to have to do something about it or else get away from it! So I finally told him, "All right. I'll do some of the things you have asked me and see how they work out."

So he asked me as my first job in the Salem United Fund if I would assume the role of the chapter chairman in our plant. In this plant we have 187 employees; this includes office girls, janitors, and everybody on the payroll. So when he got me to act as chairman I went out into the plant and picked my committee from the various departments and called them together. Then Mr. Thompson, who became president of the Salem United Fund, came over and proceeded to explain the techniques and operations of the chapter plans. We got it thoroughly in our minds that a successful chapter must have a definite quota that they must try to raise. After talking with the boys on my committee we took as our quota 2 per cent of the goal of the Salem United Fund. Mr. Mainwaring said, "You are a little optimistic." And I said, "Well, why?" He replied that under the community chest they had never reached their goal. To this I replied, "Well, if we go into the United Fund, and we go into it right, our salary structure is such in our plant that we should have no trouble in reaching the 2 per cent." "Well," he said, "you are very optimistic and I hope you can do it." I'm not bragging, but with the excellent co-operation and help that I had from other fellow employees we raised 2.5 per cent in 1952, the first year we were in.

After that he said, "Well, you have shown us that you have the ability to understand the problems in this kind of work, and I think that you should take on additional responsibilities. I kind of laughed and said, "I'll just leave that up to you." About twenty days afterward on my night off (incidentally, I do work nights) my telephone rang at home and when I answered someone said, "We're calling for the Salem United Fund and we wonder if you would accept a nomination for the board of directors?" I asked who was calling me and he replied, "Mr. Mainwaring asked me to call you." This was the only reply that I got. So I answered, "Evidently you have talked to Mr. Mainwaring, and if he thinks I can do the job I'm willing to take a crack at it, but it's going to take a lot of study on my part to fulfill the obligation that I will be taking on."

My boss backed me up 100 per cent, not only with words but with financial means. He sent me places and paid all of my luncheon expenses the first year I was in the work (that is, the report luncheons, board of directors meetings, and many others). He sent me to Portland to observe the child welfare care agencies—anything that was connected with the United Fund—even if it was on a night when I was supposed to be working. He would say, "You take off and go—here is the money. Your salary goes on just the same." Evidently I have been some good, because ever since then the [United Fund] board of directors have sent me around to these various conferences. It pleases me that they have this much confidence in me and feel that they can rely on me to attend a conference and bring back an intelligent report.

When you attend a conference whom do you represent?

I represent the Salem United Fund, but I want you to know that I'm on the board of directors to represent labor.

Will you explain your use of "labor" to me?

I'm secretary of the Pressmen and Assistants Union, so I naturally have my labor affiliations. One of the reasons why Mr. Mainwaring wanted me on the board was, and these are his words, "Labor in Salem needs some intelligent representatives on the board of directors. I class you as that." Again, that was quite a compliment to me; I'm only human after all, and you know that a pat on the back makes a fellow feel pretty good. I did get on the board of directors, and would like to tell you about the structure of the board. We have forty-two members on the board of directors, composed of businessmen, bankers, doctors, and lawyers, but labor is very capably and well represented. Out of the forty-two, there are ten members of organized labor on there, so you can see that they are well represented and have an equal share, far better than most.

How is labor attendance? Do they come to the directors' meetings?

Our records are open, and if you ever get to Salem to see them, you will see that our attendance averages 90 per cent during the entire year.

Is that high for the group?

That's high. After inquiring around the other chests and funds at these various conferences, I have found that this is an excellent attendance.

You say there are ten representatives of labor? Do you know them all?

That's right.

I wonder if you would generalize for me a little on what you would consider to be their motives? We'll start with them and then come to you, perhaps. In general, why do you suppose they are doing this?

Well, I've been connected with labor unions for the past thirty-five years in various capacities, as secretary, as president of a local, or chairman of the Tri-State Conference, and this is my opinion. Up until the last three or four years labor has had very poor public-information programs. In other words, some of the things that labor is doing now have been done in the past also, but nobody knew about it. Since the AFL-CIO merger we have what is known as a Community Services Committee on the national level. They instructed by resolutions adopted at the first meeting of the combined board of directors of the AFL-CIO held in Miami, Florida, some three years ago, that all local unions must have a committee of three people to back worthwhile civic projects in the community in which they live. They set up a ten-point program which I am sure you have seen. I feel, and the other members of the board also feel, that we have a definite responsibility to the community in which we reside and where we are making our living. But it's been pretty hard until recently for us to discharge that responsibility, because members of management can belong to the luncheon clubs, gather together an hour and a half at noon, and take on various civic projects, but a man working back in the shop in overalls can't do that. So we really didn't have any organized way to express and discharge our civic responsibility.

Now this group of union fellows that I have with me on the board you would probably consider to be "dedicated men." I would agree with you. We feel that there is a job to do, and we want to do the best that we can, and we want to interest the other members of labor to do the best that they can with this obligation that we feel that we owe. I would like to say that the Salem United Fund has co-operated with us 100 per cent. You will find members of organized labor on every committee in our fund. You will find two members of labor sitting on our budget committee. Last year, the president of our fund was Mr. Herb Barker, who was secretary-

187

treasurer of the Central Labor Council. This year, I have a job which I think is one of the most important jobs in our fund—I am chairman of the chapter relations committee. I have as members of my committee the entire forty-two members of the board of directors. At my direction they have been going out and working, and I have yet to hear one say, "Well, here we are taking orders from a union man!" Whenever I ask them to go out and do a job they discharge it. We all have the best co-operation with one another.

Let me ask you this—do you think that those ten men could do the job that they are doing at the moment just as effectively if they had been chosen (and if they thought of themselves as serving) as ordinary citizens instead of representatives of trade union and labor interests?

No, I don't think they could. And my reason is this: Run-of-the-mill union men, until three or four years ago, had more or less an inferiority complex when it came to dealing with management. They felt that management looked down on them—and that their efforts couldn't get them any place because management would just throw obstacles in their way. Through this vehicle of the Salem United Fund we have been able to prove ourselves to members of management, lawyers, and bankers. They were skeptical when they put us on—but they have gotten away from that viewpoint and they take us in and work with us "hand in glove." That was one way we had to discharge our civic responsibility, whereas we could not have done anything as individuals—we could not have gone in and talked to the president of the bank! Now any one of us out of the ten can go into the bank and the president can call us by name and we go over and chat with him. Why? Because he found out that we were human beings, just as he is.

Would you say that on any occasion anyone has ever charged one of you with "feathering his own nest" socially or politically, or (I hesitate to say) financially? Have such allegations been made in your hearing because of this activity?

Definitely! In fact, I think if the other nine fellows were here they would tell you that, when we first started in this thing, that people were very skeptical of what we were going to do. But as a group we felt that if we were ever going to overcome and break down the prejudices in our community that we had to get in and do a job. I'll assure you that the first year we really watched our P's and Q's! We were awfully careful; we didn't try to throw our weight around; and we tried not to do anything that would make people dislike us, but we observed and worked in the minor capacities that were assigned to us. They found out that they could rely on us in the small things, and then they began to give us the larger, more responsible jobs to do.

Then you feel that you and your friends are likely to maintain this interest over a rather considerable period of time.

I think without a doubt that because of the seeds planted in this group of ten men, and through them, we are succeeding in getting various other people who we think are qualified to take over some of this work when we are ready to step out —I don't mean get clear out of the thing, but we should get some new blood in. Then we will still remain in the background helping them. We're succeeding right now in getting groups of union people by our constant talking with them and telling them what is happening. They can also begin to observe things for themselves.

Now we do one other thing in Salem that I think is very important as far as labor and management is concerned. We have a Labor-Management Committee which is composed of ten members of organized labor and ten members of management. We meet and do various projects in the community. The project that we do for the Salem United Fund is to put on once a year a Labor-Management Workshop Institute.

At this Institute we have a panel of all the social work agencies that the Salem United Fund raises money for. We have the entire Labor-Management Committee there. We arrange a program where a top member of management speaks, and then a member of labor follows him. This usually gives us about an hour-and-a-half speaking program, which covers various phases of the work. At the 1957 meeting, I was assigned the task of addressing this group on "Labor's Share in the Salem United Fund." There was also a speaker who spoke for management on their role in the United Fund.

Is this a monetary "share"—the amount of money—or is this the amount of service—or is it the amount that you are going to get out of it?

Well, there are two things. We feel that we have a share in the United Fund because we feel that we should help raise the money because we live there, we like the town, and we want to do it. In doing this we feel that we can make people realize that we are a part of the community and not just a

189

group of fellows that have their hands out and are grabbing everything they can get.

I want to ask this—judging from what you hear, read, and observe in your travels, is the situation as you have described it (that is, labor participation) in Salem noticeably unusual in your state, the West, or in the nation? Or is this something that is increasingly common?

I would like to qualify the statement that I'm going to make to you in this respect—as I told you before, my board of directors have sent me to various conferences. They sent me to the National Labor-Management Conference in San Francisco three years ago; they paid the bill for me and I went down and stayed a full week. The top labor leaders from all over the country were at this meeting. I went to the conference primarily to keep my ears open and my mouth shut. I was there to learn, and I learned a great deal. And I find that in my various traveling up and down California, Oregon, Washington, and Idaho that our setup is just a little farther advanced than most of them.

At this conference, which we are attending jointly, you have heard the expression, "We can't get labor to serve on our boards, and can't get them to serve if we put them on." So I think ours is a little unusual. I lay this to my colleague, Mr. Herb Barker, secretary, Central Labor Council, who is an A-number-one fellow, who has a keen mind, a broad mind; he's willing to look at both sides of everything, and he realizes that a "pancake has two sides."

What advice would you give to labor leaders at the city level on the basis of your experience? I'm speaking now of labor leaders who have had little or no experience similar to yours.

Well, I think the only way that you can approach a problem like that is through contact with a person who has a good reputation in the community for his dealings with labor, some representative of management who, in the past, has dealt with labor and they know that he is sincere and honest in his approach to the problem. That person should visit the Central Labor Council and make himself known to the secretary and sit down and have a chat with him, and then proceed to tell him the story that the community needs the help of labor if they are going to do this thing right. He could also tell the secretary that the community not only needs labor but they also need the community, and that they would gain something out of it. They would gain recognition for what they did, because we're all human and when we do a job we like to be told that we did a "good job." This may be a selfish attitude, but this United Fund is composed of people and is for people. And union labor represents our people just like management. The only difference is the old bugaboo that labor has against management—they think when management approaches them they are out to take something away from labor, that they have a hidden motive.

It's just a question of being able to trust one another. And it's going to take time and patience on both sides to build it up. However, when the confidence of the secretary of the Central Council is built, then the secretary will be able to help by finding men from the various labor unions and getting them interested in this thing.

Management should by all means be open and above board. Labor should have every opportunity to explore everything in the setup. They must not try to keep anything hidden from them. Just lay the cards out on the table, and when the boys see that they are dealing with them honestly I'm sure that they will respond, because the boys in Salem are no different than they are anywhere else. But they have just had better opportunities than the average labor group.

Would you say that it is in any respect a fair or accurate statement that labor and management see "eye to eye" more often on fund-raising and fund distribution to voluntary agencies than they do in the state capitols on public welfare problems and health programs?

Definitely so.

Do you think that this is inevitable?

Well, it gets back to the old thing that the average union man is skeptical of anything that he knows nothing about. But in the United Fund he has a chance to find out how the budget is arrived at and how the funds are allocated after the money is raised. At the state capitol the only representation that he has is the labor lobbyist. He's always skeptical of the politicians and what they are trying to do. However, in the United Fund, labor is given a chance to know what is going on. If they don't know, all they have to do is take the time and trouble to find out.

If you were talking to a group of labor leaders at the moment and advising them, what type of voluntary welfare agency would you say is peculiarly useful to labor and, in a sense, would be its "baby"? What category of agency, without mentioning any particular names?

Most working people—and that's what organized labor people are—have a tendency to have a fairly large family, so I think that their primary interest would be in the organizations supporting youth welfare, such as your YMCA, Boy Scouts, etc., where they know that their children are definitely getting something out of it.

When you say "youth" are you including children's agencies such as Crippled Children, rehabilitation, adoption—that is, do you use "youth" as including children or excluding them?

Including them. I mean like these nursery homes that take care of them and some of the agencies you mentioned. I'd like to tell you something else. As you've probably observed I'm a Mason, and as such I've taken all the Masonic work I can get in both branches of the Masons and Shrine. And the primary reason that I wear a Shrine pin today is because I've always been intrigued with any organization that deals with crippled children. I have seen children born with club feet, children that no one had taken an interest in, and other crippled boys and girls given medical aid in the crippled children's hospitals. These children turn out to be useful citizens of the community.

Then in summary, Mr. Offenstein, you think labor participation is a growing thing—or at least that it ought to be?

I think it is definitely growing but is growing slowly. Sometimes from my viewpoint I get very impatient. But then I stop and try to realize that this thing can't be done in a day, or a year. It will have to be done with education, both of the leaders and the rank and file.

Thank you, Mr. Offenstein, for this inside view of a union leader at work in his own community.

In the acts and the points of view of men like this labor leader from the Far West may be found one of the important things organized labor can do; that is, participate in voluntary welfare at every level. A second opportunity for labor is equally important and complements the act of participation in social welfare. It is suggested that the unions might vastly increase the contribution of dollars needed to shore up the voluntary welfare structure. Briefly, the idea is this:

Union men could donate their working time for a brief period beyond the usual forty-hour week, once a year. Suppose a substantial number of the sixteen million trade-union men in the nation were to work an extra hour a day for five days a year and donate the proceeds to the united fund or community chest—or work one Saturday a year. Suppose each employer were to donate to the fund or chest as the company or corporation gift an amount equal to 50 per cent of the total employee contribution. What would this do to the financing of voluntary welfare? The firmer financial base is obvious, but the long-term values of co-operation and certainty are even more important.

Suppose seven million union men (less than one-half the national total), receiving an average of $2.50 an hour, donated five hours of extra work as suggested above. This would come to $12.50 a man and $87,500,000 as the union portion. The corporation portion would be half of this, making a joint total of $131,-250,000. Much of the total would be sheer gain for the chests and funds. Average employee giving, after all, is closer to $5.00 than $12.50, and 100 per cent participation by employees is uncommon. But, it may be asked, can funds be raised this unusual way? They can, and they have been in a few places around the country.

San Mateo County, California, in the suburbs of San Francisco, is such a place. The construction industry, that is, the contractors and the Building Trades Council of the unions, got together in 1956, and again in 1957, to see if more funds could be raised for the United Crusade by such a method. It worked. When 1,385 employees of 233 firms put in three hours each on a Saturday morning in October, the amount raised by the construction division of the united fund jumped from under $5,000 to $21,282, an increase of 353 per cent in a single year. The employer and employee shares increased proportionally.

Since seventy-five of the larger contractors did not participate in 1956 (although twenty-five did), plans for 1957 changed slightly. Instead of October, the month chosen was August—a peak time in the building industry. Rather than a Saturday morning, men were to put in an extra hour each afternoon for a five-day working week. Neighboring counties tried the idea; so did at least seven other areas in the northern part of California, as two thousand copies of a brochure about "C" Day were sent to chests and funds across the nation. The "C" Day worked better than a "C" Week, however, and 1958 witnessed a return to the Saturday morning practice. Despite employment problems in the construction industry, $2,000 more was raised the second year than in the first. Is the construction industry uniquely suited to this method? What are its virtues and defects?

I asked Jonathan Slott, director of labor-management aspects of the San Mateo united-fund drive, whether he thought there was any future in the idea of a contribution of time by employees rather than a contribution of dollars. He replied strongly in the affirmative. "The old-line union men and even the management men who were at one time union men have an antipathy toward taking anything out of the pay check," he said vigorously, "because they know there are so many deductions already." Then he continued:

> There is great resistance to having any additional taken off. When the man gives his time, however, he feels that it is just the one hour. While he does go home an hour later, nothing has come out of his total pay check. It seems to perk up these people because the philosophy of not tampering with their paycheck is a great psychological factor to them. This has been the reaction, and I'm pretty close to both the laboring force and to the management force. More and more we're trying to bring a sense of community responsibility to the employee. A lot of them have been dubious contributors; they have worked in a firm where they heard, "Well, we've got to make 100 per cent, boys." They didn't realize that their families benefited from research on the dreaded diseases, et cetera. They were under the impression that the state took care of all that sort of thing.

The San Mateo County united-fund people have stated officially that the "ingredient of faith" is most important in all this. If organized labor should be taken sincerely into partnership with management, the presumption is that its members "would accept responsibility and work constructively for the betterment of community health, welfare, and recreation agencies. . . ."

To prevent any further solicitations at work from bothering the union men, the San Mateo experiment had one particularly interesting feature. Thirty per cent of the total union contributions during the experimental period went into a newly created tax-exempt foundation under the name of the Building Trades Council. The Council could give sums from this foundation to appeals and causes of which it approved—whether they were members of the united fund or not. These grants might go to agencies of particular interest to union families (youth agencies, clinics, etc.). All grants had to be reported annually on form 990-A to the district Internal Revenue Service. Such foundations are subject to many provisions of the Internal Revenue Code.

Union leaders in this instance were naturally vigilant to see that employers did not "get away with something" in connection with what we may call the "give your time" contribution plans. Management was no doubt alert in much the same way. United-fund staff members kept a watchful eye on totals.

Finally, pay checks in the San Mateo experiment were made out jointly to the man and to the united fund. The workers promptly endorsed them over to the fund, unless they insisted on changing their minds—which remained their right.

The extra dollars which "give your time" programs of this character could provide for local and national agencies might well succeed in delaying the new fee-charging trend which could possibly destroy American charitable activity. Payment of substantial fees to the Boy Scouts, Girl Scouts, and even family-service agencies might be prevented; or, at least, fees might be kept within sensible limits. The greatly strengthened voluntary agencies would be able to do a far better job if more dollars came their way. Thus, the tide running towards mounting government social-welfare services at every level would be held in check.

Ability to utilize the "give your time" device will vary quite sharply among industries, and a number of important objections can be raised against it. Consider all these embarrassing questions:

how will workers get home when they depart an hour later or work Saturdays? Will salaried executives work, and will they donate prorated amounts? Are standard deductions and withholding taxes to come from these checks? Will overtime be paid? What about possible violations of wage and hour laws? If an industry works shifts, how will all shifts manage to do their share? If supplies are needed for production, will suppliers be working Saturdays? If a standardized process is involved, can it be lengthened profitably—or shortened for Saturday work? How, if transportation unions do not participate, will assembly-line products get out of the plant area in the customary way? With each industry selecting a peak or a slack time for this fund-supplying activity, will it not go forward irregularly all year, thus putting a burden on permanent united-fund employees and increasing overhead? Still further questions and protests along these lines could easily be devised, particularly with individual businesses or industries in mind. But even though objections to every new idea seem overwhelming at first, new ways of doing things have a habit of conquering all—that is, when they have merit. The point to remember in regard to these questions is that it did work in one industry and in one place. Time and events will tell whether the idea can spread elsewhere.

For several decades, the unions in the United States were in the forefront of the pressure groups insisting on ever-increasing welfare services from government. They turned to the employer and insisted that he provide group-benefit funds to help meet the needs of workingmen. The unions seemed to forget the existence of voluntary or private welfare agencies. This was a bad mistake, but it is one that could be corrected. Neither government nor employers should be the sole support of free and part-pay clinics, emergency financial aid, and recreational services.

Each year in recent decades, union leaders have gone before the state legislatures and the Congress to seek special services from government. In 1957, for example, the unions were represented before the House of Representatives Subcommittee on Appropriations by Hyman H. Bookbinder of AFL-CIO who submitted a long brief in support of many budget items. "In our study of the President's budget requests, we have naturally thought of the needs of the fifteen million members of the AFL-CIO and their families," he stated, adding that the general welfare of all Americans was a concern of his group. Labor and welfare activities in the budget came to $3,538,000,000, he thought, or only about 5 per cent of the total, and $20.40 per capita in the nation. His organization stood for increases of more than $40,000 for the migratory labor program, more than the $37,000 increase slated for a committee on the physically handicapped, more than the many millions scheduled for medical research, more than the already higher expenditures slated under the Hill-Burton hospital construction act (which had come to $2,500,000,000 for 3,100 projects), and more increases than those contemplated for the aging and the chronically ill. AFL-CIO wanted maximum participation by the federal government in the costs of administering public assistance programs, said Mr. Bookbinder. And all rehabilitation programs financed by tax funds should be greatly expanded. Here was organized labor's program for service from Washington for one year; similar proposals were made in state capitols. But what was organized labor planning to do "back home" for itself?

Following the passage of a labor-union reform bill by the Congress in 1959, it was insisted by some locals that their giving to united funds, community chests, and welfare agencies had been outlawed. Claiming that counsel had so advised, these union officials counted on contribution-seeking agency officials to join them in seeking repeal or modification of the law. Whatever the ultimate result of such tactics, this playing of pressure politics by withholding charitable dollars was hardly in the new spirit of community responsibility previously described.

The time has come when AFL-CIO and independent union leaders, as well as rank and file employees, should help themselves to better communities through reliance, not on government, but on themselves—through "the voluntary way." This can be done within the union or outside it. The Amalgamated Clothing Workers local in New York City has equipped the top floor of the Sidney Hillman Health Center as a recreation and health center for retired workers. Many locals of other unions have long furnished congenial surroundings in union halls for members. No doubt more of this will be done. But unions should consider carefully whether in the segregation of members and children of members from the whole community lies true wisdom. Why, after all, should union labor follow certain religious groups by building a wholly new network of charitable and health agencies?

An alternative is the strengthening and expansion of existing agencies. The donation of time, through service with voluntary agencies, and the donation of money, through what we may call "give your time" fund-raising programs, would work wonders. Leo Perlis of AFL-CIO was quite right when he said on one occasion that "posters, slogans, and gimmicks are no substitutes for sincere services given on the basis of need through democratically operated social agencies." But how are union leaders and the rank and file to get started?

Employers, in their roles as alert management and leaders on agency boards may have to start the ball rolling. (Apparently we are not going to get our Offensteins unless, to some extent, we first have our Mainwarings.) Individual union leaders will, in many instances, respond. The resulting community friendships and the subtle improvement in labor-management relations will be worthwhile by-products. The gradual but perceptible strengthening of voluntary welfare as it builds new muscles will mean much to everyone concerned. All in all, the final result of full and selfless union participation could be a genuine revolution in the extent and pattern of social-welfare activity in cities all over the United States.

CHAPTER X

The Voluntary Health Agencies:
Unify, Destroy, or Preserve?

Many diseases,
Many causes.

Multiple organizations,
Multiple dollars.

Federal research,
Voluntary research.

Raising of taxes,
Raising of funds.

Government unlimited,
Emotion unlimited.

Attacks on spending,
Attacks on agencies.

Confusion intolerable?
Suffering intolerable?

Preserve our freedom.
Preserve our health.

AMERICANS IN THE 1950's faced difficult questions posed by the
sudden growth of voluntary health agencies. The problems were
complicated by a dramatic increase in federal grants to government health research institutes. The many millions of dollars
raised by organizations like the American Cancer Society and the
National Foundation, through appeals to the public in nearly all
the counties of the nation, had joyful portents. And the men who,
financed by the federal government, performed research on diseases made important discoveries. Yet there were reasons for public concern about the field of health research—or so it seemed to
many. "Research is not a thing you can just turn on and off like
water in the spigot," the secretary of Health, Education, and Wel-

fare told Congress in 1957. "It takes a long time to develop; and, in effect, we are doubling the amount of medical research here [in the federal government] in two years' time. It is a question of whether you can go at as fast a rate as that without lowering the standards." A year later that department published, in the Bayne-Jones report, a recommendation that the federal government plan to spend one billion dollars annually for medical research. Meanwhile, the voluntary health organizations — having grown like Topsy—continued to expand their horizons. Under these circumstances some observers began to wonder if government were not going overboard, or if the time had not come to either unify or do away with some of the voluntary health agencies. Of the two propositions, the latter generated more heat in the late 1950's.

Who can quarrel either with the goals of the voluntary or government health organizations or with the results they sometimes achieve? It is easy to comprehend and to applaud the good done by the National Foundation for Infantile Paralysis through the financing of Dr. Jonas E. Salk's experiments on polio virus. After initial uncertainty and what some charged were blunders in public relations, the preventive shots met with much (though not enough) public acceptance. Paralytic polio dropped 80 per cent from 1955 to 1957. Who can say with assurance that similar scientific break-throughs will not be made at any moment because of funds contributed to American Heart Association, Muscular Dystrophy Association, or National Tuberculosis Association, or because of a fifty-thousand-dollar grant from the government's National Cancer Institute? Progress has already been made by research scientists who were financed by such health organizations as these, and additional discoveries of major importance are possible at any time. This is the attitude of highly publicity-conscious multi-million-dollar voluntary agencies and public relations officials in government. Both comprise true enough self-portraits. The value of such services to humanity should not be ignored.

Research and health education are twin services of real merit. No one will ever know how many lives have been saved by the preventive welfare work of the organizations over whose names controversy has come to swirl. The writer of a letter to the editor of the *New York Times* on February 12, 1957, urged contributions for heart research, saying, "It so happens that the money some-one gave for research in heart disease and heart surgery saved the life of the writer when he was at the point of death." The voluntary health organizations financed much research in the 1950's. They also helped physicians, medical societies, and professional associations in many educational ways. Federal health research funds, it should be noted, financed in 1958 a total of 2,329 research fellowships in 211 different institutions and 7,028 research-project grants in 699 institutions. Hundreds of pages could easily be devoted to the record of accomplishment of those occupied in research that would not have been possible without grants from voluntary and government agencies. Yet this consideration should not dissuade any who choose to take a close look at health organizations as organizational rivals, fund-raising competitors, or pressure groups. And one may at least question the appropriate-ness of earmarking a billion dollars from federal funds for annual health-research purposes at a time when so many other pressing needs deserve financial assistance from the government. Can it be that the amount of effort society intends to put into voluntary, as against government, organizations in the health field is not opti-mum? We must examine some figures on each aspect in turn.

Fund-raising figures of the eleven largest national-health groups in the voluntary field reflect their relative size and cause diverse speculation. The total figure for 1957 came to about $186,-000,000 for forty voluntary health agencies, according to the National Information Bureau, and the relative standing of the eleven was as follows:

Health Organizations	*Income* (*in millions of dollars*)
National Foundation for Infantile Paralysis	45.8
American Cancer Society	33.0
National Tuberculosis Association	26.2
American Heart Association	20.6
National Society for Crippled Children & Adults	16.0
United Cerebral Palsy Association	8.4
Muscular Dystrophy Association	4.3

National Association for Mental Health	3.8
Arthritis and Rheumatism Foundation	2.4
National Multiple Sclerosis Society	2.3
National Association for Retarded Children	1.8

These figures bear little relationship to the degree of occurrence of the indicated diseases. No particular relationship to the pain felt by patients or the loss felt by society from the incapacity of those afflicted may be discerned as one goes down the list. Nor is there any consistent relationship to death rates. For example, deaths from heart disease and diseases of the cardiovascular system stand at 515 for every 100,000 Americans; deaths from cancer, in the same ratio, come to 150. Deaths from polio rank thirtieth in such lists. Polio cases for every 100,000 people have been estimated at 7; but the number of diagnosed cancer cases may be 632, and heart disease, 5,747. Deaths from diabetes, not represented in the above list of organizations, may be 1,149; active tuberculosis, 460; cerebral palsy, 287; multiple sclerosis, 144; and muscular dystrophy, 115. Arthritis and rheumatism seem to have an incidence of 6,264, if one includes minor cases. The affluent and powerful Polio group has had few articulate friends among leaders of charitable and health agencies, for effectiveness in fund-raising is unlikely to win anything but envy from rival fund-raisers.

The problem of determining, in the abstract, an ideal ratio of funds which the voluntary health agencies should receive in accordance with the type of disease they fight is difficult. Undeterred by the practical and philosophical problems involved, however, many people, in the 1950's, held dogmatic opinions on the matter. Chief among these were the men who occupied powerful positions in the united funds in large cities. The attitudes these persons displayed toward the five largest national voluntary-health agencies were so vigorously adverse that they made newspaper headlines in many large cities.

Still, there were other and more practical reasons for this antagonism from businessmen and from social workers intent on trying to solve non-medical problems at the local level. The desire to force unity in fund-raising was not the whole story. The question they asked repeatedly was this: Are the nationally organized voluntary-health agencies obtaining money that would otherwise go to local welfare and recreation agencies? Are they taking money out of the community that would otherwise stay there? The question was most often posed in the living rooms of knowledgeable volunteer solicitors for chests, united funds, and individual agencies; only occasionally was the question actually brought out into the open.

One may certainly generalize that the "national" health agencies do not normally take more than a certain percentage of contributed funds out of the community for distribution by national headquarters. In 1959, for example, it was reported that the national v. the local and state split for the National Foundation was 62.5 to 37.5 per cent; for Heart, it was 25 to 75; Cancer, 40 to 60; Cerebral Palsy, 25 to 75; Muscular Dystrophy, 75 to 25; Arthritis and Rheumatism, 36 to 64 and Tuberculosis, 6 to 94. Few contributors are aware of these percentages.

Looking at the matter another way, how does the total figure raised by the health agencies in a town compare with the total raised for strictly local social welfare organizations and for Red Cross (which in 1959 divided its funds 47 to 53 per cent)? Here is a measure of the welfare contributions' dollar that every contributor should know and bear in mind. Unfortunately, the existence of united funds makes the computation for states difficult, since figures must be juggled to eliminate duplication of dollars. I made such a computation for California, arriving at a welfare contributions dollar, and I made a similar breakdown for every county in the state. For California, strictly local causes (arbitrarily excluding Red Cross) were getting 55.9 cents out of the contributed dollar. But in some counties, the local chest figure was noticeably better than this. In San Francisco, for example, a 69 cent figure was obtained, and Los Angeles, with over thirty chests, received 58 cents for local causes. Predominently national causes received 44.1 cents divided as follows: Red Cross, 19.7 cents; Polio, 10.9; Tuberculosis, 5.1; Cancer, 3.9; Heart, 2.6; and Crippled Children, 1.9. In rural counties this pattern was not maintained. In such places, certain highly publicized organizations with effective fund-raising machinery (particularly the

March of Dimes, Red Cross, and Christmas Seals' campaigns) raised money out of all proportion to the over-all state breakdown. But what does this mean?

The American public simply has not decided on an "ideal" proportion of the locally contributed welfare dollar that ought to go to the health agencies. Should the ratio in every state be essentially 56 per cent to local chest member agencies, 20 per cent to Red Cross, and 24 per cent to national health agencies? This was, essentially, the California ratio in 1954, but four years earlier these state totals had been 59, 22, and 19, respectively. Thus there had been a substantial percentage loss by local agencies to the national health causes during this short period.[1] It does not resolve the distribution-of-percentages problem to note that all three of these major elements in social welfare raised more money in 1954 than in 1950. They did. But Polio, Heart, and Cancer had moved into the fund-raising arena in those years with far greater success than their local chest-agency rivals. And the formation of new health agencies at the national level, in the 1950's, made this shift even more important.

Should the money contributed to fight disease and care for patients have been given, instead, to the routine community-chest agencies for expenditure by the scouts, family service agencies, and Salvation Army? Would the dollars have gone to the chest if the highly publicized health causes had not existed? Nobody knows, but my guess is: No. Perhaps some foundation and corporation and big-giver money might have shifted to this other area, but the average person probably would have been little affected in his giving. One suspects that the more varied the causes (in or out of united funds) the more likely it is that donations will be obtained. What real chance, after all, did the community-chest causes have in 1956 of talking the public into giving them even a portion of the more than fifty million dollars it chose to give the Polio organization in its peak year? One doubts that

[1] No later figures than these exist at this writing, for it took major research effort to prepare the county-by-county California breakdown, the results of which appeared in my book *California Social Welfare*, Chapter XIII.

204

abolishing such organizations would result in the smooth transfer of their annual income to local community causes.

After all this has been said, it remains desirable for community leaders to air the problem of ascertaining and planning contributing ratios: famous disease groups v. local causes of one type or another. Unless some publicity is given this matter annually, the public will have no guideposts to follow in determining whether an ominous trend has developed. Correction, in any case, could take two directions, for health agencies that came to raise far too much money in proportion to the other organizations might want to change their percentage division in such a city, rather than consent to raise less money. Basically, it is the public that gives the money; community leaders will have trouble if they crusade against Heart, Cancer, and other health groups in the light of this plain fact. And those who influence the public to cut back on contributions to disease-fighting organizations will inevitably reap a harvest of ill will in the long run.

In the 1950's government was deeply involved in the health field. The federal government spent, in the fiscal year 1958–59, about 63 per cent more for health purposes than five years earlier, for a total of $2,886,260,831. Well over another billion dollars was spent by state and local governments. Such figures indicate why people came to question the extravagant demands of some groups for immense increases in government effort in the medical field. Figures published by the Washington office of the American Medical Association in November, 1958 (Special Report 85-15) present a breakdown, in millions of dollars, for federal budgeting in the health area for the fiscal year 1958–59:

Agency	In Millions
Department of Health, Education, and Welfare	$1,116.2
Veterans Administration	843.5
Department of Defense	751.1
Atomic Energy Commission	45.5
International Co-operation Administration	39.6
Department of State	21.6
National Science Foundation	19.6
Office of Civil & Defense Mobilization	13.6

Federal Employees Health Programs	11.0
Department of Labor	8.8
Panama Canal Co. & Canal Zone Government	4.0
Department of the Treasury	4.0
Department of Justice	2.1
District of Columbia	2.0
Federal Trade Commission	1.6
Department of Commerce	1.2
Other*	.5

* Other: President's Commission for Employment of the Physically Handicapped, Small Business Administration, Department of the Interior, Selective Service, the Physician to Congress.

All but three of these items were increases over the previous year.

The financing of medical research by the federal government from tax funds increased especially in the late 1950's, as Congress gave the national institutes of health giant sums while making exceedingly few demands. Increased appropriations to its National Cancer Institute for 1959 raised that budget from $25,000,000 to $75,268,000 in two years. The National Heart Institute jumped from about $19,000,000 to $45,613,000. The Institute of Mental Health received $52,419,000; Arthritis and Metabolic Diseases, $31,215,00; and Neurology and Blindness, $29,403,000. The increase in appropriations, in two years, to all seven of the federal medical-research institutes was from $241,000,000 to $344,000,-000. Their total dollars exceeded (yet did not dwarf), the total income of voluntary national health agencies (estimated at $186,-000,000 for the top forty).

Why did federal medical research expenditures grow at a time when contribution-supported health organizations multiplied in numbers and income? A health-conscious public was responsible, of course, constantly stirred up by medical advice in immense quantities in the daily press and other units of the mass information media. Longevity made death from diseases of the aged seem a new frontier to be conquered at all costs—and at once—although there were some who questioned exactly what purpose was being served by prolonging the heartbeats of those who were otherwise ignored by society and even their own kin.

Scientific miracles, which were well publicized, brought demands for more of the same, in any event. To the hue and cry were added the astute clamorings of some persons and organizations who had long fought to socialize the state, for here they saw an opportunity to collectivize medical research. From this, they reasoned, it would be but a short step to bringing all medical activities directly or indirectly under the benevolent regimentation of government. Yet another reason existed for increased government appropriations in the health research field.

The voluntary national-disease agencies were officially nonpartisan toward government expenditures in the areas of their concern; but, in fact, their paid and unpaid officials were often to be found prominently among those urging higher expenditures on Congressional committees. This lobbying hat they wore received little publicity. The money they sought to have appropriated came to many millions of dollars, and the visits of their official or unofficial spokesmen to Washington at budgeting time came to be a regular event. Seeking giant expenditures for medical research, hospital construction, and welfare activities, the health-agency people were sometimes joined by powerful medical, dental, hospital, and nurses associations (at least some of which profess to be great opponents of socialized medicine). Economy-minded congressmen felt, on occasion, that they were being overwhelmed with a united front of health experts when they received the persuasive, humanitarian pleas and listened to the emotional testimony of organization executives. Many examples of this lobbying could be given, but here is part of the story for the 1957 session of Congress:

Urging that the federal budget continue to contain an item of $24,000,000 for the government's National Arthritis Institute, the president of the National Arthritis and Rheumatism Foundation wrote the Congress that "no better investment can be made than in arthritis research." The figure he asked was termed "minimum." (This official doubled as "public member" of the government's Institute.) The administrator for research of the American Cancer Society, which he properly identified in his testimony as "a voluntary fund-granting agency," presented Congress with what he called "a line-by-line justification of a recommended budget for the National Cancer Institute." It came to a 20 per cent increase in a year. "It is my considered judgment," he said, "that the amount of funds available for the support of research in any field must always be greater than the amount actually expended, if we are to encourage the development of the best possible plans for imaginative and productive research." Since the Congress had followed this philosophy in 1956, he noted, a full $5,000,000 budgeted for cancer research had been left over. At this, Congressman John Taber observed, "It looks like Congress was too liberal with you last year." Be that as it may, here was an official of a $33,-000,000 voluntary health agency seeking to enlarge a $48,000,000 government rival—or at least keep its budget from being cut.

The medical director of the New England chapter of the Arthritis and Rheumatism Foundation asked Congress to grant $14,000,000 for research projects on arthritis and metabolic diseases. Moreover, the National Tuberculosis Association urged approval of the $17,400,000 budget of the Institute of Allergy and Infectious Diseases, especially the $7,000,000 for "the tuberculosis program." The secretary-treasurer of the American Venereal Disease Association asked Congress to continue its support of Public Health Service activities both in personnel and in project grants. Asked if he thought the proposed appropriation for the coming year would be adequate, this official replied candidly, "I am not familiar with the amount asked for." The American Social Hygiene Association also lobbied for this program.

The American Hospital Association, a membership and pressure group rather than a health agency as the term is used here, chose at that session of Congress to endorse a major project to spend federal funds to evaluate drugs in cardiovascular therapy, stating: "Guiding principles and policy decisions will be made by an advisory board composed of prominent medical scientists. The membership of the board will be drawn from members of the American Medical Association and the American Heart Association. The advisory board will authorize all subgrants of research money to the physician teams."

The director of research for the American Hospital Association was, interestingly enough, to be "the principal investigator" for the project. The American Public Health Association sought, at the time, a federal program to support states and localities in their treatment of chronic illness among older persons. Its resolution urging this expenditure was only one of many that this government-minded group sent to Congress. What are we, in summary, to think of the type of activity we have noted in these pages?

While the several associations are financed by their members, and one naturally expects pressure activities to be both important and routine for them, the national health agencies solicit their funds from the general public in the name of "the voluntary way." In few of the examples given did the agency officials go out of their way to make it clear that they spoke for themselves or, officially, for the agency. Opinions will no doubt differ on whether these leaders engage in a dubious activity on the occasions when they lobby for large research expenditures, using the public's money to do so, and when they speak with the force of a nationwide organization. Some would say, perhaps unfairly, that through dual office-holding and simply ex officio, senior officials of the disease-research societies may, on occasion, profit personally by the receipt of grants or their administration, or may gain in authority or prestige by accepting unpaid policy-making posts with the national institutes in question. How can these men possibly be "public" members of such bodies, considering their orientation toward fighting specific diseases or furthering special causes? Others will argue that expenditures by government for disease research ought to be sought by conscientious voluntary-agency officials as part of their over-all duty to further, at all costs, the public health. Lobbying, furthermore, is an educational function upon which legislators rely heavily; certainly the Congressmen showed real interest in the testimony of these well-prepared administrators of health agencies. One is puzzled when contemplating this problem. Yet it must be remembered that money contributed by the public built up the giant voluntary-health organizations. If they are to retain public confidence (and one certainly wishes them well), their officials will want to be cautious not to use official funds for the support of rival organizations in the government itself.

Multiple duplication clearly existed among health agencies in the 1950's. As in the United States, duplication of effort occurred in Great Britain as indicated by an advertisement in the *Listener* and other British publications on behalf of the Imperial Cancer Research Fund, which "carries out cancer research in its own laboratories without State aid." In this country, the Damon Runyon Memorial Fund for Cancer Research, aided mightily by the sincerely emotional pleas of Walter Winchell, realized $885,-000 in 1958 at a time when the American Cancer Society had an income of nearly $34,000,000.

Small but enthusiastic disease-research organizations were also prevalent in the 1950's. In 1958, the Allergy Foundation realized $134,000; the Common Cold Foundation, $63,000; the Cystic Fibrosis Research Foundation, $276,000; and the National Parkinson's Foundation, $32,000—just to mention a few. In addition, there were voluntary organizations working to rid mankind of hemophilia, diabetes, myasthenia gravis, epilepsy, and kidney disease. What, if anything, should be done about the multi-organizational pattern that developed in the 1950's in the health field? It may be said that it would be a wise first step to have at least a few of the big national voluntary health agencies consolidate. This possibility deserves attention here, whatever explosive emotions may generate from the idea.

Consolidation of the major voluntary health agencies could take one of two forms: administrative or fund-raising. Those who call for unity seldom make it clear which of these they seek, but the predominant force seems to be in favor of unity in fund-raising. "I feel very strongly that some unification of these health causes should be accomplished," said Harry L. Jackson, Director of Community Relations for Lubrizol Corporation and vice-president of the vigorously united fund-minded National Solicitations Conference at that group's 1959 meeting. Clearly representing the consensus of his companions, he added, "We can't conduct a health-agency drive in the plant every week of the year. There ought to be a trend toward unification of these agencies—at least at the fund-raising level." Earlier in the decade Leo Perlis of the AFL-CIO Community Services Committee had said trenchantly, "We should put the human body back together again and stop appealing for funds for heart, limbs, and lungs separately"; and he continued with the prediction that "a National Health Fund is not only necessary but will become a reality within the next five years." Thus these two gentlemen expressed the desire for unity in fund-raising. But is it possible without a parallel administrative unity? And what is the opinion of the voluntary health agencies on that?

A number of the larger national groups expressed their attitude on full administrative unification in the Gunn and Platt report of 1944-45. In 1954-55, I asked several of the larger groups if their opinions toward unification had changed after a decade. I asked them the same question again in 1959, but only a few changed their forthright opinions.

During World War II, thirteen health agencies had replied to the question: "Can you see any advantages in one unified national health agency over the present situation, provided adequate financial support was assured, and each special health interest was as well represented as it is today?" The result was that two gave an unqualified "yes"; six, a qualified "yes"; four, "no"; and one was vague. A decade later, the seven replies obtained from these same agencies added up to a unanimous and emphatic "no."

The national health agencies want no part of unification. Those previously voting "no" stated that their present attitude would be even more strongly negative than before. The following excerpts from letters I received from highly placed administrators and officials in these groups indicate how they feel about losing organizational autonomy and independent action.

The national president of Muscular Dystrophy Associations of America stated:

> It is our feeling that one of the most significant justifica-
> tions for numerous voluntary health agencies is that they give
> rise to greater drive and initiative. They are part of the very
> fabric of the American way of free enterprise and independ-

211

ent action. It is very possible that this basic concept could be
diluted or lost in one united national health agency . . . .

The executive vice-president of the American Cancer Society
replied in 1954 in vigorous language, and re-emphasized his answer again in 1959:

> What is best for cancer control is the sole concern of the
> American Cancer Society. We can see no advantage, under
> any conditions, in a unified national agency. Wide experience
> with local united funds seems to have demonstrated clearly
> that the fight against cancer is stronger when carried out by
> our Society acting as an independent in fund-raising, and
> planning its own research, education, and service activities.
> Naturally we co-operate with other voluntary groups and
> with medical societies, but we are convinced that our growth
> and our effectiveness depend on our independence.

National Tuberculosis Association replied, in 1955, through
its managing director that the whole idea of unification was "unrealistic," and these comments held good four years later:

> If it were possible to create such a single national health
> agency, I think it would mean the end of the dynamic, pro-
> gressive voluntary health agencies as we know them in the
> United States of America. These agencies have made a tre-
> mendous contribution to the advances in the health of the
> citizens of the United States, and their dissolution would be
> a tragedy.
> Actually I think the question is quite academic since from
> practical experience in exploring the possibility of combining
> only two national voluntary health agencies, I am certain
> that it will never be possible to combine all of them into one
> agency. There is, however, a need for exchange of informa-
> tion and joint planning between the various national health
> agencies, both voluntary and official. The National Tubercu-
> losis Association itself is very much aware of its need to know
> what the other health agencies are doing and to work closely
> with them. We maintain very close relationships with the
> United States Public Health Service, the Veterans Adminis-
> tration, the Office of Vocational Rehabilitation, and other

H. Armstrong Roberts, Philadelphia

The heights of happiness scaled by those who are aided in adopting a child legally, safely, and with competent guidance can scarcely be known to the outsider.

Photograph by the author

Discouragement is a daily companion of the unemployed.

official agencies of the Federal Government and voluntary agencies whose activities are concerned directly or indirectly with the control of tuberculosis.

The giant National Foundation for Infantile Paralysis had been able to see in 1944 "no advantage" in unification, feeling then that it would "interfere with and minimize the strength of individual services now in operation." Ten years later its president, Basil O'Connor, defended independence of action as follows, reaffirming for a renamed National Foundation his view in 1959:

> Our answer today would be the same and, if possible, stronger. We believe that the voluntary national health agencies have provided a dynamic leadership that would be lost or dissipated in as wide a program as a single national health agency would involve. Certainly, the focusing of interest on individual health problems by these voluntary agencies has been instrumental in making the general public aware of the health needs in the various fields and in securing active public support in meeting these needs.
>
> We realize that a great deal can be gained by co-operative efforts on the part of the voluntary national health agencies. There are certainly definite areas in the health field which have benefited by an exchange of information and joint planning of the various health agencies, whether they are voluntary or governmental. The National Foundation has always made a great effort to participate in and assist in such efforts.

The Arthritis and Rheumatism Foundation's executive director replied, in 1955:

> We do not think that one unified national health agency would be feasible. Public education is a very important part of an individual health agency's program. The individual agency at present utilizes the campaign period to focus public attention on the work it is doing, and the campaign offers an excellent means of educating the public regarding its particular health program. We do not feel that a unified health agency can do this important job effectively for the individual agency. It is also impractical to believe that any one agency

213

could raise sufficient funds to adequately satisfy the needs
of all the health agencies.

At the close of the decade this particular agency was struggling
to maintain its program and income in the face of the expansionist program of a National Foundation no longer limited in its activities to polio alone.

The executive director of the National Society for Crippled
Children and Adults stated:

> The National Society does not believe that one unified
> national health agency could possibly be created which would
> provide adequate financial support or assure the continuance
> of the dynamic programs of the separate health interests rep-
> resented by the independent agencies of today. The Society
> would see more disadvantages than advantages in any at-
> tempt to create such an agency. . . . We can visualize no con-
> ditions under which a national health agency could assume
> the responsibilities which the Society has of conducting a
> nationwide program of education services and research, on
> behalf of the crippled.

The executive director of the American Heart Association
called attention, in 1955, to a printed policy statement on co-operation at the local level with planning bodies and welfare agencies, adding that "the Heart Association encourages active co-operation among all organizations, official and voluntary, concerned
with problems of health." A fully official answer would require
action by the board of directors, but it was this Heart official's
personal opinion that "effective co-operation among the major
health agencies is preferable to an organic union of those agencies." He believed, finally, that "the contribution made to the
nation's health by the individual agencies is likely, in the long
run, to be greater operating individually, but co-operatively, than
would be the case if they were all merged into one." This summary again met with the approval of the Heart Association in the
year 1959.

The meaning of these several judgments is clear. The researchers on health agencies during World War II wrote that the

replies they gathered reflected "principally the opinion of the executive and cannot be considered as committing the organizations." This may be technically true of some of the answers quoted here. Yet these replies were received only after the lapse of from one to eight months; they were signed by presidents or executive directors. In the letter of inquiry, it was made clear that the replies would be quoted in print, and they stood the test of renewed inquiry in 1959. They, therefore, seem reasonably official— enough for the purpose at hand.

The statement of the earlier researchers was that "practically and realistically considered, unification seems so fraught with uncertainties, unknowns and difficulties that the boards of national associations are not likely to take any steps whatever." This judgment seems equally valid as a summary of most recent reactions of the spokesmen for the voluntary health agencies. Unification was not imminent in the early 1960's, at any rate. "We are not ready for it yet," said Dr. Paul Dudley White in July, 1957, urging an audience to continue to support the Heart Association. Yet, as he said this, the united-fund movement was nearing the close of its first decade in the nation, and the National War Fund of World War II lay far behind. It was in 1945 that a vice-president of Metropolitan Life Insurance Company called for extensive unification in these words:

> It is not too much to hope that as the wisdom of working in close coordination is demonstrated, the National Tuberculosis Association, the National Foundation for Infantile Paralysis, and perhaps even the American Red Cross, will combine forces with the rest to become one united association, with branches and services everywhere. This would prove a worthy partner of a co-ordinated and well-supported health department in the Federal Government.

From this, he hoped, would come substantial savings and public acclaim for the resulting "relief from multiple appeals for funds."

One rejoices that such unification did not take place. Domination of the whole area of giant national social welfare, government and voluntary, from Washington, D. C. would have proved intolerable. Much of the nation would have been just as un-happy if the voluntary area had been unified under the control of people in a suite of offices in New York City. Enough organiza-tional unification of the large health agencies had, by the close of the 1950's, come to be found within the National Health Council. The man who would become its national president in 1960, James E. Perkins, M.D., wrote to me in March, 1959, that almost every national health agency held membership in the Council, since both the American Medical Association and the American Hos-pital Association had joined in the recent past. He continued:

> The National Health Council is playing a progressively more important role in utilizing the combined efforts of the member agencies to further certain objectives of common concern and interest, such as a health careers project de-signed to interest young people in entering into some career in health to help relieve the serious shortage of trained per-sonnel in the health field; the work of the National Advisory Committee on Local Health Departments, sponsored by the National Health Council; the holding of annual National Health Forums on major problems in the health field of con-cern to the entire United States public, etc.

Effective though this council may become, however, the cries for more visible unity will still be heard. One reason is the prolifera-tion of more and yet more health agencies.

Disease-oriented agencies with high hopes of "going nation-al" continue to be born and to solicit funds with emotional cam-paigns. While it is true that, in a free country, distraught parents should be allowed to organize in order to interest strangers in giving money to seek a cure for any rare ailment afflicting their children, this sort of thing can get out of hand. The spread of the practice of founding voluntary health groups on ever narrower bases is clearly to be deplored. Dr. Perkins puts it well when he says that "any textbook on medicine or pathology will reveal that there are hundreds upon hundreds of relatively rare medical con-ditions which, although causing great grief and sorrow to those afflicted and their close relations, can scarcely be considered important health problems from an over-all viewpoint . . . ." If each should develop its own voluntary health agency, the result would be "further annoyance" to the contributing public and tremendous confusion, added this official, who is the managing director of the National Tuberculosis Association.

When one considers the extent of giant research expenditures of government, universities, hospitals and existing health agencies—all of them in the interest of conquering disease—one is tempted to oppose the founding of any more health groups with ambitions for national solicitation. Misgivings occur, however, when one reflects that a similar philosophy held only a few years ago would have prevented the birth of many of the effective health groups now in existence. It is all very puzzling, but surely the existing fund-raising and administrative machinery ought to give pause to those who continue to place want-ads for still more fund-raisers and administrators.

Implacable war between the united funds and the most powerful disease agencies was being waged in many cities at the close of the 1950's. The intensity of feeling was unknown to the general public, although editorials in some newspapers made the issues plain. Every trick in the book was being used in cities like Pittsburgh in an effort to crush the independence of the physician-dominated Cancer and Heart organizations. In the *Executive Newsletter*, a secret avenue of national communication for directors of united funds, each apparent tactical triumph was, in 1957–59, proclaimed as a battlefield success. Defeats were invariably greeted with stony silence. United Community Funds and Councils of America, Inc., in New York City, served as general headquarters for the federated fund leaders, and from it poured a stream of literature designed to strengthen the backs of united-fund leaders from San Diego to Cleveland. Such activity, of course, was vigorously and bitterly resented. The president of the American Heart Association, Robert F. Watkins, told one state-wide group of Heart executives in the summer of 1958: "Most federated funds are run and controlled by big businessmen who are used to having their own way and who become frustrated and angry when opposed. This is why they are attacking us so bitterly and using methods which constitute blackmail to prevent our leaving the united funds . . . ."

Faced with the problem of disposing of health contributions, the united funds contrived to by-pass the voluntary health agencies by giving to local health foundations. However, giving the money to these local agencies presented more of a problem than the united funds had anticipated; and, after some delay, it was arranged to turn a large portion of this money over to the National Fund for Medical Education. This money was to be used for basic research. As a result of this endowment, some people urged that a new national commission to consolidate all health research be set up. However, these people met with little success.

It was true that those who controlled the united funds focused their strongest ammunition on Cancer and Heart. There was no hope or serious thought of forcing an end to the Christmas Seal campaign of Tuberculosis, while the strength of the National Foundation with an emotional public prevented many open attacks on the organization headed imaginatively by Franklin D. Roosevelt's former law partner, Basil O'Connor. Behind the scenes, however, the polio, arthritis, and birth-defects group was the recipient of tirades delivered impromptu by men of affairs from industrial America. A 1959 article in *Harpers Magazine* (quickly reprinted in *Reader's Digest*) attacked the health agencies. It was immediately made available in reprint form by United Community Funds and Councils at twenty dollars per thousand, and fifty thousand copies went out at once. Unafraid, the National Foundation issued, in 1958, a statement blistering the united funds, saying in part that "they have become so vicious in their tactics that they leave us no choice but to oppose them. The system they advocate and the methods they use are so bad, so contrary to voluntary giving and voluntary association, so violently different from our concept of the American way of life that we now must oppose them both in principle and in practice."

Robert H. MacRae, later to be president of the National Conference for Social Welfare, said as early as 1957 in an address in his home city of Chicago:

218

I would hope united funds would become less bemused with the idea of creating a monopoly in community fund raising. In a pluralistic society such as ours there is a place for the agency that chooses to go it alone. Such an agency should not be subjected to castigation and abuse. It has long seemed to me the practice of some united funds in raising funds for "causes" [like a "heart" or "cancer" fund] to exercise pressure on recalcitrant agencies is an ugly manifestation of monopoly mindedness. It is a far from wholesome development based upon principles of voluntary co-operation.

Considering the normal perils of prediction and the powerful resources of the combatants, I can only suggest that the independent survival of the National Foundation, Heart, Cancer, Tuberculosis, Crippled Children, and others among the large national health groups seemed certain as the 1950's ended. Resistance from grass-roots givers to these famous, reputable, normally well-administered, and dedicated groups simply did not exist. The effort by the New York co-ordinating group for united funds to magnify a well publicized, and, no doubt, carefully engineered Cleveland suburban volunteer solicitors' "revolt" against multiple soliciting for health agencies into a nationwide movement, failed dismally. The Cleveland-oriented and big business-dominated National Solicitations Conference was founded, in large part, to strengthen the united fund movement by one device or another, but by its sixth annual meeting, in 1959, it showed no signs of progress in attracting additional people to its always friendly meetings—sessions where the only literature distributed was that of the National Information Bureau, chiefly supported by business organizations, and the New York State Department on Solicitations, a growing regulatory body. The early hope of some over-eager united fund enthusiasts to expand iron-fisted governmental regulatory bodies (like that in Los Angeles) to the point where harassment of health agencies and other independent campaigners might force them into united funds proved illusory, although fund-raising regulation was spreading. There remained potential danger to fundamental freedoms in proposals for state-wide and even federal controls. Properly organized and operated, however, these public units sometimes did good work in reducing charity frauds, and only comprehensive research would reveal the balance between dangers and benefits in such activity.

In summary, the health agencies, on the eve of the 1960's, showed no signs of succumbing to the harassment of united funds, chambers of commerce, better business bureaus, or the gradually growing machinery of government regulation at various levels. The campaign against their independent activity had reached proportions that should have been alarming to all who believe in freedom of association, independence from uncalled-for government intervention, and the clear right of the American public to choose which deserving social welfare causes should live—and which should die of financial strangulation.

If those who hold positions of leadership in American communities should triumph over the voluntary health agencies in spite of these considerations and force them into a position where the price of survival seems to be joining the united fund, perhaps the agencies should first consider the alternative of banding together to campaign once a year in a semi-unified health drive— six months after the close of the united drive. I have gradually come to doubt the wisdom of this maneuver, and would urge it only as the price for regaining in-plant solicitation or for maintaining the independence of the health agencies from the virtually monopolistic aspirations of the unified drive powers-that-be. There will prove to be little magic in "Give Twice"—or little sense. It would be more sensible to split the united drive at the same time, converting to "Give Three Times," in the idea that each drive would be representative of one of the three main facets of social welfare: health, charity, and recreation. This would give the public a clearer choice and greatly ease the publicity problem faced by the chests and united funds in the past. The American National Red Cross, being deeply involved in each of these three areas, might, in such an event, participate in all the drives, stressing the particular facet of service appropriate to the occasion.

If businessmen, to save the costs of multiple campaigns in their plants and offices, stifle the solicitations of the voluntary national health agencies and create, in their stead, various ineffectual local health "foundations" devoid of talented staff, they can and should anticipate results they will not like. The 1958 Bayne-Jones report of a committee of the Department of Health, Education, and Welfare called for building the National Institutes of Health into annual billion-dollar disbursing agencies. In spite of what was said earlier about the occasional lobbying tendencies of voluntary health officials, it is perfectly clear that the true self-interest of Heart, Cancer, and the other independent agencies lies in some important limitation of government activity in the health field. The voluntary groups are pioneers; they are yardsticks; they live on contributions—not taxes. Are the corporation executives who fight them tooth and nail absolutely certain that they want to maim them? One doubts that they have thought the problem through as they struggle to keep Heart and Cancer from soliciting funds in their factories and offices. If anything is clear, it is this: by their penny-pinching conduct in this respect they are furthering the socialization of American medicine. Perhaps instead of making annual corporation-dollar contributions to these and other health causes, they should give the voluntary health agencies a gift "in kind"—that is, the underwriting of the costs of helping these groups solicit once a year in their plants. Yet the further spread of the in-plant solicitation method with additional payroll deductions, convenient though it would be for the health agencies, is not something to be lightly advocated. Perhaps, after all, the best thing the business community can do to preserve the voluntary groups as a counterpart of federal activity (and, possibly, government monopoly) is to cast off the boxing gloves and extend a genuinely friendly hand. It is high time.

When all is said in criticism of the medical fund-raising and organizational scene of the 1950's, one key truth remains to be noted. All mankind was being served with American research dollars. An interchange on heart disease between Dr. Paul Dudley White, the physician who treated the President's heart condition, and a Congressman, in 1957, showed the relationship between money and results. The legislator inquired if Dr. White thought that the expenditure of over $130,000,000 in federal funds for heart research in eight years had been "a wise expenditure" of government funds. The doctor replied:

> In ten years there has been, partly through this very program, I would think, as much advance as almost in the hundreds of years before. Cardiovascular surgery has all developed in this time, and that is just one example; and these researches that are now beginning to be worldwide—most of them have come since that time, although, happily, private funds are helping, too. I think they should go hand in hand always. . . . It takes time and money. . . . The most important advice I give to people around the country now is: If you want to protect the youth of today from heart disease of tomorrow, support our research.

Other spokesmen in the health field have said similar things; for example, the president of the Muscular Dystrophy Association states hopefully, "Our research program has brought us to the threshold of a whole series of significant discoveries in muscle function and structure." Yet so much remains to be done. A national official of the small Multiple Sclerosis Society says about his terrible disease, "We don't know its cause, we have no specific diagnosis test, and we have no specific treatment."

The public should applaud past accomplishment and hope for future results. Less carping criticism of fund-raising techniques would be a step in the right direction. Still problems of administrative procedure, fund-raising methods, and organizational structure will continue to exist, whatever results may be obtained. Well-meaning protagonists of special causes have sometimes closed their eyes to the broad picture and reverted to provincialism. And peculiar things have taken place from time to time.

It seems incredible that, in the light of the statistics on federal and voluntary medical research expenditures given here, there should have been, in 1957, in California, a request to the legislature by two medical school physicians (one a dean) for three hundred thousand dollars in state funds for new medical research sponsorship. But there it was. New York City inaugurated a medical research program, in 1958, with five hundred thousand dollars, which was applauded by the metropolitan press, politicians, and a large number of initially appointed committee members and potential recipients of the money. Any attempt to co-ordinate the intelligent spending of federal, voluntary, state, and even city funds for medical research would present serious problems. Further, private efforts are being made in medical research. For example, the pharmaceutical industry spends millions of dollars annually in this respect. Although there is a temptation to be overwhelmed by this duplication of effort and to clamor for the formation of a giant regulatory and planning body, perhaps one should go slow. Who, after all, calls the tune in industrial research? To whom are we willing to delegate czarist powers over social-science research? Should the liberal arts be supervised to prevent two researchers in semantics from exploring the same communications problems? And has the situation in medical research really gotten out of hand?

Still some restraint in making rapidly scheduled grants in the health field may be in order. The proposal, in 1959, for a new National Institute of International Medical Research, to cost $50,000,000 a year (an idea widely praised), nevertheless gave rise to the quite proper public protest by Basil O'Connor: "The amount of money that can be intelligently spent on scientific research, medical or otherwise, depends solely on the number of people competent to use that money intelligently." The bill as passed in 1960 was much watered-down.

The public will do well to watch thoughtfully the actions of those seeking to help what some call "forgotten patients" by making duplication of research effort in this extraordinarily expensive field a three or four-way socket. Those in high office were, in the 1950's, genuinely upset by what Marion B. Folsom chose to call, in 1956, a "serious lack of joint planning and co-ordination between public and private agencies"; but few, at the time, were willing to delegate power to government to regulate, regiment, or destroy private agencies, and government officials were naturally reluctant to permit private officials to censor their actions. We may surmise that the financial entry of the federal government into the medical-research field—one in earlier years dominated by the Rockefeller Foundation, the Mayos, and others—will lead at length to ever increasing co-ordination of effort under federal leadership. To say this is certainly not to agree that this is desirable. But faced by the blank-check riches of the federal research institutes, the far poorer voluntary agencies will, in coming years, have to choose between co-ordination and war. Considering American experience with the growth of public-utilities regulatory bodies and innumerable federal administrative agencies, charged with responsibilities for the stock market, railroads, and the airwaves, one can guess what is inevitably ahead. As it comes, let it be in the calm spirit expressed so well by C. Ward Crampton, M.D., who, writing on "Contra-Senescence" in *New York Medicine*, said:

> In the body there are no isolationist organs. Disease may have as many causes as a tree has roots. The heart is served or damaged by the liver, kidney, stomach, and the wisdom and the stupidity of the mind of man. Similarly, there are no isolationist organs in the body politic and by the same token, none in the practice of medicine and all the organizations that work for health. Teamwork is the principle, and the word "together" is its spirit.

Certainly this spirit is essential in the field of fund-raising for health agencies across the fifty states, for there are very real limitations to the use of the mass-communication media in this area. A spokesman for the Advertising Council quite properly warned that full co-operation by his powerful group with each and every health agency could turn America into a nation of hypochondriacs. Should our motto ever become "Every man his own diagnostician"? By attempting to save people from dread diseases, should we worry them to death?

The various views presented here have been arrived at in an effort to accomplish one primary objective in particular: the preservation of "the voluntary way" in social welfare as a permanent part of the American pattern. That objective outweighed, for me, all of the arguments I have heard for inflicting fund-shrinking unity on the voluntary health organizations, for destroying them, or for supplanting them by government bodies. They should be preserved. Even if, through research successes, one or more of them may seem to solve certain facets of the major disease whose name they bear, new tasks will remain for decades to come. Built through years of effort and millions of dollars, the national health agencies should not be liquidated without first making every effort to convert them (as in the case of the Polio group) to still other tasks on behalf of humanity.

The national health agencies developed, in the 1950's, into gifted problem children, to be sure. And one result of their successes and their constant agitation through the mass-communication media was the development of a popular psychology which facilitated the sudden growth of governmental rivals. Another result was the perhaps inevitable creation of enemies, some of whom sought for other social-service causes the dollars the health groups obtained from the public. Others saw in them a threat to old power patterns in charity and health in the community. Still others merely regarded them as items of business overhead on the assembly line at fund-raising time. But opponents and friends alike agreed on one thing: as individuals, all were willing to have their own lives made more livable by the scientific and medical discoveries made with the help of the dollars the agencies obtained from the public and turned over to the experts in research centers and on university campuses.

On the question, "Unify, destroy, or preserve?" I want to recommend a decision. The voluntary national health organizations are still young; they deserve, and they ought to be allowed to enjoy, the freedom to grow into long-lived, useful, and dynamic adults. Nothing is to be gained by hastening their death. And, in cities where the united fund-health agency battle rages, there is no excuse whatever for any who have at heart the total welfare of society to stand by silently while the voluntary health agencies are starved into second-class citizenship by powerful leaders who should know better.

CHAPTER XI

Social Workers: An Appraisal

Dedicated, and
Educated—sometimes.
Humanitarian
Pioneers.

Useful and
Practical. Yet
Otherworldly
And jargonal.

Check-payers and
Philosophers.
Building, but maybe
Undermining.

Respected, though
(By some) despised.
Chips on shoulders,
Striking back.

Directionless on ultimates?
Changing—yet content.
Idealistic, full of purpose.
Always trying.

WRITERS ON THE THEME of social work have trouble whenever they try to define the terms "social work" or "social worker." The public also reveals its puzzlement. An authoritative publication in the field of social work education has noted "a lack of concensus among welfare workers as to what agencies and programs constitute the field of social work, and . . . who is entitled to be called a social worker." As an afterthought, the article states that, in their evolution, the older professions had been equally uncertain as to their nature and boundaries. One thing seems sure: a social worker does social work. But what does this mean?

One definition of social work which enjoys certain reputability is noble in sentiment but is not likely to be of any real service

to the inquiring layman. "Social work" is thought to be "a professional service rendered to people for the purpose of assisting them
as individuals or in groups to attain satisfying relationships and
standards of life in accordance with their particular wishes and
capacities and in harmony with those of the community." Elsewhere, social work has been called "the adjustment of men to
their environment." This stupid definition would have social
workers adjusting skid-row habitués to live in the gutter and
like it!

Here are two other definitions sometimes heard: "the art of
adjusting personal relationships and reorganizing social groups"
and "the practice of the art of helpfulness for its own sake." A
wordy but descriptive definition by a United Nations group makes
social work a "helping activity" and a "social activity," as well as a
"liaison activity" which strives to assist people, to integrate assisting organizations, and to act as a "social diagnostician" for the
community.

Yet an occupation as well known as "social worker" must
have some generally accepted characteristics. The term was defined in the statutes of California, in 1948, under the guidance of
professional social-work leaders, and in that state it became a
matter of law, as follows:

> . . . the term "social worker" means a person whose primary
> professional task . . . [is] the rehabilitation of the individual
> or group in adjustment to society and includes a person en-
> gaged in social work, social group work, social research, the
> teaching of social work and community organization for so-
> cial welfare . . . . A person employed in a general recreation
> program which was without discernible group work or case
> work content shall not be considered a "social worker."

A definition in an ordinance of the city of San Diego, California,
passed after guidance by the local chapter of the American Association of Social Workers, was framed in an effort to discourage
amateurs from practicing social work to make a quick and, possibly, an undeserved profit. It is of real interest because of its
list of excluded groups. In San Diego, at least:

Social Worker shall mean a person who practices in the non-medical field of human adjustment, who holds himself out to the public as a Social Worker, who, by the use of social case work techniques, interviews, community resources and skills in inter-personal relations, counsels or assists people with social, personal, emotional, marital, familial or employment problems. Social Worker shall not include members of the clergy, religious practitioners in the performance of their duties, attorneys at law, physicians, surgeons, osteopaths, chiropractors, employees of colleges, public agencies or social agencies, students matriculated in a chartered college or university where such activities constitute a part of their supervised course of study, employees of organizations using social case work techniques and skills for counseling or assisting their own employees.

Part of the difficulty of defining the term "social worker" lies in the great diversity of work practiced by the men and women who labor in the field. If definition is difficult, listing and describing the subdivisions of social work and the types of activity engaged in by its practitioners is staggering. One authoritative list contains 152 occupations classified under the following fourteen major headings:

Administrative and Special Positions
Public Assistance
Other [Agency] Services to Individuals or Families
Child Welfare [except Court Work]
Court Services for Children
Visiting Teacher or School Social Worker
Mental Hygiene Services
Hospital or Medical Clinic Services
Rehabilitation Services for Physically Handicapped
Work With Adult Offenders
Miscellaneous Services to Individuals and Families
Group Work and Informal Education Services
Community Organization Programs
Teaching Social Work

The rapid growth of the field is such that even authorities are by no means agreed on whether or not this list is too brief or too comprehensive.

AMERICAN NATIONAL RED CROSS

MOBILE ⊕STER CANTEEN

GOOD THINGS HAPPEN WHEN YOU GIVE
Support Your Red Cross

American National Red Cross

The AFL-CIO donated four mobile canteens for disaster relief purposes to the American National Red Cross in 1957. They were placed in service in St. Louis, Alexandria, Virginia, Los Angeles, and Atlanta.

Social Security Administration

The new federal Social Security Building, Baltimore, Maryland, holds the work histories of over 130,000,000 Americans.

Contact between the workers in public welfare and those in voluntary agencies is not frequent, on the whole. Despite pleasantries at conventions and meetings it hardly exists at all during the daily routine. Yet some trained workers have shifted readily from the one field to the other. Caseworkers trained in social-work schools can make the change from a public-welfare department to a private family and children's agency without undue problems. Yet the daily paper work of the strange field may worry the newcomer for a considerable time, especially since some caseworkers put in as much time with paper work as they do interviewing or visiting their "clients."

Social workers may be classified in accordance with the amount of their formal training or the nature of their daily work. Sometimes they classify themselves according to the ages of the persons they try to help—"work with aged" or with children, for example. They may term themselves "medical social workers" or "group social workers." They may be sharply divided into religious and secular schools of thought and procedure, so that communication between employees of Catholic, Salvation Army, and government agencies is often somewhat formal or even strained, with the contempt of one group for the techniques of the other only thinly veiled. The value of religion and of guidance in the spiritual realm has long been a sharp bone of contention. Other barriers to unity come from striking differences in the working environment. Thus there are workers in huge institutions, many in small offices, and still others who visit people in their homes or even, in New York City, walk back streets seeking to serve. Some run up huge mileages in county automobiles in the process of bringing services to the common man and his family wherever they may be.

It should be clear by now that social workers do not engage in a single occupation with a settled daily routine, uniformly required educational preparation, standard job satisfactions, minimum mental and physical requirements, or even stabilized goals. How, then, can one ever train to enter such a diverse, complicated, and fluid field?

A recruiting leaflet issued to persuade young people to choose social work as a career begins with these warm and persuasive words:

If you like people and want to help them, social work may be the career for you. Thousands of young men and women are choosing social work because it offers rewards that few other professions can match. As one social worker put it: "There are more than five hundred families in my town who are happier today because they solved problems with my help. Not that I was the only one who gave them a hand. I worked with doctors, teachers, psychiatrists, judges, probation officers, employers, newspapermen, public officials and other social workers." . . .

Although many social workers earn more than bank managers, teachers and other white collar workers, this profession is not the quick route to wealth. What social work offers is almost unlimited personal satisfaction for men and women who enjoy helping others.

Here is a forthright appeal to one's social-service instincts. It would tempt many of those with some of the personal characteristics set forth by Leonard W. Mayo, formerly dean of a school of social work. He told a young man, in 1956, that these are: "a liking for people, a healthy amount of self-respect, a willingness to work hard, a willingness and ability to remain in the background when that is indicated, poise, warmth, and personal convictions and ideals." Quite an order.

Social workers are noticeably variable in formal education. Fully 60 per cent of all social workers in the United States have had no graduate work, while 21 per cent have had some graduate work but received no degree. Only a meager 4 per cent have one-year degrees, and 15 per cent have two-year degrees. The number achieving the doctorate has been, and clearly will remain, negligible (far less than 1 per cent).

The bottom group of social workers has had very little formal education. Nearly 10 per cent of all social workers have had only a high-school education or even less. Another 7 per cent did not complete two years of college. Eleven per cent took more than two years of college, but did not obtain a degree. Here are discouraging figures for the formally educated social worker to live with, but many vocal partisans find it easy to ignore such facts.

The fifty-five accredited social-work graduate schools in the

United States have made variable progress in recent years in their efforts to train more students to fill growing job vacancies (said to number ten thousand in early 1959). Enrollments in the schools rose from 3,716, in 1948, to 4,551, ten years later, possibly in response to intensified recruiting efforts, the certainty of employment in an understaffed field, and national growth. But the number of graduates of the two-year curriculum remained almost stationary, the 1948 figure being 1,759; and the 1958 figure being only 1,744.

There were 654 full-time faculty members in the social-work graduate schools in 1958, and 552 part-time teachers. The schools have admitted that they could enroll over eight hundred more students per year than they have. In these statistics we have an unfortunate manpower situation. The big schools, in decreasing order of 1958 full-time graduate student enrollment, were: New York School (Columbia), 302; Pennsylvania, 170; Fordham, 167; California (Berkeley), 161; Chicago, 159; Michigan, 144; Smith, 136; and Southern California, 111. Washington, Tulane, New York University, and Boston had 104 each. There had been considerable change in enrollments in these and other social-work schools in a two-year period, with Pennsylvania and Michigan gaining substantially. Some states in the nation furnished these graduate schools very few students, while one-sixth of all social-work graduate students in the nation have called New York State their home.

The results of one study indicated that of a group of 432 applicants for public-welfare jobs, only 6 per cent had close relatives engaged in social work. Indicative of the extraordinary mobility of mankind in response to financial grants by government and private foundations, there were, in 1958, among full-time enrollees in the nation's social-work schools, 31 students from Latin America, 42 from Europe, 18 from the Middle East, 10 from Africa, and 107 from the Far East. Canada's seven schools had their own separate enrollment of 398, among which were doubtless many citizens of the United States.

Training of social workers has become standardized since the schools got together on a "Basic Eight" minimum curriculum of subject-matter areas. The eight fields in the 1950's were: social casework, social group work, community organization, public welfare, social administration, social research, medical information, and psychiatric information. A revised policy statement, in 1952, was important, but substantial curriculum revision, in the 1960's, was likely in view of an intensive self-examination conducted by the Council on Social Work Education. As the decade came to an end, many authorities considered social-work training unrealistic, in terms of the diversity of employment possibilities and the needs of public-welfare departments in particular.

While no school's graduate program could be termed "typical," the basic first-year program at one major school of social work consisted, in the 1950's, of the following units:

Law and Social Welfare	1
Social Case Work *or* Group Work	4
Growth and Change of the Individual	4
Social Welfare Organization	2
Social Welfare and Income Maintenance	2
Social Welfare Research	2
Field Work	8

Elective units could be taken from among six other courses, but some variations might be made "in accordance with individual preparation and needs." Students choosing to stay for a second year of work could specialize in one of six areas of interest: corrections, family and child welfare, medical or psychiatric social work, administration, group work, or research.

There is no language requirement for the two-year Master of Social Work degree in any graduate school of social work. A thesis is optional at many, with students electing to take four extra units of casework instead. At the University of California, Berkeley, and perhaps elsewhere, an attempt is made to guarantee that, when the thesis is omitted, some co-operative research experience is included. Such "group research projects" (social work students working together under faculty direction) have included studies of the use of leisure time by employed men, the exploitation of census data in social work research, changing family trends, civil rights in housing, and "the layman's stereotype" of the social worker.

Nineteen different courses have been offered in social welfare at one school, with additional classes in "special studies," "research," and "field work" available to interested students. Some schools offer more courses than this, while others give less. Of course, there is nothing unusual in such educational diversity. By spreading one's work over a period of years it is often possible to hold a job while earning the M.S.W. degree. Here again the social work field resembles other specialized areas.

Doctoral graduates in social work are so rare that only eight registered social workers in California had Ph.D.'s with social-work specializations in 1950. This situation is likely to change very little, since in the school year 1957–58, only seventeen doctorates in this specialty were awarded in the entire nation. Serious doctoral work is centered at a few universities where academic standards are normally high.

It seems almost safe to say that the social-work schools, when compared with the law and medical schools, are not really obtaining and turning out young men and women prepared to assume important leadership roles in our communities. The big executive plums in social-welfare organizations are going to experienced administrators from other fields, to graduates of business schools, to financiers, and to others who drift into the social-work area for a single task, only to remain. As early as 1928, the layman president of the National Association of Community Chests wrote that "chests are becoming more strongly convinced of the importance of requiring for executive community leadership the rare combination of a welfare strategist and a financial expert." The development of large-scale organizations has increased the need for social-work executives to have a knowledge of economics, political science, and journalism; meanwhile, the social-work school faculties persist in emphasizing social-work vocational techniques—like psychiatric casework and group-work devices.

Scholarships for study are small but plentiful. Forty-one hundred and sixty-seven grants were being used late in 1958, which means that only a handful of the nation's enrolled social-work students were not receiving some kind of grant. Awards were derived more often from tax funds than from school or agency sources. (The distribution: government funds 2,643, university funds 459, private 1,065.) Perhaps scholarships carrying higher figures would increase enrollments in these schools; a small portion of the amounts so generously donated by corporations for engineering and applied science might do wonders. Only a very few of the scholarships now offered would allow a married man to support his family during a year of graduate training. A Lilly Endowment grant of one hundred fifty thousand dollars recently made for post-master's degree study, field training, scholarships, and recruiting of personnel was a small and tentative step in the direction of increasing educational qualifications in the social-work field, and a projected United Community Funds and Councils program of "long-range training and recruitment," aimed at personnel problems in the community organizations area, held some promise if adequate financial support could be found.

Employment opportunities in social work remain more than plentiful. One university records the diversity of jobs:

> Professional social workers are in demand for public welfare departments, employment services and social security agencies, private family and children's agencies, mental hygiene societies, public and private child guidance and psychiatric clinics, hospitals, health centers and clinics, boards of education, municipal and county recreation services, public health departments, housing authorities, juvenile and adult courts, and correctional institutions, probation and parole services, social group work agencies and settlements, councils of social agencies, and community chests.

Corporations are increasingly engaging social workers to smooth out their relations with employees.

One reason for the abundance of employment opportunities in social work is the high rate of resignations. I have often met men whose wives "used to be social workers." A study of reasons for the resignation of social workers from the county welfare departments of one state in one five-month period showed that the most frequent reasons were (in order of frequency): (1) salary too low, (2) future too limited, (3) returning to school, and (4) work-load too heavy. Is there anything unique in all this? Who can say? Many young women who finish a year of graduate social work training enter the labor force with the same attitude taken by many elementary school teachers, to wit, "This interesting non-secretarial job will do until the right man comes along." And come he does—for a great many.

Divorced and bereaved women in great numbers also labor devotedly in the social work vineyard. One wonders sometimes how much marital advice is being passed out by well-meaning women who did not retain their own husbands and by young women who have not yet married. This is a subject for research to be undertaken at one's peril. We know that there were seventy-five thousand persons in the nation listed as social workers at mid-century, 70 per cent of them women. The median age of the whole group was forty.

Most social workers at mid-century were employed by government. The over-all distribution was 62 per cent by state, county and local governments, 35 per cent by private agencies, and only 3 per cent directly by the federal government (which actually financed the salaries of many workers in local government jobs). The judgment of two acknowledged experts on such statistics should be noted:

> It is understatement to say the statistics on social work and social workers are incomplete, unreliable, and generally chaotic. This situation stems from the rapid development of the field and a lack of concensus among welfare workers as to what agencies and programs constitute the field of social work, and as to who is entitled to be called a social worker.

Of the public assistance workers, practically none are federally employed. Family-service workers with M.S.W. degrees are normally affiliated with private agencies but a rising number may be found in public welfare departments. The three Pacific states had fifty-seven social workers per hundred thousand persons as late as 1950. This was a figure exceeded only by the Middle Atlantic states with sixty-seven. The Southeast had only thirty-four. The other sections: New England, fifty-four; Great Lakes, fifty-one; Middle West, forty-four; Mountain, forty-two; Border, forty; and the Southwest had thirty-six.

To return to a tender subject, there can be no question that salaried social work is a favorite occupation for many older women who have lost their husbands through death or court decrees. Among the women of all ages working in the field, 45 per cent are single, 38 per cent are married, and 17 per cent are widowed, divorced, or separated. These figures are entirely at variance with those for men, which are 16, 81, and 3 per cent respectively. Many of the best administrative jobs are held by men. A definite shortage of highly trained and experienced women executives is a factor that has become increasingly troublesome in this occupation.

Social workers (like teachers and, no doubt, everybody else) feel underpaid. The men make more money than the women—as is true in many other lines of endeavor. Salaries have been substantially higher on the Pacific Coast than in any other region. The best salaries have been paid by the federal government, however, followed by the private agencies, and then by other branches of government. Salaries for typists and clerks in the voluntary welfare field are much lower than those for private industry, a fact easily verified by examination of budgets of welfare agencies. Yet clerical salaries in state and county welfare departments may be scaled with salaries in other parts of local government.

Social workers clearly seek to be considered members of a profession having the respectability of law, medicine, and the ministry. The formation of dozens of nationwide and even international associations, and of still others within states and cities, has tended to increase group consciousness. Well-attended conventions and frequent meetings, with "societal" programs carefully "structured" into "meaningfully dynamic" or "ongoing" patterns, also increase the "functional" homogeneity of the group. Tracing the changes in one state association over a sixty-year period will show something about social work and workers in our century.

It was in Oakland, California, in January, 1901, that a

California State Conference of Charities and Corrections was founded. After meetings in various cities, which discussed juvenile court work, child welfare, and related topics of the day, the seventh conference in Fresno, in 1911, changed the name of the association to California State Conference of Social Agencies. By the close of World War I it was common for a handful of specialized associations to meet concurrently with the group. At the Riverside meeting, in 1920, were the California Probation Officers' Association, California Society for Mental Hygiene, the Red Cross, California Library Association, and the Association of Collegiate Alumni. Co-operating groups were the Tuberculosis Association, Psychopathic Association, and the Federation of Women's Clubs. Under the names California Conference of Social Welfare, California Conference of Social Work, and finally California Association of Health and Welfare, the state group met regularly through the years. Numerous changes of name were justified on the ground of "flexibility" and regarded as consistent with the changing times.

This organization of social workers and sympathetic lay people, under whatever name, has not had the state welfare field entirely to itself. A California Taxpayers Association tries to keep a watchful eye on public-assistance expenditures. The George McLain "old age pension" organization, the Institute for Social Welfare, has lobbied successfully for higher pensions for aging citizens and for liberalization of numerous legal phrases touching on the subject. Also important, but across the fence, is a County Supervisors Association, which with a small permanent staff has maintained close liaison with county welfare directors and the county officials who hire—and fire—them. Its meetings and conventions are places where decisions of real importance to future legislation are made behind the scenes. The cause served by the county group is economy for the county governments. This has not been the same as over-all governmental economy, for to crush public-aid programs would by no means serve the re-election interests of a county supervisor.

Also active in California is a County Welfare Directors Association, complete with a confidential bulletin which communicates plans and ideas. Sometimes this group meets jointly with the County Supervisors Association. Several small organizations of public welfare and/or voluntary-agency employees exist from time to time, hoping to increase wages, but no labor union has had much success in organizing white-collar welfare workers. The memory of the 1930's, when ideologies of the left often lay behind unionization attempts and exposed social workers of the nation to their critics, has hurt organizational attempts. Constant staff turnover also hurts. Constant yearnings toward "professionalization" give advocates of unionization the same headache suffered by organizers who seek to enroll teachers into militant unions. Both the teachers and the social workers feel that union membership is not a "proper" activity for professional persons.

From time to time in the various states, there has been agitation by social work leaders to license social workers, the hope being to legislate the group into "professional" status. This agitation has been without tangible results except in California. Long agitation for licensing proved ineffectual when the 1959 Legislature failed to pass a bill which had been long discussed and much amended.

For the previous two decades, some social workers in California had tried, unsuccessfully, to persuade the Legislature to pass a bill requiring the licensing of social workers. After special efforts in 1929 and 1939 proved fruitless, the lobbying machinery of the California Conference of Social Welfare obtained, in 1945, the passage of a bill providing for voluntary registration of social workers.

The California law did not prevent any person from engaging in social work, but it did restrict the use of the letters "R.S.W." to two groups—the many "blanketed in" until 1947, and to all who passed an examination thereafter. R.S.W. was neither a degree (like M.D.) nor a license. It amounted to recognition of some ability, experience, and/or education in social-work procedures. A bill to abolish the whole program was unsuccessful in the Legislature in 1957. Attacks on the costs of the program and prospective deficits forced increases in fees for registration and renewal in the 1960's (to ten and five dollars, respectively). If the public and voluntary agencies had promptly insisted on possession of the R.S.W. as a condition of employment, registration could have become, in effect, a license. But agencies showed little tendency to choose experienced workers with R.S.W. over those without it. In 1953, an effort was made to legislate a licensing provision which would have made it a misdemeanor for any person not having the R.S.W. to use the title "social worker." This section never passed, the candid explanation of the Board of Social Work Examiners being that "because of the opposition to this section, the board offered an author's amendment deleting this section when the bill came up for hearing in the Committee on Social Welfare."

California's unique registration program has attracted national interest. Between 1932 and 1945, the California Conference of Social Welfare conducted its own voluntary plan of registration and, at the time the R.S.W. bill passed had 2,665 workers registered out of the state's 6,000 social workers. Of the 2,665, 72 per cent retained their registration under the new law. By July 1, 1947, there were 4,098 R.S.W.'s in the state.

"We Reach Our Goal! State Registration of Social Workers," the periodical of the social workers of California had announced in 1945. To every R.S.W. under the voluntary plan was sent a post card beginning "Victory Is Ours!" Governor Earl Warren soon appointed the seven members of the new Board of Social Work Examiners, five university-trained practicing social workers and two laymen, as prescribed by the law.

California law provided for the Board of Social Work Examiners to give candidates for R.S.W. a written examination, based on federal and state welfare laws, social-welfare literature, "basic information in related fields of the sciences pertaining to social welfare," and "current events and developments affecting social well-being." From 1948 to 1953 there were 1,299 social workers scheduled to take the examination. Of these, 954 took it and passed, while 78 failed. Those familiar with law and medical examinations in various states will want to make comparisons with their own experience in this variable field.

Where do the candidates for this West Coast examination

do their training? In one two-year period, those eligible had attended forty different schools of social work. The top three were in the state: University of Southern California, 111; University of California, 79; and University of California at Los Angeles, 53. The next three were: University of Chicago, 46; Atlanta University, 22 and New York School, 22. Such worker mobility would not surprise California readers. Of the whole group, 35 per cent had two-year master's degrees (Master of Social Work). In the two-year period, 1958–59, education of applicants for the examination revealed 2 with three years of graduate work, 168 with two years, and 190 with one year. The group was two-thirds female. In another examination group of 84, 42 had one year of graduate preparation, 9 had two years, and 33 had the M.S.W. Exactly half were still students; only 9 of the non-students were not employed at the time.

The mechanics of the R.S.W. examination are simple. Applicants desiring to take the examinations given by the Board of Social Work Examiners in California fill out a form which asks for data on education, professional social-work training, social-work experience, memberships in social-work organizations, citizenship, and length of residence in the state. A three-page reading list of books and periodicals is given applicants as a basis for reviewing for the examination. The reading materials are classified under the following headings: Field of Social Work, Social Welfare Laws, Social Casework, Social Group Work, Community Organization, Child Welfare, Medical and Psychiatric Information, Probation and Parole, Social Welfare Administration, Public Health and Medical Care, Social Insurance, Research and Statistics, and miscellaneous.

The examinations given the prospective R.S.W. are prepared by the Board of Social Work Examiners. The Board has announced that its aim is to give "an objective examination that will test the basic knowledge, skill and attitudes that should qualify a person to practice social work after the completion of the minimum of one year of professional education." The examination is tailored to what is taught in the first year of graduate work by members of the American Association of Schools of Social Work.

While test items are compiled from private sources (individual social workers, teachers, former Board members), items, on occasion, have been submitted for review to faculty members in social work schools. The 150-question multiple choice and matching tests have been reviewed by several experts including a test-construction specialist of the State Personnel Board (who sometimes revises or eliminates a few items). The Board explains that items in the main are "generic" and cover basic material in social work fields involving the techniques of casework, group work, child welfare, community organization, administration, research, and statistics. Candidates are told whether they passed or not (passing grade: 70 per cent) but no grades are released.

Prospective R.S.W.'s must have had graduate study in social work to be eligible for the examination. Yet there is serious doubt that any bill containing a requirement for graduate study could have passed the Legislature, since graduate work has been so uncommon. At its first meeting the new Board arbitrarily established a requirement that all applicants for registration after January 1, 1947, would have to have completed one year of full-time graduate study in an "approved" school of social work. Fifty-five schools have met the accrediting requirements of the Council of Social Work Education and thereby of the Board, while eleven offer a Doctor of Philosophy degree in social work and a Doctor of Social Work degree. Yet 146 universities in the country have been offering Doctor of Philosophy degrees. At least fifteen of the institutions with approved schools of social work do not graduate Ph.D.'s in any field. Harvard, Yale, Princeton, Stanford, and other famous universities do not have schools of social work. Degrees from these universities give no eligibility to take the Registered Social Worker examination, even though the would-be candidate might have majored in sociology, psychology, anthropology, education, or some useful combination of advanced courses like these. Creation of social-work undergraduate curricula in California state colleges, in the late 1950's, will probably lead to pressure to modify the R.S.W. educational requirement.

A survey of the Registered Social Workers of California was undertaken at mid-century by the Board of Social Work Examiners. Hoping to show "evidence of the growth and maturity of social work as a profession," the Board prepared a number of tables and graphs from the 2,900 replies received from questionnaires mailed to the 4,113 R.S.W.'s of that day (1959: only 3,816 in a state with an exploding population). The value of the survey was diminished somewhat by the Board's evident desire to show the Registered Social Worker program in the best possible light. It pointed out proudly in its survey report that "California pioneered this registration—first under voluntary auspices, then under state law." The omission from the survey of information from several thousand practicing social workers who were not R.S.W.'s naturally made many of its findings invalid for social workers as a whole. Members of the unregistered group clearly had fewer years of formal education, made less money, were more likely to work only part time, and were less likely to write articles for social work journals.

The survey of the registered group, both the old timers originally "blanketed in" and those admitted since 1945 by examination, revealed significant differences between the R.S.W. group and social workers in the Pacific states as a whole, even though the former group was included in the latter. Comparison showed, for example, that males constituted 21 per cent of R.S.W .and 31 per cent of Pacific states.

The predominantly female R.S.W. group had more years of formal education than social workers in general, 43 per cent of them having one or more years of graduate work. (The figure for all social workers in the Pacific states was only 29 per cent; and, for the nation, it was 27 per cent.) The California R.S.W. was clearly, by salary and education, something of an elite. Seeking to account for the failure of R.S.W.'s to grow in numbers, the Board explained, in mid-1959, that " the educational requirement and the relatively small number of potential social workers attending the graduate schools of social work have been major factors in the numerical stability of the program." Even giving the examination on occasion in Hawaii and in Washington, D. C. failed to help very much.

It may be that an R.S.W. program in all the states would

have merit. Preparation for a state examination has some value in itself and does not hurt those preparing. The annual California overhead of about twenty-five thousand dollars (coming from fees) need not be a general experience, although some executive and clerical costs are inevitable. But social-work leaders will have to give recognition to "R.S.W." before it will really amount to much. So far, the genuine degree M.S.W. has quite properly meant far more. The California Board said plaintively, in 1959, that it had "continued to urge" that employing agencies use registration as one test for prospective employees; but, since the Board candidly reported that "recruitment efforts are a constant concern of employing agencies," the R.S.W., in my opinion, must not be serving as either an asset when present or a liability when absent— whatever boost it may give the morale of the holders. The social-work group will have to work this problem out for itself, with the over-all interests of the "profession" in mind.

A social planning official of national stature made, in 1956, a keen analysis of his motives for engaging in social-work planning, asking, "Why, in spite of some frustrations, disappointments, and harassments have I continued in the chest-council field?" Robert H. MacRae, executive director of the Welfare Council of Metropolitan Chicago, outlined eight reasons: The work involved ceaseless change, with "no dull days." His was an observation point from which to view social work. Here could be found priceless experience in working with the top leadership of business, labor, and the professions. The opportunities to lead in "development and growth" of community services, he thought, were outstanding. Two other reasons were: belief in the principle of voluntarism and exercise in "practical working idealism." Then there was the privilege of "having a part in the ongoing process of healing and protection, equalization of opportunity, social change and the enrichment of the human spirit." Finally, this official found his work to be fun, yet he could cling to "personal ideals of service." Who would not be glad to gain such diverse pleasures from the task of earning one's daily bread?

Social work is hard work. Heavy stress is placed on one's emotions by days spent immersed in the often unsolvable problems of

243

others. Even though far too many are hit or miss in their formal education, social workers, as a group, clearly deserve infinitely more respect and open-handed friendship from the public than they get, regardless of whether theirs is a "profession" or not. The best social workers are undoubtedly, as the title of a banquet staged in their honor in one city put it so well, "giants of the community."

CHAPTER XII

Social Work: Potential Profession

Do we not all seek to be professional,
To have degrees and status, and respect?
To feel the world's esteem and know that
All one does is right and good and just?

Institutionalization, tradition, ethics, income—
These go with the word "profession," so 'tis said.
A word with magic, to roll upon the tongue,
To tell one's children, to tell one's self.

Why not make social work professional?
No doubt it can be done. We live surrounded
By a vast array of experts. Let us then
Make our social workers expert, too.

But much must first be done before the word
"Profession" can be truly won. To that task
Let the intellectuals and the worthy leaders
Give their all. Then shall we not applaud?

Is SOCIAL WORK a profession? This question is a vital and yet painful subject, one made no easier to discuss by the world-wide disagreement over which occupations are professions. Clear thinking on the nature of professions in fluid societies appeared in an editorial in a British periodical in 1957. Certain vital characteristics were noted. Professions have been "the repositories of particular virtues upon which liberal civilization rests." These occupations have "mastered the art of combining personal independence with public service based on a freely accepted corporate discipline." Their practitioners, moreover, are "devoted to a craft practiced according to principles which are unaffected by calculations of social unity."

In the United States the professions are by no means easily or sharply distinguished from other vocations or occupations. An acknowledged expert wrote in the preface to *Education for the Professions*, in 1955, that "the professions are the occupations through which people obtain the highly specialized intellectual services." While small numbers of people engage in them, the nation depends on professionals to design machines, protect human rights, heal and teach, provide moral and spiritual guidance, and help us all in a hundred ways to live happier and more satisfying lives. Without the professions, civilized society could not be maintained on the present basis. Social workers and their work may be judged by such standards, with one eye on attorneys, physicians, and ministers as representative professional people.

A definition of "profession" which I find appealing is that of the *Dictionary of Education*: "an occupation involving relatively long and specialized preparation on the level of higher education and governed by a special code of ethics." Lloyd E. Blanch has observed that the professional man or woman is sustained by the satisfaction obtained from rendering a service well, from gaining the esteem of his fellow professionals, from living up to the solidly established tradition of the little society or professional group of which he is a member, and from discharging faithfully the high professional obligation in which he has been indoctrinated. A truly professional man is said to be a dedicated man, one who espouses a high ideal of service to his fellow man. He need not make much money. His professional organizations distinguish the qualified from the unqualified by admitting to their membership only those who measure up to acceptable standards. Codes of ethics are said to be characteristic of all well-established professions. And professional persons usually establish and maintain schools, foster and support research, engage in clinics and seminars, and attend conferences.

If social work is not yet a profession, the odds seem to be very much in its favor. Has not the word been diluted? And the bars have gone down. The mid-century census disclosed that 3,813,770 persons, or 6.4 per cent of the national labor force, were engaged in twenty-three "professions" in America. The percentage in 1850 had been only 1.9, a figure which grew to 3.8 in 1900. While the working force of the nation grew eight times from 1850 to 1950, "professional" people grew nearly twenty-six times.

Social workers say with much justice that if newspapermen can consider themselves professionals without regard to gradua tion from journalism school, while insurance agents and real estate men often speak of their "professions," then they, too, are entitled to use the ego-satisfying word. The social workers have a point. Perhaps we need a new and narrower word. Social work certainly comes close to being a profession by the present use—or abuse—of the word. But we must pause.

The historian of the National Education Association, Edgar B. Wesley, in his *NEA: The First Hundred Years,* has described the slow advances made by teachers toward the ultimate goal of professionalization. In 1870, he states, many educators were calling their activity a "profession" and one optimist called it a "science." Nevertheless, it was neither at that time. "Educators saw the necessity of a profession of teaching and boldly proclaimed its advent nearly a hundred years before its actual arrival," he writes. Have social-work leaders been doing the same? Over and over the teachers called themselves a profession; but only time, great tasks, stress, co-operation, better education, and standards which rose higher and became stricter brought status before the bar of the American public.

After a lifetime of association with teachers, Professor Wesley suggests that a profession consists of members who have acquired, by training and experience, some specialized techniques that are basically intellectual in nature; they form associations and are largely unified in purposes and procedures; they enforce standards of practice, "usually embodied in a proclaimed code of ethics," and guarantee the competence of newcomers to the group. Yet individual autonomy exists. These professional persons "place altruism, service, and social welfare ahead of personal gain," even though they promote the personal welfare of their own members. Co-operating with other professions and counseling the government regarding their own, they inform the public in such a way as to make sure that laymen know what to expect of the group.

What single factor, in and of itself, makes a profession? Is it state licensing? Well, barbers are licensed, and some have not even taken the usual six months of barbers-college training. Surely social workers need not wait until state legislatures pass social work licensing laws. And far too many occupations are licensed now to make the licensing act convey prestige. Can a "profession" be recognized by the size of the group? Is size any indication of professional stature? Some social-work leaders seem to have been misled by this standard, allowing the mere growth of social work activity to color their feelings in the matter. Then is it social significance? Whatever this may mean, one would quickly protest that enlisted soldiers and sailors have, for two decades, been socially significant. This standard of measurement leads far afield. Is a profession to be recognized by the degree of formal or technical education required to achieve competence? Those who repair the new electronic brains like Univac engage in constant on-the-job training, but are these persons really much more than carefully trained mechanics? Yet three or four years of graduate work do seem related to professional activity. What is missing? Why is a physician with an M.D. commonly thought to be a professional man while a labor-union leader or businessman of worldwide power is not?

If social workers want to be members of a profession they must give far more attention than they have to such questions as these. One truth of the matter seems to be that it is partly ethical standards—well recognized by the group and rigidly followed by the practitioner—that make most of the difference between a profession and a mere occupation. The medical doctor has his renowned Oath of Hippocrates and powerful medical associations, working in league with the power of the fifty states, trying to enforce the important provisions of the code of ethics recognized by the group. Even the general public seems to sense the vital difference between the bona fide physician and the medical quack. A formal minimum curriculum of medical education has now become mandatory—all know this. But the public feels, in addition, that punishment for violations of ethical practices will be inflicted promptly and surely by the group. People seem to have somewhat the same presumptions about dentists, university professors, lawyers, and ministers, despite variable enforcement of group discipline.

What the public thinks about social workers, on the other hand, is a trial and a tribulation to many who labor in the vine-

yard. There can be little doubt that the public does not feel protected from being questioned, misguided, controlled, or supervised by an incompetent, otherworldly, unethical, or irresponsible
social worker. It was in depressed 1939 that an accountant employed by a state relief organization summed up his doubts about
social workers in words which too many would still find very easy
to endorse:

> The social workers have too much theory and are definitely
> lacking in practical knowledge, or the value of the dollar, or
> the source of the relief dollars. The case workers go on the
> prerogative that they are hired to spend the money; in fact,
> to give it away, just as fast as possible.

There are still workers like these in public-welfare departments
across the nation, are there not? Whose fault it is?

Part of the blame must rest on the often fuzzy economic
theories underlying many articles in social work magazines; some
blame rests on the shoulders of certain social-work school faculty
members, some of whom (zealous missionaries) seem to feel a
mandate to ingrain unrealistic preconceptions about society in
the minds of students as part of the standard curriculum. Mis-
education takes years to wear off.

Assignment of further blame for the employment of untrained and maleducated persons is perhaps fruitless in view of
shortages in the field. If it continues the blame will rest largely on
the lack of appeal that social work has for college undergraduates;
but executive directors of private social-work agencies, those who
hire and fire for government welfare departments, and highly
placed educators in and spokesmen for the social-work group are
not blameless. This is so because these persons have insisted that
almost anyone who works in the social-welfare field, in whatever
capacity, is a social worker. Totally untrained persons have been
employed by public-welfare departments at regular salaries and
turned loose on a completely unsuspecting public. These amateurs engage in counseling and guidance, meddle in family situations of the utmost delicacy, and advise on employment—even
though they may be very young women in the first year of their

first jobs. Other persons direct group work and recreation with no special training beyond a pleasing personality, a few courses in education and general subjects, and a brief career in college basketball. Sometimes such untrained persons rise to administer sections or even whole divisions of large welfare organizations, without background in business and little course work in sociology, psychology, or public administration.

Social-work leaders say that good personnel is a matter of money; that is, the public does not contribute enough money to the voluntary agencies and does not force legislators to support public programs with sufficient tax funds. Yet the blame must rest on both the public and social-work leaders. The academically trained and the untrained have not been clearly segregated in many salary schedules drawn up for public-welfare departments; neither has the presence or absence of advanced and specialized university training been made an absolute dividing line between "social workers" and clerks. Telephone operators, receptionists, typists, bookkeepers, and the janitor are by no means social workers, but the public is not always clearly alerted on this in many agencies, especially in the super-secret public-welfare departments, where even departmental doors bear no labels much of the time. When transferring "clients" or the public to better trained persons within an agency, the staff is not normally instructed to say in so many words, "I will have to call in one of our social workers." Or, "Mrs. Jones holds a Master of Social Work degree; let's ask her what she thinks." Desk signs indicating titles and/or degrees held are infrequently seen in welfare agencies, possibly in the overly democratic attempt to soothe the feelings of the untrained at adjacent desks. Such equalitarianism is costing the social work "profession" dearly. There is some basis for hope in governmentally subsidized in-service training programs, however, and some counties are even sending career workers back to college for a year, in an effort to get these people to lift themselves by their own bootstraps. Supervisors of caseworkers often put in vast numbers of hours of seminar-like instruction, thwarted in part by the employment turnover of a few years.

What can be done about the worker in a giant public-welfare

department who has gained several years of experience in the paper work of her job but has no formal educational preparation in social work whatsoever? Facts ascertained about 2,000 of the 3,600 employees of California county welfare departments through a state survey are relevant.A majority of those replying to a questionnaire would have liked taking social-work training in college if they had had the chance. Yet 88 per cent had "no definite plans" for taking any, and only two out of every hundred were taking courses at the time. Most hoped that courses could be made available in the town where they worked and that someone else would pay the cost of their attendance at classes. Two-thirds of 1,566 said that they would need financial help to take social-work training, and many felt that they had deep roots in the county and could not go away for training.

Those responsible for this survey clearly hope that tax funds will be made available for sending workers to college for social-work courses. Yet there are problems. Many of these employees indicated that, if this happened, they would want a different daily work assignment on their return and a different program division. The popularity of adoptions duty and child-welfare work was clearly discernible in these caseworkers and supervisors, while full-time Old Age Assistance and county-relief workers were far from willing to go back to their assigned fields. Apparently bright-eyed children are one thing; discouraged and even dirty adults and old people are something else again. How can departmental administration be improved by training people who transfer to other specializations?

The survey can also be interpreted as an indication that altogether too many workers who handle the problems of adults wish that they had more romantic jobs in social work. Who can say if this is affecting the caliber of the work being done in the nation's county-welfare departments? In a profession, not everyone can have the more glamorous jobs. Somebody must do the dirty work with real satisfaction and strive constantly to do it better—not just hope to improve to the point where present tasks need never be done again.

If the trained and the untrained in welfare agencies are, in fact, of equal competence after a few years of work (and this is given as a reason for not separating the trained from the untrained in duties and salaries), can it honestly be said that all is well in social-work education? Is such course work worth the effort? Furthermore, if the untrained person is doing "just as good a job" as the trained and is said to be entitled to virtually equal salary on this ground, how can we maintain that the occupation of social work is really complex enough to be called a profession? These are discouraging questions for the leaders sincerely interested in raising standards in the social-work personnel field.

It is with the word "standards," moreover, that we touch upon the crucial matter. Social workers have not faced squarely the unification of their group behind a simple code of ethical practices, the violation of which would be viewed as a serious matter by one's colleagues. One group, the American Association of Workers for the Blind, has created a code of good practice to govern its less than one thousand members, but this excellent example has been followed by too few groups. In the field of fund-raising (the "profession of fund-raising," according to over-enthusiastic participants), the social workers have left the matter of ethics to various outside groups representing businessmen: the solid National Information Bureau, the urban Better Business Bureaus, the new National Solicitations Conference, a tiny Association of Fund-Raising Counsel, and local chambers of commerce. These have prepared codes and standards by which the ethical can be separated from the unethical, the honest from the dishonest, and, to a far lesser degree, the wise from the foolish. Not having engaged in self-regulation, some directors of social work agencies seem to resent the efforts of large givers to protect themselves from rackets through reliance on such organizations or on the local police. There is a void in this area which can only be filled by community leaders capable of imaginative effort.

Social workers across the nation were disturbed and embarrassed by an article about them which appeared in *Harpers Magazine* in the spring of 1957. Almost any other group would have ignored criticism in a popular magazine. Yet in California, for example, the article was dignified by a full reply at the annual dinner of the state social-workers convention, and an official publication noted that "some social workers are laughing, some are burning, and some are taking pen in hand to reply." (The essay was on the reserve book shelf for graduate students of social service at the University of Chicago in the winter of 1959.)

The article attacked the "group" en masse for its habit of using big words borrowed from psychiatry, for its concentration on casework, and for allegedly lying down on the job of reordering society. Bureaucratic tendencies and what was called lack of concentration on public-welfare programs were also mentioned. The charges, while not original, did have some merit. Yet contemporary social work cannot be written off so breezily.

It is well known that social workers are of mixed educational backgrounds, purposes, activities, and employment. Here is a basic fact for all critics to remember. Those who generalize often do so with the stereotype of a family agency caseworker in mind. These often psychiatrically trained persons can be very trying conversationalists for the layman, but they do get results, and they are not necessarily any worse companions at a community or social gathering than many an M.D., grade or high school principal, C.P.A., or you and I. Other people's specialties have always annoyed many of the uninformed, and they probably always will. Still, caseworkers could easily make converts among the most skeptical, provided they could point to their successful cases by name, describe the beginning symptoms and distress of the individual, and summarize with pride the happy consequences. But all is confidential, by practice and by law. So it is that the government-employed caseworker, in particular, writhes in pain as the layman denies the possibility of results which the professional knows can be, and have been, obtained. So the caseworker turns to sarcasm or irony and retires to her own kind for comfort.

A word of advice could be given to caseworkers: To be treated as a professional person who has really mastered technical subject matter and who produces first-class results as a matter of routine, three things seem to be necessary:

(1) Make sure that mastery of the subject and the achievement of results both actually exist.

(2) When and if they do, be convinced that this is the case; talk and act as though you believe the matter no longer needs proof.

(3) Have authentic facts and figures at hand to prove your case.

Social workers take criticism very badly, as a rule. Breathe a word of doubt or criticism near the average social-work school graduate and be prepared to duck!

The first three sentences in Esther Lucile Brown's *Social Work as a Profession* are: "No profession ever makes its appearance full grown and mature. Like all biological organisms, it must undergo augmentation and development. Social work is no exception." The social-work people would do well to roll with the punches. But the spirit of fundamental inquiry is really not welcome in many social-work circles. They prefer the critic to be objective within "a social-work orientation." A number of social-work authors, in the book *New Issues in Social Work* (1959), offered criticisms of the field which made an ugly pattern, but what effect these may have is uncertain. Co-ordination and policy-setting in the field of social-work education has been, since 1952, the special province of the Council on Social Work Education. Resulting from a merger of two older groups, it is described in the *Social Work Yearbook* as "an educational agency with authority to speak and act for the social-work profession on all educational matters." I well know the meaning of that mandate. The executive director of the Council, Ernest F. Witte, informed me that my proposed circulation of a brief questionnaire to the nation's graduate schools of social work was out of the question. He wrote, after seeing the simple two-page completion form:

> It is the usual practice for schools of social work to get in touch with our organization when they receive questionnaires which appear to require considerable "digging out" of facts and figures to see whether or not we have endorsed the study or inquiry. It would be necessary for us to say in relation to your study that we have not endorsed it and would need to know much more about it before asking the schools to undertake the detailed work which many of your questions would

254

require. There are several reasons for this. First, we do not see the immediate value of a quantitative study of this kind as the basis for an essay. Second, and this is a more practical reason, the schools of social work are currently involved with us in a comprehensive three-year curriculum study. This requires their active participation in supplying information and completing questionnaires. Until this study is completed, it is highly unlikely that we shall endorse questionnaires from other sources unless the value of the study is beyond question.

As a monopoly organization, therefore, this Council is in a position to quash comprehensive investigation of social-work education before it ever gets off the ground. This seems to be an unhealthy situation and one unlikely to "enlist the understanding and support of the general public. . . ." An effort to distribute a questionnaire among research workers in agencies by using the handy mailing list of the National Association of Social Workers failed in 1959 when the price per name (for some 650 names) was placed at what amounted to a freeze-out figure: fifty cents each.

Now for some words of possible wisdom for the average citizen. Social workers, in my experience, really enjoy developing close friendships with laymen; but more than most specialists, they must be approached initially with genuine care. They have a mental list of things they want done in the world—or the community—and they are prepared to classify most outsiders at the outset as foes of their ideals. They look for hints of incipient opposition in the manner customary with new converts. The layman must either ask individual social workers what they want society to be, or he must come to sense it by their specialities or activities. The inquiring citizen will more than likely find that he is in distinct sympathy with at least some of these goals. (When it comes to means, or "specifics" as social-work convention speakers say, paths may well part.) The average social worker can forgive and forget routine differences of opinion; she cannot ignore and will not abide much divergence on goals. Her goals and means are invariably "societally structured" and fully in accordance with human values. The outsider's ideas (the ones that clash with hers) are "typical of the lay mind" and full of "unresolved dichotomies." Her goals were in past years all too often a first order of business in the social-work schools; indeed, the provision of a locale for their indoctrination seems to have been a chief reason why some of these vocationally oriented schools were created as separate entities in the first place. Fortunately, this situation was not universal.

An uncritical friend is often one's worst enemy. Thus one charge in particular must be levied against many social-work leaders, both salaried and volunteer. It is that they soothe each other at innumerable luncheons, conferences, and conventions with uncontroverted reassurances while eschewing the society of outspoken critics like the plague. Having defined an "enemy," they fear to expose themselves to his probing, even though it might strengthen their own strategy, tactics, and daily functioning. The critics they invite to address their meetings are "friendly critics" or—too often—uninformed ones. The danger that potent leaders of the opposition might carry the day is considered too great. Nor do critics seem to have gained entree into social work journals, judging from the uniform lack of articles or reprinted speeches in the latter attacking hallowed fundamentals. Their book reviews judge books chiefly by two major criteria: Does the volume favor the "welfare state"? and, second, Is it enthusiastic about social case work in theory and in fact?

Can it not be said, in summary, that some social-work leaders need to revise their attitude toward critics, granting them some small measure of humanitarian motivation? Outsiders need the chance to present their ideas orally and in print to rank-and-file case workers and agency administrators. Certainly much of the bitterness felt by critics of social work as an activity stems from their feeling that they have no audience among social workers for their ideas and criticisms. And they are right.

The young social-work school graduate tends initially to be a radical without knowing it and a reformer operating outside all existing political parties. Never having taken course work in political theory, philosophy, or logic, as a rule, he is, at first, a young citizen lacking an orderly pattern of economic, political, and social doctrines. He is a proclaimed "humanitarian." The world to

the beginning case worker is a place full of unhappy and unful-
filled lives, where money and opportunity are not at all well-dis-
tributed, and where the layman (and especially the businessman)
is shockingly indifferent to his fellow creatures. However, this
young person has decided, with ample federal funds expended
under enthusiastic socio-oriented leadership, all will come out all
right and new patterns in society will emerge.

The young social worker fully expects to furnish the leadership. Unfortunately for such plans, top lay leaders in the community usually prove indifferent or recalcitrant. They are often
the products of rugged academic programs in the universities.
Logic and philosophy, political and economic theory, physics, corporation finance and accounting, and Shakespeare; American history, public administration, law, medicine, and chemistry were
among the undergraduate or graduate courses taken by these "lay
citizens." They consequently prove to be no pushovers. Not well
oriented in child psychology, they can still hold their own in debate on tax rates, legislation, and community planning. Years
pass before even a few of the beginning social workers (too few
of whom were campus "big wheels" or straight-A people) find it
possible to overpower, with their personalities or their fund of
knowledge, these citizen-roadblocks to their dreams of utopia.
Small wonder social workers sometimes turn edgy, cynical, or
scheming as they irritably contemplate a world apparently bent on
thwarting their well-meant plans to do good on a wholesale basis—
and to do it *now*.

Social workers intent on social action in a hurry, when
stopped at the center of the line, sometimes run around the end,
resort to passing that is unwise, and rely on trick plays. The sched-
uling of many meetings of local organizations provides a tailor-
made source of press releases on "grass-roots demands" to solve
imperative community "needs" by new expenditures. A community council, not well financed and lacking power to act force-
fully on anything significant without nearly unanimous agreement
(worked out over a period of years), issues emotional pronounce-
ments on the failures of the community to care for its own.
Laymen of power or wealth are cultivated and flattered into lend-

ing their names to the cause. These busy persons are repeatedly named to committees which officially endorse surveys carefully "socio-oriented" by semi-professional hands. Announcements of newly discovered human needs and of anticipated governmental action come right on schedule from these busy senior citizens, too many of whom scarcely read what they so casually endorse. Shortly before a banquet, these irresponsible benefactors pick up, for the first time, the heart of the speeches they are to give. They stumble a bit as they recite the audience into a stupor, although many listeners grow restive at such duplicity—which I have so often witnessed at close range.

An important public-assistance official once said in my hearing, "If you ever see my name in the paper in connection with a program or social problem you'll know I've slipped." He works night and day, normally behind the scenes, and nearly always effectively. Such anonymous roles are much cherished by the really powerful professional executives in the social-work field. They pull the daily strings, and they get weekly and monthly results. They attend meetings, but they say little. They draft model bills for the legislature, but they never take credit or speak publicly in favor of them. They hand-pick speakers and organize conferences, but they shun the limelight. Government social-welfare officials in particular fit this description, finding their technical area of operations well suited to backstage tactics. The working press seems almost totally unable to grasp the meaning of proposals made in the public-assistance area; therefore, the public remains uninformed.

Social-work leaders know full well that they have powerful opponents to their plans to enlarge certain government expenditures for the benefit of the several needy groups in the state. They try to leave little to chance. Letters to the editor, signed by obscure people, will be carefully planted in newspaper offices at the right time (a tactic suggested in at least one book on public relations for social workers). Extreme examples of human poverty or degradation (or whatever the cause may require) seem to make news about the time an important committee vote is scheduled at the capital. All this is no accident. The "right" people get notices well in advance about legislative committee hearings; the opposition, often badly organized, reads about it in the morning papers. Post-card campaigns may be attempted through organizations of social workers, while these and related membership groups send telegrams purporting to represent the views of vast numbers of people at the grass roots. (In all fairness, however, it should be pointed out that violent opponents of welfare experiments have read public-relations books, too, and their tactics may readily be viewed in various realms of American life today.)

Social-work groups do a great deal of lobbying in Washington, D.C. and in the state capitals. Executive secretaries and "public information" officials of these groups are very active indeed. Because these officials are usually armed with quickie "surveys" of various sorts, they are very effective. They are also greatly aided by the direction many of these committee hearings seem to take sooner or later; that is, the social-work organizations assume the role of spokesmen for humanity and the underdog, while the opposition ends up speaking ineptly for economy or "leave well enough alone."

Seldom is the opposition prepared to recognize the problem while, at the same time, urging alternative, nongovernmental, less bureaucratic, or less expensive solutions. More often they simply deny the existence of a very evident problem and lamely attack the "welfare state" or the social-work spokesmen. Small wonder that program after program clears legislative committees with relative ease. The battle is between lobbying groups; the public is unheard. When the bill is finally passed and the legislature adjourns, the losers vainly cry "socialism," thereby gaining headlines but little else. Neither the legislators nor the public, throughout the life of such controversies, get the all-important and impartial facts sorely needed for making right decisions.

If one of the earmarks of a profession is its engagement in rigorous self-analysis and self-regulation, then the social-work group has a long way to go. The constant assertions that social work is already a profession, accompanied by extravagant claims of accomplishments and a superior attitude toward the layman, do not serve to bring the day of recognition as a profession any nearer. What should social-work leaders do to bring the public around to believing that theirs is a profession? The answer is clear: they must take some increasingly aggressive steps to make it one. This means:

(1) Social-work journals must begin to carry critical articles about the failures and successes of specific agencies and particular programs, governmental and voluntary alike. Comparisons and contrasts need to be stressed. This will necessitate a revolutionary change in present editorial policies, which seem to recognize more "sacred cows" than even the most timid newspaper possesses.

(2) When a technical jargon is really essential to the daily work of certain agencies or social workers, its employment among professionals is unobjectionable. But jargon used in public to impress laymen (who remain quite depressed by the practice) is out of place. Fortunately, the practice is already declining. The late Professor Harry M. Cassidy used to tell his social-work graduate students, "Unfortunately, precision of terminology is not characteristic of social work today. Key words and phrases are used very indefinitely, the same term often being employed in several different senses."

(3) Deans and professors should stop offering watered down versions of regular courses in sociology, psychology, anthropology, political science, and economics in the curricula of social-work schools. Social-work graduate students should sink or swim in the main stream. At the same time, any tendency to turn particular social-work graduate schools into trade and vocational schools devoid of course work in theory ought to be arrested. If the business and engineering schools have felt that they must give "practical" vocational courses geared to specific corporation needs, this is probably a trend neither to be admired nor to be emulated. Is field work—apparently one-third of the graduate curriculum— being overdone in so short a program? Social-work education should be primarily in theory, history, and facts, not in daily procedures that can be acquired quickly on the job. (Schools of education have been severely criticized for going too far in the direction of "how to do it" at the expense of subject matter.)

(4) The social-work group should discuss ethics repeatedly

at social-work conventions and gatherings until a consensus emerges on what is honorable and proper ethical conduct—and what is not. Then codification will be in order. But, some will say, all social workers are dedicated people. They are never tempted to cut corners or abuse their authority. If so, social work is a far less demanding and socially responsible field than it has been painted, and it would scarcely deserve to be called a profession. Should a formal oath of dedication, like the medical oath, be incorporated into the graduation ceremony of social workers at the Master-of-Social-Work level? This would probably be impressive to graduates in social work and observers as well. Such an oath, to have any important national effect, should be one agreed upon by outstanding people in the field and leaders of public thought, as well. It should not be merely a codification of existing across-the-board practices—good, bad, and indifferent alike. This means that any forthcoming social work pledge should be lofty enough in its idealism to be incapable of absolute accomplishment by more than a very few. A low order of idealism will not do.

(5) Social work needs an insigne; but far more important is a professional reality to be symbolized.

(6) A true profession is a demanding occupation. During the period of preparation, it is usual for many to fail and fall by the wayside. However, there is little evidence that the schools of social work have proved so difficult that an appreciable number of students fail to obtain admission. Nor are many who are admitted to study dropped later for scholastic or temperamental unsuitability. Law and medicine have fairly good records in this respect; the mortality for the Doctor of Philosophy degree is normally high; and even at the Master of Arts level at the better universities and colleges, more than the mere desire to "stay on" for a year after the B.A. is needed to obtain permission to do so from the faculty. Advanced degrees in engineering, physics, biology, and theology are known to be demanding.

When rumors are commonly heard on our campuses that "the social-work curriculum is really rugged" (and these rumors are backed up by significant numbers of rejections for scholastic reasons—not "aptitude"—at various stages of the graduate training program) real progress will have been made. Social work will never be respected as a profession as long as many of its fifty-five graduate schools accept and graduate almost all humanity-oriented comers, justifying their course with the sentiment that there is a real shortage of personnel to fill job vacancies. Perhaps university senates and administrative officials should gather facts on this matter, compare their graduate schools, and then act when a need for improvement is indicated.

(7) Social workers ought to bear in mind that they serve the general public as well as their "clients." The public pays both their salaries and the benefit checks they issue to those thought to be in need. Social-work leaders have stressed over and over the importance of recruiting social workers with a "social conscience." While there is merit in this idea, it may have been carried too far. The Children's Bureau of the Social Security Administration mailed out in 1956 an authoritative booklet, *Interviewing for Staff Selection in Public Welfare*, which described as essential in employees "a social conscience, which includes concern for all people and the impulse to better social conditions, as well as the desire to help on an individual basis." The twenty-nine social-work leaders who were responsible for this document felt that "over-intellectualization" was "a danger signal." The "ability to involve himself emotionally" was the key quality to uncover when selecting a new staff member. (The task of successful applicants, it will be noted, would be to decide, in the light of law and administrative provisions, whether or not to give individual applicants from eighty to three hundred fifty dollars a month of the taxpayers' money for indefinite periods.) The booklet dwelt on its theme:

> Experience has shown that professional knowledge alone does not assure competence in social work. State welfare agencies have long recognized that certain personality qualities, such as ability to relate purposefully and with self-discipline to individuals and groups in a helping role and emotional maturity and flexibility, are essential for successful performance in social work. . . .
>
> In order to help others it is essential that a person be able

to relate to a wide range of people, to those in authority, those who are dependent, to one's peers, to persons of the same sex, of the opposite sex, to children and to adults. He must have the ability to reach out to people and to *feel* with people.

Here were pleas for Christian characteristics, to be sure. But behind these statements is an unexpressed idea to which some public-assistance social workers give voice in private. Their job, as they tend to see it, is to make an effort to arrange things so that applicants for public aid are found eligible for it. Presumably an employee with the characteristics most desired by the social-work authorities would find it extremely difficult to say "no" to any who want aid. The enthusiasm of leaders for a social worker who gets involved emotionally, coupled with their expressed disinterest in one with intellect and "professional knowledge," are real danger signals in an occupation longing to be a profession. How can the public really respect a group with tendencies toward elevating bias above brains and emotional desires above the plain demands of the law?

In summary, the ability to consider and implement such suggestions as these for change in the social-work field lies peculiarly within the province of present-day social work leadership. These men and women can rise to their responsibilities for action, or they can continue to insist that theirs is a profession—and continue to be covertly smiled at by academic colleagues and by many practitioners of the older, already recognized, professions.

There has been genuine accomplishment in social work. Trained and dedicated workers may be found at every level. But there are significant defects, failures, and unresolved problems that offset some of the positive aspects of professional social work. The truth is that all who yearn to be members of a profession must first become professional, and only then can they anticipate general recognition from a skeptical public.

CHAPTER XIII

On Radicalism, Pressure, and Planning

To change the world
To do it
In one generation. There's
An objective worth having!

Shall we achieve it then
By revolution?
No. Too messy, brutal,
And impractical.

Propaganda; pressure
On legislators;
Orienting the community; even
Loading the dice:

There are methods that
May work! But
Let us make haste. For
Time is short.

EVER SINCE THE TIME when men and women first engaged in social work as a way of making a living, the proper relationship between social workers and society has been a matter for debate. The basic question has remained, "Should social workers exert an effort to change the total environment, or should they limit their reforming efforts to individuals"? Social action in matters of legislation, a highly controversial subject, will be examined here, for the nature and significance of that activity by social workers and its influence on American society have lasting interest.

Is social work radical or conservative? Should the public look on its social workers as knowing or unwitting allies of socialists and communists or as cohorts of vested financial and business interests? These questions have to be faced, for among men of power, wealth, and affairs are some who call career social workers enemies of "the American way of life."

Everyone must grant, at the outset, that many social workers have been antagonistic towards the rich and towards businessmen.

These workers, often prime believers in "social action," have demanded an ever more powerful state. One social-work leader at the beginning of the Depression cried out that "the old unchecked individualism has failed. The family movement accepts the fact," he continued, "that it can and must contribute to the development of a more sensible economic and industrial system." At the same meeting of the National Conference of Social Work where this warning was uttered, another social worker called on his associates to attack with relentlessness "the roots of the evil whose fruits we are now called upon to harvest." The passage of years, especially years of postwar prosperity, have reduced in numbers and effect such forthright cries by social workers for fundamental changes in the economic system.

The truth is that proposals for basic revision in "the system" are quite out of keeping with what social workers try to do. The carefully trained and highly motivated social worker is one of the important lubricants necessary to keep the capitalistic machine going. Any economy, whether based on the profit motive or not, inevitably fails, on occasion, to facilitate even the minimum desires of some who are unable or unwilling to fend for themselves. Such thwarted persons could easily develop into malcontents, and they could become dangerous ones. While communists have often rejoiced at any increases in unemployment and misery in Western nations—seeing in these symptoms the imminent collapse of the capitalistic system—the best social workers continue to work daily to ease the lot of the unfortunates of society. Their finger is in the dike.

Potential instigators of violence in the nation are quieted not only by unemployment benefits and public assistance but by the work of the Salvation Army and the St. Vincent de Paul Society, and by county relief payments. The social worker takes special pride in converting individual misfits into useful gears in the machine of a dynamic society. Social workers certainly do not try deliberately to worsen the lot of anyone. They do not try to increase personal problems; they do not conspire to magnify discontent among unfortunates. Why should they?

Social work in a capitalistic society is really a mighty conservative movement—whether the rank and file of social workers or the uninformed public realizes it or not. When the economic system of the nation develops a hotbox, the social worker does more than his share to get the train running again. The steam hisses from an obscure crack in the system; the social worker hastens to apply a patch. Sometimes he gets burned for his pains, but the career worker carries on, anyway. Social disaster is always a possibility in a nation unless there is constant vigilance and preventive maintenance. The capitalistic system can carry on unscathed as long as its wounds are bound up regularly and carefully. True friends of capitalism should be very careful before they lash out to destroy practitioners of social work.

There are grounds for saying that if there are still social workers in the United States who are communists, they are remarkably contradictory or unusually stupid people. For what they do to earn a living as social workers every working day of their lives pushes farther off the day when "the workers" could possibly recognize themselves as irrevocably exploited and throw off their "bonds." Few persons seem to realize this. Still fewer say anything about it.

Some years ago one radical social worker sensed this situation. She exclaimed in despair to a national convention audience that the social work of her day was, in truth, a "salvage operation." It only attenuated the ruthlessness of the representatives of economic militarism, she thought morosely. Had not social workers of her day been caught in an essential contradiction? She continued morosely:

> The more effective our service became the more we allayed popular unrest and assuaged the spirit of rebellion. Unconsciously and unwillingly we became the allies of a predatory system, the instruments of reaction. Organized charity stands today [1932] between our discredited economic system and revolution. This is as much an indictment as it is a tribute.

The daily tasks of social workers continue to block the bumpy road that could lead to drastic change in the American economic system. All of them may not be overly fond of this role, but they are playing it anyway. If they pay lip service to radical doctrines of equalitarian upheaval, or lend themselves actively to the furthering of such causes while carrying on their social work duties, they are involved, as has been indicted, in a serious contradiction.

So far we have been speaking entirely of extremes, of those who advocate a communistic or socialistic state—that is, a workers' state which amounts, in fact, to an ownership state. If the United States has very few social workers who long for such an extreme, it has thousands, on the other hand, who rejoice at each financial and administrative extension of the already long arm of government. The appropriated dollar is more important than political theory for such persons—especially a dollar from the federal government which matches state welfare expenditures. Almost equally sought after is a state dollar appropriated to match county and/or city welfare and health expenditures. While taxpayers themselves, these government-welfare-minded men and women can see no good reason for not pleading for ever larger appropriations by federal, state, and county governments. They decry the warnings of all who insist on economy at the cost of welfare items in the budget. Above all, they equate governmental action with humanitarianism. This is the foundation of their social-action structure.

Focusing on the asserted needs of the recipients of government bounty, the social workers of whom we speak seem oblivious to the needs of other middle-class wage earners who pay increasing tax bills. One wonders, sometimes, if satisfaction will come to these propagandists only as the residual incomes of Americans begin to reach a dead level. Few tears are shed in certain social-work circles over such a possibility. If the national debt continues to rise as government expands indefinitely, the prospect of leveling is almost a foregone conclusion.

What seems to be desired is government paternalism on the installment plan. Far from being aimed only at the "needy," as the word was once used, it is increasingly beamed toward the middle class. The concept of a "needy person" has to be revised substantially if we are to call some of the proposals for additional federal activities in the medical field "social welfare." The idea seems to be that if the middle class finds it hard to save for old age, the federal government will handle all the problems of the individual, disadvantaged or not, in his senior years.

To the down-and-out, and to an ever increasing number of persons who, by no stretch of the imagination, are down-and-out, the advanced planners are saying in effect, "We will see to it that society, through benevolent government, meets your every need." These advocates of the glorified service-state share a common disregard for the financial hopes of the industrious and ambitious among their peers in the citizenry. Constant and unremitting solicitude for people known to be in trouble, in despair, or in degradation is to be expected of a social worker. But are these the only people with inalienable rights? When social workers assumed an obligation to serve society, they took on the burden of serving more than merely those who hit bottom.

Contemplating this, we are reminded of the football fan who focuses his ultra-powerful binoculars on an inept guard, a partially injured tackle, and a careless end—all on the weak side of the line. Finally, he exclaims at the close of the contest that the game was unfair and one-sided and that his team must have better training, more expensive coaches, and an immense athletic-scholarship program. This spectator has, in this instance, a bad case of tunnel vision. Overlooked on his team during the game was an All-American backfield. Dedicated and talented persons on the other end of the line had covered themselves with glory. And the game had been won 45 to 9. Frequent substitutions for veteran players had been possible, so that the total fund of talent was developed and strengthened. Onlookers from distant places were inspired throughout most of the game.

Skid row is not the story of America, nor are alcoholics and the unfortunates in trouble the only elements of society worthy of consideration.

Part of the "social action" difficulty seems to come from patterns of thinking derived from religious or moral teaching, which, through the years, has become distorted. Most social workers take seriously the parable of Jesus on the lost sheep. He began by remarking that he had come to save that which was lost. "How think ye?" he asked. "If a man have a hundred sheep and one of them be gone astray, doth he not leave the ninety and nine, and goeth into the mountains, and seeketh that which is gone astray? Even so it is not the will of your Father which is in heaven, that one of these little ones should perish." Here was a clear injunction to concentrate one's efforts on the underprivileged minority at some expense, if need be, of the majority. This seems to be part of the moral.

Social workers have always been on firm ground in making attention to the unfortunate minority their life's work. But should we, perhaps, bear in mind that in this example the underprivileged was one out of one hundred? Some people in American society, social workers among them, have long since enlarged the lost-sheep category beyond all common sense. Are there really so many lost sheep among us? Soon it will be contended perhaps that we are all lost sheep, and that we must all rely on government as an intermediary in an effort to remedy all problems. Does the mighty injunction to seek the one that has gone astray mean that such a one is thereby entitled to an extraordinary variety of complex services and monetary payments over an extended period—almost as a reward for straying?

Many in our republic believe that a giant regulatory, and even paternalistic, state is a menace to be feared only slightly less than a so-called workers' state or a property-ownership state. From the standpoint of these apprehensive persons, the never ceasing pressure to augment state programs and build state powers seems neither humanitarian nor conservative. Quite the contrary. Here they find radicalism. Because modern cries for all-encompassing government action appear to be rooted in altruistic idealism, they are hard to combat. (The idealism of many foes of big government is hard to demonstrate, as a rule, for it often rests in concern over the ultimate rather than the immediate, and the total rather than the part.)

Some social workers hold attitudes toward government that are directly contrary to those of their colleagues discussed above. The leaders in the voluntary field who want government to absorb their programs are not the only spokesmen from this occupation.

A substantial number in the voluntary group feel, with great pride, that their own organizations are (when reasonably well-financed) satisfactory vehicles of social service. By and large, individuals of this persuasion are quite common among leaders and workers for the Salvation Army, Red Cross, and many Catholic and Jewish agencies. They spend little time trying to build up government programs to parallel or supersede their own. Some eager group-work and family-service leaders are not so self-sufficient, however, and tend to pressure legislators at every session to enlarge the area of publicly financed social service. Let it be said, however, that they visualize their role in all this as one of great public service and both a necessary and proper activity for persons in their calling.

In an organized society it is not surprising to find that those who lobby for government programs have organized together for the task. It is only natural to find social workers' groups zealously guarding their self-interest at every turn. Fully 78 per cent of the local chapters of the National Association of Social Workers have committees on "social policy." Some pressure for expanded government programs is undoubtedly the result of the search for better jobs and status. In 1957 the accredited lobbyist for the National Association of Social Workers appeared before the House Appropriations Subcommittee on behalf of his group—"an association of social workers employed in governmental agencies, federal, state, and local voluntary agencies, sectarian and non-sectarian,"—as he described it. He wanted a 10 per cent increase in Children's Bureau personnel and an 18 per cent staff increase for the Bureau of Public Assistance. He sought $10,000,000 for a training and research program rather than the $4,500,000 scheduled. In passing, he admitted that "we have a lot of interest, our particular organization, in both training and research grants. . . ." And he urged that training be offered primarily to social workers already employed in the field (a not particularly defensible position in view of the acute scarcity of trained social workers across the nation). Whether this was a disinterested voice cannot be said with assurance.

I watched a delegation from a united fund while it stood in

the chambers of a county board of supervisors, pressuring to have a new "voluntary" homemaker service housed in public welfare department offices. These lay and social-work leaders would put up three thousand dollars of united fund money; the immediate cost to the county, they explained a bit too smoothly, would be small (for a year, it turned out). In ensuing years, program costs of several hundred thousand dollars would result. County taxes would have to meet these costs.

The scene was not unusual. The Hill-Burton Act accustomed private hospitals to look to government for millions of dollars in federal funds. Payments by state mental-health departments to nongovernmental agencies are spreading; allocations by government to voluntary agencies for vocational rehabilitation are becoming commonplace. The California Council for the Blind took notice of a new proposal in this area in April, 1957, when it urged that subsidies not be made by the state to "privately operated sheltered shops" as provided by two bills before the legislature. "Experience has shown clearly that such shops do not usually promote the rehabilitation of blind and other disabled persons working in them, but rather instill defeatism and discouragement in many, and pay wages that keep blind people at an extremely low plane of living . . . ," said this official (and unusual) resolution. Whatever the validity of this argument, it was the kind of dissent on method commonly heard in social work circles but seldom heard in legislative halls—where social workers try to agree, not disagree.

Omnibus social-welfare expenditures by government, when poorly considered and hastily enacted under pressure, can bring bad results in spite of the humanitarian intentions of legislators. Social action by government is never easy, and the representatives of the public find themselves confused on many occasions. They depend heavily on advice from interest groups, and among these the social work bodies figure prominently.

Whatever has been said in criticism of unrestrained government intervention in the social-service field, the fact remains that many government services are proper, necessary, and must continue indefinitely. Opponents who speak in condemnatory gen-

271

eralizations need to understand this. Unemployment-benefit payments are, for many in depressed economic areas, the staff of a minimum life, and public-assistance payments are very often the cement that keeps families together. "Hope is the anchor of life," reads the motto of the United States Department of Health, Education and Welfare. Even in our nation, voluntary charity could never produce the staggering billion-dollar sums needed to do the job that must be done, even in times of great prosperity. So much is clear. There are compelling reasons why the opponents of public assistance and unemployment benefits should beware of overselling their case.

No matter how antagonistic he may be toward "give-away programs," an executive in the financial or business community should recognize that there is a connection between profits in a capitalistic economy, on the one hand, and social welfare programs on the other. Welfare payments and health and recreation services affect visibly the financial and business climate of a community. Old-Age and Survivors Insurance payments, Old Age Assistance checks, Unemployment Insurance benefits, and other relief and aid checks, coupled with charitable payments made by churches and voluntary agencies, amount to a sizable sum. Payments of this type have a considerable impact on local purchasing power. Nor is this the whole story.

Social work makes many tangible and intangible contributions to society beyond the payment of cash. Character building and recreation agencies keep youths out of trouble with the law. They preserve young people as future productive workers and citizens in the community. Guidance, counseling, and case-work procedures by family-service agencies can prevent families from going on the public aid rolls—or take them off. By forestalling divorces and even violent deeds (including suicides), welfare agencies can preserve family units as happy elements in the community. Many health agencies, such as public nursing units, make it possible for wage earners to report daily for work. Homemaker programs, while perhaps too expensive for indiscriminate use, can relieve men from their household duties in time of critical family illness, thus keeping them at work in the factory. Management's personnel officials know (or ought to know) these things. The case for free and part-pay physical and mental health clinics is being pushed vigorously in some states; such government facilities, especially if they include treatment for alcoholics, will serve business at the same time they serve its employees. Whether business would find it cheaper and wiser to seek other solutions to such employee problems is another matter.

There can be no doubt that organized social work today, while it is often portrayed solely from the standpoint of cost, is an important factor in preserving the profits of industry and commerce. It affords many a hard-boiled case for charitable giving by corporations. The Red Cross, by its specialized services, has long saved the military the expense of courts martial, extra military police, personnel officers, chaplains, investigative machinery, lost-duty time by personnel, and endless correspondence. That these services constitute a considerable saving to taxpayers, corporate and otherwise, is too obvious to require comment.

Some of the pressure for augmented government social-work programs seems to be coming from management people who see the advantage to business in having employees' whole needs cared for by the state rather than by additional clauses in union-benefit contracts. Thus social work financed by government—and to a lesser extent by contributed funds—becomes a service to American business, one financed by the whole public.

If American commercial and industrial leaders voice the suspicion, on occasion, that they are not benefiting from their contributions for voluntary welfare and the percentage of their tax dollars allocated to public welfare they are largely mistaken. With all the alleged (and real) failures, follies, and futilities of social-service programs, social workers are still giving the businessman a pretty good return on his minority share in the total investment. This may be hard-boiled language, but the universal and unqualified character of the attacks on the "welfare state" which are made by some of these indirect business beneficiaries and their agents have often deserved just such a rebuttal. For it is clear that the self-interest of banks, corporations, and all well-to-do persons in having a nation where none starve and most are happy is a very desirable thing.

273

Conservative forces in the United States should want to preserve the portion of our existing public and private welfare system
that serves real and important needs. For them it is the path of
enlightened self-interest. Persons who work for indiscriminate
abandonment of all organized social-welfare work are, without
any doubt, among the most dangerous radicals we have.

To summarize the answer to our original question, "Is social
work radical?" one must say that it is—and it is not. The intention
of some social workers is that drastic changes be made in the
American way of life. This is particularly true of a few social work
professors at a handful of the larger graduate schools and officials
of certain social-work interest groups. Yet at the grass roots, where
social workers practice their daily tasks, this is not normally the
case. Radical social-work mariners navigate for unknown shores,
but their anchor drags on the bottom and the crew is unknowing
or indifferent.

The intent of a great many social wokers is that their occupation shore up the existing timbers of a capitalistic system which
they would not change or modify in any important way—even if
they could. These perform their daily jobs as a humanitarian service to improve the lot of mankind. They give little thought to the
ideological impact of what they do. In this casual disregard for
ultimates they are by no means alone. Yet the majority of social
workers, like most Americans, have long believed in progress. The
confident belief that there will always be appreciable progress from
year to year has sustained them.

It seems reasonably clear to me that whether rank-and-file
social workers know it or not, the majority of them think the
capitalistic economy can succeed and wish it well. If more of the
men and women who work for our welfare agencies realized their
position (and if more of their vigorous enemies understood it),
the whole field of social welfare in the United States would gradually become healthier and more effective.

The fact that social workers and social-work volunteers try
to plan has misled some critics into thinking that here is sure proof
of radicalism. No doubt this suspicion dates back many decades—
to fear of the Progressive Movement for some, to fear of the New

Deal or Fair Deal for others. But planning is not conspiratorial. And it is nonpolitical by nature. The most conservative as well as the most radical groups plan and urge their ordered ideas on society. The community-welfare planning councils of the nation cannot be defended or attacked, in all fairness, simply because they try to plan. Rather, the councils can be criticized most appropriately on the basis that they do not face squarely the major problems around them and cannot act on behalf of the whole community. Before considering further the role of councils in our society, the assets of voluntary welfare must be examined once again.

A vigorous defender of voluntary private-welfare organizations has suggested an "S.E.C." system of showing the superiority of these organizations over their governmental companions. "S" stands for "starting." Programs freely begun by voluntary agencies presumably reflect the wishes of community leaders. Such programs are said to begin at the time they are wanted. Government is likely to be slower, waiting for the desires of all the public to be made clear. "This freedom to start anything is something precious and peculiar to private charity . . . ," wrote Alan Gregg of the Rockefeller Foundation. His next letter, "E," is for "experimenting." Government is said to envy the voluntary field this freedom to try and try again. And "C," in "S.E.C.," stands for "changing," for adaptation or adjustment. This may be easily accomplished in sensitive response to changing circumstances. The private agencies "can even die more gracefully and promptly than governmental agencies." In summary, the three advantages are the ability (1) to start new work, (2) to experiment, and (3) to change.

In years past there was much to this theme. But is it entirely true of voluntary welfare today? As ideals, "starting," "experimenting," and "changing" are highly desirable. But where is all the starting, experimenting, and changing in the voluntary field in our day? If these words comprised, in 1949, a good description of the voluntary field in many cities (and one may well reserve judgment), there are grounds for doubting if the passing years have brought marked spread of the gospel.

A voluntary agency, once created and financed for two years, is likely to last for a long, long time. Embarked on a program which is financed by a chest, a private agency can endure, and probably will, for decades. Perhaps the details of daily practice will shift from time to time; but without a change in executive directors even this is unlikely, especially if the same handful of regular attenders at board of directors' meetings remains firmly in control. And this is the custom. Many voluntary agencies in America do so much bragging in press releases and annual reports about their "dynamic role in the community" that the lay leaders who support them hesitate either to sponsor or even to permit sudden change. To do so would be to admit previous error. This would indicate initial stupidity on their part, they seem to feel. Is this too strong an indictment? Perhaps so. But the all-embracing claims of enthusiasts for voluntary welfare have been increasingly unrealistic ever since certain professional public-relations people moved into the field and drowned it in a sea of flattering adjectives.

The truth is that neither government nor private programs evolve rapidly enough to meet changing social and economic conditions. Part of the blame for this rests in the complacent public. Part is the fault of an uncritical press, which prints verbatim, or in somewhat shortened form, almost any nonsense given it as a press release by a leading charitable agency. Part of the trouble lies with the welfare planning councils of our communities. These have assumed responsibility but are not prepared to exercise it.

We have had quite enough praise of councils since the first ones were founded in Pittsburgh and Milwaukee in 1909. Most textbooks on community organization are more than charitable toward councils. Indeed, they are the darlings of social-work literature. They can do much good in a community, but the positive has been considerably over-sold. Realistic reservations on the community council were mixed with praise by insider Frank J. Bruno, who reminded his readers in *Trends in Social Work, 1874–1956*, that "its method of arriving at judgments through conferences shared by the forces concerned is too slow and sometimes too timid to suit those impatient for decisive results. . . ."

What the councils try to do may be seen, from their own point of view, in the expressed objectives of the Welfare Council of Chicago, which terms itself "Watchdog of Your Welfare Dollar." This council: (1) tries to guard against duplicating services and wasted money; (2) hopes to spot immediate human needs and encourage new services, perhaps adjusting present services to cope with needs; and (3) attempts to set measurement standards so that agencies can be held accountable for performance. All this is a big order. Without considering specifically the performance of the well-financed Chicago group, the way that most councils meet their assumed obligations must be commented upon.

Nearly all community planning councils lack the power to carry through on plans as elaborate as those indicated. How many councils can abolish a branch YWCA, even after much discussion, and convert the building to some other use? How many can force or persuade the Girl Scouts and Camp Fire Girls to stress work among teenagers rather than among the seven- to ten-year-old group? What active and aggressive council can really boast that it enjoys the confidence of both the local social workers' organization and the county taxpayers' association? Some can, perhaps, but not very many. Council action, when taken, is often too one-sided for this. What council fights publicly against increases in old-age benefit payments in order to spend available tax money for recreation for youth—or ventures to take an opposite stand? Certainly very few councils are so bold. Most of them customarily evade or straddle the really "hot" issues to debate the creation of a small nursery school out by the city limits.

Real power simply does not rest in the hands of councils. And, considering the matter more closely, this is just as well. Voting procedures within these bodies seldom reflect the possession of any capacity to shape community destinies. The Salvation Army—a very large group—and the tiny Legal Aid Society, with its staff of two, often have equal voting strength in a council. Red Cross may have one vote, while many large national agencies which solicit and spend money locally are often not represented on a community council. How many votes should Heart, Polio, or Cancer have in a local council? Of such reflections debates are made.

County public-welfare departments, it has been urged increasingly, should play a role in community-council activities. There are grounds for suspecting that this agitation in social-work circles has been chiefly a device to justify applications for government fund grants to councils. Such grants have been obtained in Tampa, Florida; Stockton, California; and elsewhere. In twenty-three major cities, in 1955, however, only a meager 2 per cent of chest, council, and united-fund administrative financing came from government sources. This was 2 per cent too much!

Many executive directors of councils would say "amen" to the late social work Professor Bruno's judgment that "council financing has always been bothersome." When I questioned the director of one large community council on what basis he had for urging public-welfare department participation in a council, he declared before an audience of social workers that the county welfare department ought to be included for two reasons: (1) it has a large staff of welfare workers, and (2) it pays out large sums of money in aid checks. "Does this mean that its power in the council should be scaled in accordance with either of these"? Plainly surprised, the speaker replied in the negative. "Then should the manager of the local branch office of the federal Old-Age and Survivors Insurance office be included on a community council? How about all the other local representatives of federal and state health, welfare, and recreation bureaus? And should these be prorated in voting strength"? Clearly, the questions had entered an area new to many social workers. Council voting procedures have been of little interest because councils have been accustomed to making such minor decisions that voting procedures make little difference. As a rule, councils arrive at virtually unanimous votes on perfectly obvious and almost innocuous "needs" for new services. They leave major programs and large agencies alone. Welfare councils tend to be glorified debating societies.

Yet community councils are by no means valueless. Their debates do illuminate issues under discussion; the exchange of views is valuable; rapport is established; and valuable friendships develop (along with some new enmities). The councils often prepare and publish directories of community services, and these are essential to any metropolitan area. Research surveys of value can be carried on by council staffs. Some feel, however, that these surveys are too often undertaken for the sole purpose of buttressing decisions already reached by leaders "in the know." This procedure undoubtedly varies from place to place.

Lay representation on community-welfare councils is seldom truly representative of elements in a community who are suspicious of public aid and of government financed programs. This means that council decisions, when finally reached after months and years of discussion, must often be debated all over again in the forum of the greater community. Perhaps there is no other alternative. It has been evident in many cities, however, that the people who control the united-fund drives and the volunteers who rule in the planning realm have not been one and the same. (Here, let it be surmised in passing, is an important reason for the niggardly financing which many councils get from the chest or united fund; naturally, the councils have turned toward tax fund-sources for new financing.) If the men of corporate management are increasingly overrepresented in fund-raising machinery, they are often grossly under-represented—and almost excluded—from the planning councils. Dr. Stephen Fleck of Yale University School of Medicine told the National Conference of Social Work in 1956:

> Rare is the larger community that has not had or is not having a battle between its Council and its Chest or Fund— . . . the "professionals" in the Council against the "volunteers" responsible for the fund drive. Often these controversies reflect in part divergent sectarian interests within a community as well as conflicting local and national concerns.

The American people certainly stand to profit from the preparation of plans which outline possible courses of action. When government expenditures are in order, it is well that the council planners remember that the elected representatives of the whole people at state, county, and city levels are chosen to be planners, too. In their planning of a city, county, or state budget calling for heavy expenditures for health, welfare, and recreation, the councilmen, supervisors, representatives, and senators—and their appointees—must remember both the people who will pay and those who will receive. If government agencies are, for some reason, to be represented on what were hitherto independent and private social planning bodies, there is grave doubt whether an appointed administrator—like the director of the county-welfare department—is the proper official to sit with them as they plan the spending of thousands of dollars of tax funds. Financial policy is a function of elected county boards of supervisors. No administrator with common sense would try to sway county governmental policy through his council membership. After all, tomorrow the council will be putting pressure on the supervisors. "Wanted: new director of public welfare" will be the wording of the advertisement.

What, indeed, is the proper representation basis for a community council? Does the hit-or-miss method of one representative for each charitable agency, free and part-pay clinic, and recreation group in the city—augmented perhaps by three ministers, an educator, and a trade union man to represent "working elements"—really provide any guarantee that the whole people are being represented? We may well doubt it. Admittedly, there is assurance that persons presumably interested in the needs of "people" will be planning to meet what they consider to be "needs." but many councils are open to the charge that there has been no really careful attempt to arrange scaled representation of the various population centers, age groups, and economic interests of the area covered. It can be argued that a council is private and a law unto itself. In that case there need be no such representation, but then the council can speak only for itself. The pretense of popular consensus must go. Cross-representation of chest and united-fund board members on councils will give them strength, but there are dangers in this.

280

Only by genuine representation of the whole people and by equitable voting procedures can welfare planning bodies achieve the power, the community respect, and the better financing that they crave. It takes more than the use of a city name attached to the magical word "planning" and the final word "council" to bestow the right to reorganize the environment and the lives of a free people. Councils have tried to earn the right to power by wise decisions. Their first and wisest decision, however, ought to be to make sure that they are not really the creatures of large agencies or special interest groups with axes to grind.

When councils sponsor research surveys of community needs they will gain greater public acceptance if they begin with impartial fact-finding and then make these facts generally available in unvarnished form. In this way all proponents of special points of view can reorganize and rearrange the facts to "prove the truth" as they see it. The one-sided nature of far too many social "surveys" has been close to scandalous in various parts of the nation. Only because this type of inspired investigation is often "in a good cause" (and because few scholars read surveys anyway), have many of the "needs" surveys avoided the general attacks they invite and richly deserve.

Many councils seem to have been addicted to the kind of research investigation that starts with a hypothesis and then proceeds to prove it—by leaving out adverse facts and through careful presentation of data through pictographs. The trained persons who do this type of research for the councils know better. But they, too, are obsessed with the absolute necessity of selling the community on the need for quick action. It is easy for them to justify on humanitarian grounds what amounts, in extreme cases, to falsification of evidence. Omission of the negative is more common, however. By not putting their names on the covers of such surveys, the researchers who do the work find it possible to soothe their consciences.

There is room for special-pleading treatises in our society. Agencies and lobbying groups will, no doubt, find many occasions when one-sided studies need to be prepared and circulated to counteract the arrant propaganda of others. But a council which claims to be representative of a whole community should zealously guard any reputation for fairness it may enjoy. One way it can do this is by giving the people authentic facts in a fair-minded package which all can open and share.

Having attacked the councils for what seems to me to be a substantial failure to serve the best interests of society, it still may be urged that citizens join these bodies and serve diligently. The councils may be weak (and in extreme cases conspiratorial) but what other independent body is available? Some of them, on occasion, turn propagandist; but can this tendency best be arrested from the outside—or the inside? If councils are sometimes lightheaded, a good counterweight would be the addition of solid thinkers and additional men and women of real substance in "our town." We can abolish our councils; or we can make them a greater force for changing, starting, and experimenting. The latter course is the one most likely to give both governmental and voluntary-welfare agencies and programs of specialized services a much needed shot in the arm.

When finally satisfied with the above paragraphs, I showed them to Robert H. MacRae, executive director of one of the nation's largest councils, and solicited his written reaction. Granting the validity of most points, he had reservations on others, saying, "Some of my disagreement is a matter of emphasis rather than of substance."

> In keeping with your request I have read the section on community welfare councils with particular care. I have to confess, reluctantly and unhappily, that your indictment of councils on the charge of ineffectiveness is true all too frequently.... [Yet] Councils have performed with some degree of adequacy the clearing house, co-ordination, and common service functions assigned to them. While performance has been uneven certainly, it has not been grossly inadequate. It is in relation to the planning function that councils have failed most clearly.

This failure, he thought, stemmed in part from the fact that the majority of councils continue to be councils of agencies rather than community-welfare councils. This tends to tie them to the status quo and to immobilize them from proposing drastic changes. Furthermore, it tends to keep representation too largely "in the family," and to exclude important social forces outside the family of agencies. The fact that the majority of the councils are closely identified with community chests causes them to be regarded as simply adjuncts of the chests. As a result, the participation of government agencies and non-chest voluntary agencies is all too frequently limited in nature. While councils must maintain close relationships with chests, Mr. MacRae wrote, it is the independent councils that tend to be the more effective. Summarizing his experience in the council field, he said:

> Probably it is fair to say the majority of councils have not yet moved very far toward becoming effective planning bodies in the full sense of that term. There is evidence, however, of strengthening of staffing and financing of councils and of new understanding of the role of councils which should lead to greater effectiveness. As yet we would have to admit the council movement reflects an unrealized potential for serious planning in health and welfare.

One cannot improve on this series of acute observations.

A former dean of a school of social work has written that "social work is concerned with the whole person." By this, he said he meant that social work deals with the adjustment of an individual in his family circle, in his job, and in the community. Such an interpretation, written for the benefit of the readers of the national *P.T.A Magazine*, sounds suspiciously like the sloganeering of progressive education. Perhaps it is significant that the late magazine *Progressive Education* printed, about the same time, an article calling for close liaison at the community level between teachers and social workers. The goal of the proposed collaboration would be "social reconstruction."

Is the reconstruction of society what we want as the end result of our social work and social-welfare programs? Perhaps it is all a matter of semantics, but it would not occur to most laymen to phrase any but equalitarian objectives in such a way. And there is nothing conservative about this idea, as some persons seek to bring it to pass by governmental action. Rehabilitation of the individual is one thing, and it is wholly proper as a goal for social work, provided the problem of individual consent has been solved and not ignored. But many will feel that there is little about current social-work education or the daily duties of social workers to lead one to believe that either is uniquely well-suited to perform the reconstruction of American and world society into a better pattern.

As a citizen, a social worker has a perfect right to work peacefully toward the realization of whatever ultimate goals he may choose. But he should not mind if other citizens—outsiders to his field—concede to him and to his technical work area no special status in the task of building a new and better universe. Here is a task for a political philosopher, a social-economist, a statesman, and a sage! And it cuts across the labels "radical" and "conservative."

Must one agree that social workers are particularly well-equipped for the task of "reconstructing" and "reordering" the society of which they are a part? Consider the remarks of three authorities in social work: H. L. Lurie has written, "Social work is . . . a contemporary aspect of the perennial attempts that man has made to improve the conditions of life and promote the general well-being." It may be, as Professor Herbert Stroup hopes, that social work will respond to the challenges of the day with "conceptual structures and social programs which will help the general citizenry to extend even further the full meaning of democracy in American life." Possibly it could be true, as Sanford Solender has written in Social Work Yearbook, 1957, that "social work's preoccupation with the whole person and the total environment results in a breadth of social concern which is uncommon among the professions." Few citizens observing the contemporary scene will grant that either social work or social workers have, as yet, come to rest on so exalted a level as is postulated by many social-work leaders from metropolitan America.

One agrees with an authority that "social action," in the hands of social workers, should be "informed, constructive, dignified, and courageous." The public can insist on this from an aspiring professional group; it cannot demand that anyone's views be either radical or conservative. Perhaps the best of our social workers may come, in time, fully to deserve the label "social statesman." It is greatly to be hoped, in any case, that leaders in social work will not be so eager to become "a positive social and cultural force" that they will line themselves up permanently with one political party in opposition to other elements in American society. If they should do so, the result would be a disservice to social welfare, to social workers, and to the needy persons these leaders aspire to serve. Social work can serve society, but doctrinaire radicalism, a tunnel-visioned picture of human need, and constant focus on social reconstruction will not accomplish maximum results. Truly humanitarian results from the hands of contemporary social workers are most likely to come, slowly and painfully, through the rehabilitation of individuals.

CHAPTER XIV

The American Pattern in Social Welfare

Government and voluntary, acting in parallel,
     sometimes competing,
Taxes and pledges, dollars in tandem,
     vastly extensive,
Giving in secret, giving through churches,
Organizations, heady publicity,
Salaried employees, technical programs.
Service to others.
Service to God.

Patterns emerging, solidification,
Trust funds, foundations; unity, diversity.
No turning back (but longing for old days).
Urbanization.
Big population.
Structuring needs never dreamed of before.

Social insurance—pay for the trip in advance!
Public assistance—no one must starve!
Voluntary organizations. Fund-raising. Planning.
Personal doing of good.
Social welfare; an American pattern,
Federal, local; complicated, simple.
Service to others.
Service to God.

CHANGE HAS BEEN THE GENERAL RULE in twentieth-century America. Our people have accepted this and come to live with it. The temptation is great when studying and writing about any aspect of life in these fluid years to say, in effect, "there was the great change." Books on science say this; so, too, volumes on industrial relations, on communications, on warfare, and on literature. Nothing escapes this tendency.

One of the most significant changes in social welfare, beyond any doubt, was the vast multiplication of welfare organizations serving the needy. This phenomenon was apparent at the national, state, and local levels alike. The building of voluntary organizations sufficient in extent to be household words in every state is amazing, until one thinks of the development of the mass communication media during the same period.

The shift from individual charity to voluntary organizations, and the rise of governmental supremacy in money expended marked the first half of the century. Somehow, the incidence of purely religious motivation among those engaging in full-time social work declined and, in many instances, disappeared. Once Americans helped people because they were convinced that it was the necessary and proper thing for a Christian or a follower of Maimonides to do, not because one found in textbooks in graduate schools of social work that certain "on-going programs" constitute the work of particular agencies and that, by formal training, one could make such work a rewarding career. Americans of the old school and the modern world both found the lot of the unfortunate something to be ameliorated through effort. But, over the years, that effort became collective rather than individual. Charity became organized, and recreation became therapeutic. Health was everybody's business and something to be pursued with the same spirit shown by the forty-niner in search of nuggets.

The machinery of government proved a convenient vehicle for administering vast programs of cash payment. Whether by outright gifts from general tax funds, payments for specified numbers of weeks from funds built up by taxes on employers, or regular forwarding of benefit checks from social-insurance programs, government, as administrator, was a gigantic reality toward the middle of the century. There was an acceleration in the transition from public aid to social insurance. While both remained important, that shift of emphasis was clearly one of the most significant developments in social welfare after World War II.

The ultimate effect that so much social-welfare activity might have on the American spirit has inspired little research and has been little understood. Most of the public has seemed to hope for the best, pleased to be the recipients of program benefits but often critical of benefits paid others. There has been blind trust that those who have led their fellow citizens along unknown paths have not been merely transplanting European ideas into American soil without distinguishing between weeds and flowers.

Some have said that so much activity on behalf of "security" will destroy initiative; others have hoped or believed that absence from worry will lead to longer life and increased productivity. There has been no meeting ground in ideology, party politics, or judgment of human nature.

New programs have multiplied until special courses in "community organization" have become necessary to inform graduate students of the vastness of the social-service field. Agency names listed in alphabetical order in the classified section of telephone books under "social-service organizations," or equivalent headings, fill inches of space, and many cities are issuing directories of such agencies for the information of judges, attorneys, physicians, policemen, and specialists.

Government regulation of voluntary organizations has increased gradually but noticeably. While this has encouraged those concerned with "charity rackets"—a subject to which much contrived publicity has been given with too little thought—it has not, by the dawn of the 1960's frightened persons who have normally sought to keep government power within strict boundaries. The irony of the regulatory development, as it came with sharp teeth at local levels and at state levels in a few instances, rested in the fact that, for several decades, social workers were among the most vigorous advocates of positive government. They said they desired a powerful management state. Somehow they seem to have expected that voluntary welfare organizations would be left free of state control. They expected too much, because the business community—operating through better business bureaus and chambers of commerce—gradually come to exercise a life and death grip over solicitation of funds by agencies and groups in many towns; and, in other places, businessmen encouraged the police department or special city bureaus to adopt arbitrary rules and regulations. Agencies with religious affiliations often escaped the net (although some of these certainly deserved regulation as much as the often casually administered "veterans" causes).

Theodore Roosevelt had once camped in the Dakotas oblivious of the whims of the government bureaucrats in his day; but, by 1957, the twelve thousand resident camps of the nation were subjected to regulatory codes in thirty states, laws that an expert claimed were becoming more and more stringent. So it has been that, in the name of health, safety, and welfare, even the virgin forests have yielded to the superior force of government.

Could every man become his own social worker? Some who have attacked full-time social workers at every turn have acted as though it were possible to do away with the specialization entirely. But to any who have taken time to inspect agencies and investigate programs, it has been abundantly clear that the social-work group has achieved routine results in many areas of effort toward which the benevolently inclined of the nineteenth century only shook their heads. Skid row still stands forth against the social worker—unapproachable, pitiable, and defiant. And "rehabilitation"—although the favorite word of social workers from coast to coast—has been all too seldom a measurable reality. A popular word of the times, however, is "prevention"; and in the name of this potent term, much vigorous and highly effective effort has been expended by government and voluntary organizations alike.

International social work has seemed, to close observers, to be a field of great promise for the second half of the century. A leading figure of the 1950's, Charles I. Schottland, has predicted the future:

> A new group of alphabetical agencies has arisen, many of them still unfamiliar to most of us. ECOSOC, WHO, ILO, IRO, UNICEF, FAO, UNESCO, UNRRA, ECA, CRALOG, LARA—these are but a few of the strange sounds now being heard on the new international social work frontier. Social welfare is taking its place on the international scene as another force to bring about international co-operation in a common effort to raise the standard of living of all peoples and alleviate poverty, suffering, and distress wherever they may exist.

Although many nations have contributed to United Nations' activities since World War II, by and large the world of international social work has been American financed. Thus has been continued a long tradition of missionaries and philanthropists from the United States seeking to "do good" in foreign lands. The

Rockefeller Foundation, since 1913, alone has spent half a billion dollars, much of it abroad. Social workers from Europe and Asia came to the United States after World War II in an effort to learn from the experience of their colleagues in Chicago and New York City, and in graduate schools of social work, how problems in their own countries might be solved or ameliorated.

American social work has come to bear the aspect of a bright star for the rest of the world. But not long ago men and women from the United States sought to learn from Sweden, England, or the Soviet Union. The attraction of foreign experience has continued; but increasingly the social work intellectuals from the nation who go abroad have spent their more serious hours lecturing and demonstrating what they already know and have found that there is an immense eagerness on the part of others to learn.

In the day of the total-service state in many European countries, atrophy in private philanthropy and nongovernmental social-service work has become evident to the observer from this side of the Atlantic. Fund-raising has become a church monopoly or a rare phenomenon, while pioneering organizations like YMCA and YWCA and the Scouts have found state-created and sometimes state-indoctrinated youth groups tough competition. This lesson has not been lost on Americans who can remember photographs of the raised hand salutes once directed toward Hitler and Mussolini—and Stalin.

Voluntary welfare in the United States seemed for a time to lack articulate and dedicated spokesmen, as the ocean of dollars from the federal government reached high tide. Leaders in voluntary welfare were reduced to a state of stupefied awe. But the founding of a tiny Foundation for Voluntary Welfare in the 1950's, and what seemed to be the building of at least a temporary monetary floor under voluntary agencies by new (although often domineering) methods of financing, encouraged those who had temporarily lost hope—or the courage to defend principles in which they had never ceased to believe.

Hazardous, and often thankless, is the task of peering into the future. Yet, to act wisely, society must from time to time consult the facts at hand, make educated guesses about possible directions, and, only then, choose among alternative courses of action. In the social-welfare field, first priority may well be given to predicting the relationship which may come to exist between tax- and contribution-supported welfare, health, and recreation organizations and programs.

In measuring this relationship, one is almost forced to resort to counting the dollars expended, respectively, by government and voluntary agencies. Still, services can sometimes be counted, and so can hours spent by paid and unpaid social-service workers. In terms of dollars, what ratio will exist between voluntary programs, supported by charitable giving and other income, and government programs, financed by taxes and fees? Will the proportion of 5.44 to 1 (government expenditures to voluntary agencies' income), which I discovered to exist in 1954 in the metropolitan San Francisco Bay Area, continue to be found there? When similarly exhaustive studies are made in other parts of the nation, if they are, will similar ratios be found? Points of view will certainly differ on whether such a balance should be maintained or modified. For example, the lobbyist for the National Association of Social Workers gave Congress, in 1957, his views on the paramount importance of government welfare:

> Inadequacies in our public programs for families and children—and there are many—as anyone who will take the time to examine the program in his local community will soon discover—these inadequacies produce a basic neglect of people that cannot be compensated for in other ways—the excellent though financially limited programs of our voluntary agencies notwithstanding.

For him, and for persons of similar views, the future is inevitable: government has the money; voluntary agencies do not.

Such wishful oversimplification makes clear that a key problem of public policy, to which the layman has given too little thought, is the relative roles the two welfare forces should play. A straddle has already suggested itself to some clever social-work intellectuals. It is: Destroy the boundaries between public aid and private charity by a simple device. Just put voluntary social-work agencies increasingly on the public payroll. Social work will then be "unified" as never before, and the outer manifestations of the problem will allegedly disappear! Social-Work School Dean Emeritus Arlien Johnson cheerfully admitted to a national conference in 1959 that "where money goes, control follows, is an axiom of public administration" and asked, "When public funds pay for the cost of almost every child in the care of a voluntary agency, for example, at what point does the public welfare authority take over entirely?" The ever-increasing government subsidy alternative should be rejected except as a last resort. Its only justification would be to prevent the complete extinction of voluntary-agencies at some future date if they face financial bankruptcy. National disaster could present another occasion for a merger with government.

One speculates, in connection with the giving of government money to voluntary social agencies (those engaged in rehabilitation, for example), whether a private organization which gradually begins to live off large grants of federal funds is still a "voluntary" agency, as that term has been used here. Is it not quasi-public? Can it still be uncompromisingly sectarian? Officials, after all, are supposed to follow their grants with a certain amount of regulation and inspection and awareness of policy. Only in this fashion can the normal interests of the taxpayer be served. But to do this might well destroy the free and voluntary nature of a social-service agency. How could it be otherwise?

Testifying before Congress in 1957, Miss Mary E. Switzer, the head of the United States Office of Vocational Rehabilitation (an organization with nine regional offices at the time), stated the case for giving federal funds to voluntary social-service agencies in order to accomplish results:

> Experience during the past two years has demonstrated overwhelmingly that national voluntary organizations, through their local affiliates, are ready and willing to pool their resources with those of the state and federal governments to extend rehabilitation services for persons who have been difficult to reach under the public program alone. At the same time these projects will provide community re-

sources and experience upon which State programs can draw to extend services to greater numbers of the more difficult cases.

Listing problems requiring more staff participation by her department, she included "the need for improved relations with and greater use of state and local rehabilitation groups, both public and private." Can we discern from her testimony whether the federal government is to be a senior or a junior partner in such alliances? Yes. OVR hoped for heavy increases in staff. Its executive head, commenting on the two-million-dollar research, training, and trusteeship program, complained that it was being run by only three persons. This limited "to a dangerous degree the first-hand observations of proposals and projects, on the site, by OVR staff. . . . We should assure ourselves, from direct observation and consultation, that the purposes of the projects are being carried out. . . ." For these reasons new staff people for OVR were thought essential. In conclusion, this federal official, in this representative instance of government welfare, judged succinctly, "Sound and effective administration at the federal level will play a major part in determining the direction, scope, and success of the total program." Could the role of government, in following its financing with control of voluntary social agencies, be made any plainer? Clearly, federal funds in private agency hands can mean federal initiative in program determination, constant supervision and inspection, and, in the last analysis, full control—for better or worse. If this happens, it should be intentional—not accidental.

It is submitted that the alternative of "splitting the difference" by pumping tax funds into Goodwill Industries, Salvation Army, or St. Vincent de Paul rehabilitation centers to "improve their rehabilitation programs"—if it comes to this—will be most undesirable. Yet these agencies are as entitled to such grants as the private rehabilitation clinics, mental clinics, and training centers that began to get such funds in the 1950's, or the voluntary child-care agencies that have had public subsidies for many years. Such payments, however, convert voluntary social-work organizations into quasi-governmental groups spending tax funds. Yet their top administrators will not enjoy civil service. First their budgets and later their policies and programs will become responsive to Washington legislation and administrative decision.

Justification for this financial and program conversion has been claimed, however. Through articles and speeches, supporters of conversion have made elaborate claims of ultimate tax savings when an individual on public-aid rolls can be rehabilitated into an employed taxpayer. While some of these protestations have been overly enthusiastic (one signed article by a layman in *Journal of the American Medical Association* in 1958 eliminated from the costs column such items of expense to the taxpayer as education under the GI Bill and veterans' disability benefits), something can be said, in many cases, for the proposition advanced by Dr. Howard A. Rusk that for every federal dollar invested in vocational rehabilitation a disabled person will pay back ten in federal income taxes. What if the government had not helped half a million disabled veterans with vocational and rehabilitation service? The accomplishments have been real. But the toll road to accomplishment in rehabilitation ought to be routed around the heart of the voluntary way in social welfare—for the ultimate good of society as a whole.

Church groups, thinking of Hill-Burton hospital construction funds, have in many cases furthered the idea of "purchase of services" by government. That is the pleasant name they have grown accustomed to hearing—not "government subsidies" or "payments." Nor do the church-oriented agencies like to think of themselves as on the federal payroll in such instances, even temporarily. It has been tempting to solve financial dilemmas and accomplish quick results by closing private hands around public funds. Yet "no rose without thorns," says an old proverb, and serious thought should be given to such propositions as these. One of the greatest temptations in the voluntary area of social welfare will always be the deceiving ease with which immediate results can be accomplished if only the government will pass a subsidy-granting law or allow a bureau administrator to make a determination. And in rebellion against diversity—often confusing and sometimes inefficient—it is all too easy to allow social service to come gradually under the umbrella of government at various levels, particularly federal.

A defender of independent voluntary agencies, Sol Morton Isaac, has written in their behalf: "The forces that would destroy our democratic form of society—be they totalitarian of any cast—must, among the first things they do, dispose of the voluntary social agency." This sentiment illustrates the depth of feeling once commonly held by sectarian and non-sectarian leaders in the voluntary field. To continue to argue that voluntary welfare and health and recreation agencies are good because they are voluntary and independent, and then to turn the other cheek and insist that it does no harm to a charitable agency with a budget of half a million dollars to accept (and ultimately depend on) an annual one-hundred-thousand-dollar grant from the county, state, or federal treasuries, is self-deceptive reasoning. It seems the point of wisdom, all things considered, to keep voluntary agencies as voluntary as possible.

The community councils of the nation have been looking longingly toward local government for additional financing. At a meeting of council officials in 1957, a speaker extolled the virtues of getting local government to help finance a community-welfare council, a triumph just "put over" in Tampa, Florida. Can local government give fifteen thousand dollars or more annually to a planning body of this type without demanding a role in governing expenditures, without having delegates on controlling committees, without participating in discussions, and without seeking to protect government activities from interference from the planners? What happens when the council concludes that the time has come to spend a few million dollars for a new park or to increase general relief payments by one-third?

The professional council people, lacking enthusiastic support from united-fund layman directors as a rule, seem to want public funds for councils without strings. Privately, many of these council planning officials stand for "sky's the limit" government expenditures for health, welfare, and recreation. They, therefore, see no objections to placing officials of local government on their planning committees. Aggressive in enlarging government, the

295

council executives are happy to get intelligent public-welfare officials to serve on their boards, wholly aside from any monetary income that may be obtained from the county or city fathers. Why the latter should be willing to give councils money in the first place is a mystery, since many councils in their enthusiasm for "improving" the community stand consistently for enlarged expenditures across the board, so much so that they take on the aspect of a lobbying group. It is improper for government to help in financing any organization that comes to wear this face. Should a taxpayers organization receive appropriations from county government?

Money is the real key to the amount and quality of social-welfare services. All who pondered recently the dilemma of public v. voluntary organizations were, if alert, concerned over who is to pay, how much will be paid, and what organizations, government or voluntary, will end up with the money. The problem of money in the form of appropriations, contributions, and fee or endowment income deeply concerns pressure groups—and it ought to.

The management executives of corporations and the highly placed community leaders who now spark the united-fund campaigns or community-chest drives, which finance much of the needs of voluntary-welfare agencies in urban America, find themselves in a curious corner as they face the future. On the one hand, they and their companies have to pay a considerable tax burden. In 1955–56, corporations paid $21,300,000,000 of the $75,100,-000,000 in taxes collected by the federal government. Corporation management is aware that a portion of its tax dollar goes to finance the welfare, health, and recreation agencies of government. (Welfare is for many counties the largest budget item, or is second only to highways.) On the other hand, business leaders have been working in recent years to put the financing of private charitable activities on a "businesslike" basis. "Ability to pay" has become the criterion, coming dangerously close to displacing "desire to give." Those solicited where they work are expected to co-operate.

Some thoughtful people feel that a thin line separates an annual, scaled, almost-but-not-quite mandatory "contribution" obtained by moral suasion in October from an annual, scaled, mandatory tax payment to government in April. In both cases the "giver" is out of pocket. There is ample reason to believe that he might prefer to keep the money himself, have it go to certain non-welfare activities of government, give it directly to special causes, or put it in the hands of the church of his choice.

This being the case, some leading citizens who set the annual goals for large fund drives are deeply torn within. Every year, in an inflationary era, the voluntary agencies continue to insist on more and yet more money to make ends meet. (The nation is growing! The dollar is shrinking! Horizons are expanding! Yesterday's luxuries are today's necessities!) Naturally, the welfare-agency people would like to meet their own desires for higher salaries and for better working conditions at the same time.

The fund-drive lay leaders find it hard to oppose the idea of raising more money each year. Some are really anxious as a matter of personal prestige to lead "the best community campaign" yet seen. Higher goals can only come from higher corporate and in-plant contributions, carefully prorated. Each division must do well. Results are almost mandatory. From such considerations comes the pressure on the contributor.

Meanwhile, the lay fund leaders sometimes have unpublicized misgivings. Suppose too much money is raised, far more than ever before? Won't this result in bigger and looser welfare programs? Excess money resting in the hands of social workers could mean new and untried activities and experimentation with crazy new programs. And the meaning of experimentation? Keen observers of the welfare scene know full well that, tomorrow, some of the most articulate voluntary-agency executives will be lobbying for the government to put money into the field of the successful service experiment, thus setting the stage for higher taxes in the future. And who made it possible?

These leaders have other grave doubts about annually increased goals in voluntary fund-raising. Deep inside, many an executive in the financial or business world really questions the desirability of building bigger voluntary agencies and programs (the Boy Scouts, of course, being "different"). One fund-raising volunteer, after studying figures proving that a given community chest had increased agency financing very little in thirty years, observed slyly to me, "After all, our government welfare activity has increased many times in these years. The need of voluntary agencies for funds simply isn't there. Maybe we should lower our annual fund drive quotas and eliminate certain agencies, instead of building ever greater empires." The president of a giant chemical company challenged a top-level national conference in Detroit in 1957 to prove to his satisfaction that the need for ever increasing fund-drive quotas was real. Effective replies were made, but his question will appear again and again.

Impressed with the immensity of a welfare pattern composed of government plus voluntary, and effectively thwarted, as a rule, from cutting anything substantial from government aid and service programs, some men of affairs facing the 1960's were greatly tempted to cut services and costs in the voluntary-agency field. After all, they rationalized, they had the power to do as they pleased. Since they were faced in Congress and state legislatures with representatives of the many voters who regularly rode the welfare train as a convenient vehicle to re-election, these lay leaders drifted rather strangely into cutting "the welfare state" at the voluntary agency grass roots, thereby furthering individualism in the ordinary citizen. Somehow, these leaders never quite saw themselves as hurting the character-building of young people in the community or making still more difficult the lot of unfortunates. On the contrary, they said and they believed that they were "merely applying tested methods of business management" to the administration and financing of social-service work. When the time might be ripe, the same procedures would be applied to government welfare. (But in the meantime, government stepped neatly into the voids that appeared with every cutback in voluntary welfare and every failure to seize responsibility for lack of funds.)

Perhaps it was the impersonality of federation in fund-raising, the "one big give," that facilitated ideas of economy. Efficient collections on the installment plan, complete with IBM forms, bills, and receipts, gave the illusion that, in the area once called charity, one merely played the usual economic game of buying and selling and administration. Hugh R. Jones, president in 1959 of the New York State Welfare Conference, pointed out, "We must not let fund-raising become an annual tax. . . ." To this official the distance between giver and receiver was ever-widening.

Social welfare simply must not be depersonalized any further. To do so would be to take it a thousand miles from the soul-searching approach to charity and the doing of good that once characterized the United States. Behind the unmet goals on the accounting forms, the agency deficits, the staff not retained or never hired, and the programs that remain strictly marginal will be the understaffed scouting organizations, tired old settlement buildings, and sad dormitories on skid row. How can this reality born of underfinancing be driven home to the overweight lay-man, cutting the lawn of his suburban home with a new power mower? Jonathan Swift put it well when he wrote, "Nothing is so hard for those who abound in riches as to conceive how others can be in want." Potential givers and those who set quotas must be propagandized to some extent if charity is to continue in sufficient strength to do the job in an expanding society. Here, however, as everywhere else, moderation is a virtue. The banner of social welfare can be hoisted too high, especially when government attempts to enforce "giving" on the reluctant taxpayer, and highly organized fund-raising groups attempt to do much the same thing.

There is wide divergence of opinion on how many and what kind of programs ought to exist for the benefit of the needy persons of society. We are never likely to be in fundamental agreement on what percentage of the population is to be included in the lost-sheep category. What shall be our social goal? Shall it be one-half caring for the other half? A wage-earning 20 per cent supporting 80 per cent? Or shall 90 per cent pay for the daily needs of 10 per cent? There is no agreement.

To put this problem another way: Shall equalitarianism be the goal, or is it more realistic, in the light of the nature of mankind, to expect some to subsist on each of several economic plateaus? The question has not been faced squarely by many in society. To me, the following proposition is acceptable: Americans

299

should not have to live under any firm national policy that would call for constant redistribution of property among the haves and have nots in the name of "social welfare."

What worries some men of position as they survey the contemporary social-welfare scene in the United States is this: How real is the actual difference between the following two states of society? In one, ample opportunity exists to make money, but government takes a high percentage for redistribution. In the second, the right to rise to monetary pre-eminence is denied at the outset. The first would purport to be an ultimate form of welfare capitalism. The second is communitarianism—or communism. Successful people, who hope that their children will be able to duplicate or surpass their own careers, are wondering if the unexpressed, uncodified, and even uncomprehended motto of too many about them—including some in social-service work—is in essence, "From each according to his abilities; to each according to his needs." And there are some planners who have devised "needs" which go far beyond the previously held minimum obligations toward the stranger.

Cradle to the grave, government-guaranteed, social and economic security financed by taxes has been in twentieth-century America the national direction. Citizens who have continued, in spite of this, to give priority to charity-begins-at-home obligations to a wife, children, and aged parents, have found the prospect of so much social service to strangers not a little alarming.

Responsible members of society (in the nineteenth-century sense) paid twice—once for their family needs; and again for some other family's needs. All this costs money. The wage earner from the middle class tends to react as follows: first, he attacks government expenditures in general. Then, contemplating an inability to save money for his own and his wife's old age, for catastrophic illness, and for the provision of a college education for his children, he turns, paradoxically, to government to help solve his problems. He becomes an advocate of an expanded welfare state, dimly perceiving that higher tax payments will inevitably accompany his every demand from government. State-financed medical care, vastly increased old-age benefits, and a program of government scholarships for his children will not come cheap, he knows; but, in the light of existing tax rates, how can he save? Heavy government taxation to finance security programs, far from bringing him a solid sense of security, as was the intention, makes him feel economically and socially insecure.

In his dilemma this American citizen reconciles the cost of more services as an extension of the familiar installment plan for doing things. Government will have to be both collection agent and benefit administrator. Social welfare seems, in this remarkable vignette, to have come full cycle. Once charity for a few in real trouble—that is, largesse from the have's to the have-not's—it now becomes transformed into benefits-for-all-to-be-paid-for-by-all. Government is to be the intermediary, a presumably efficient and faceless IBM machine, emotionless as it collects from all and dispenses to almost all. By using the term "social insurance" and collecting compulsory tax payments from individuals or businesses, much of the taint of benefit receipts almost seems removed. Elderly people, who paid in moderate amounts to social security, quite properly cry out against dollar inflation; but the ethics of their demands for increased payments and services (for which, incidentally, they did not pay) is open to question.

All realize, to some small extent, that government cannot create any of the benefits it pays in neat green checks to its citizens. Even in the role of employer of men and women in and out of uniform, the state pays only the money it gets from the whole public though taxes and loans. Nothing is solved, financially, when citizens band together in interest groups to say "let the government do it." But when this has been said, it must be added that there are at all times small numbers of truly needy people for whom extensive services may have to be provided for at least a time. Citizens sensitive to the needs of the human spirit will never forget this plain truth.

The following credo, recently delivered by a co-ordinator for the Conference of State Taxpayer Associations to the Oklahoma Welfare Association, is refreshing:

I contend that in a country as wealthy as the United States

of America there is no rhyme, no reason, no excuse for any
American to be denied the necessities and a few of the luxuries of life. But I also contend there is no rhyme, reason, or
excuse for burdening society as a whole with the maintenance
of any individual or family until that unit of our society has
exerted every possible effort and exhausted every resource, in
the attempt to care for itself.

The speaker, Steve Stahl, went on to say that "the American people as a whole want an adequate, even generous system of social
welfare based on humane and enlightened considerations of need.
Less than this they will not condone; more, they will not long
support."

American society has erected in our century a complex social-
welfare structure whereby the individual will be, in almost any
eventuality, the responsibility of some voluntary agency or some
program of government. A democratic society with a republican
form of government and a capitalistic economy has, through planning and chance, cast a friendly cloak about each of its members.
The cost of creating and maintaining such social protection has
not been borne equally in the past. The trend of the times, however, has been for the burden on each person to increase regularly
in proportion to the growth in welfare services. We thus have
something vastly different from the public aid and private charity
of earlier years, both of which still linger on in public assistance
and in agency cash-benefit payments.

The welfare of all our citizens transcends party politics, even
if methods of reaching goals do not. President Eisenhower said
on February 28, 1957, in opening the Red Cross drive, "The concept of neighbor, 'good neighbor,' is part of the American heritage.
We are a nation of neighbors and we live in a world of neighbors.
And the way we give effective testimony to this principle is by
freely sharing our skills and resources with others needing them."
Adlai E. Stevenson outlined in eloquent words his hopes for a
New America in his Boston speech of October 29, 1956. "We
know what we want America to be," he said, "and we mean to
make it what we want it to be." Most Americans would find it
easy to endorse his goals:

We mean to make it a land where everyone has a decent roof over his head and can feed and clothe his children properly; a land where children can learn from good teachers in good schools; a land where the doors of opportunity are open to all alike.

We mean to make it a land where the sick can find adequate medical care, whether they are rich or poor; a land where we can all look forward to a tranquil security in the last years of our lives; where everyone who wants to work can find a job; where savings and pensions will not be washed away in a tide of rising prices.

Paths clearly diverge, however, as soon as leaders begin to outline their programs for reaching goals. And uncertainties multiply. Yet we must continue to outline problems and make suggestions unless the future is to come, willy-nilly, without any architectural plans whatever.

Must it be predicted that both voluntary and government social welfare will not be able to obtain from the public the annual increases in financing necessary to take care of inevitable population growth, dollar inflation, and expanding demands? A downturn in the economy with increased suffering would quickly change this. And can it be that the short work week of the future, with its augmentation of leisure time, will make possible immense increases in volunteer service to agencies? If children grow up with a feeling for community responsibilities, it is just barely possible that voluntary welfare may flower—not wither, expand—not contract. But such results cannot be attained by a voluntary-welfare system that may fall into the hands of small minds thinking in terms of holding the line, converting to the public payroll, or just living on with weak leadership, confused programs, and dilapidated buildings. The current population of 180,000,000 could grow to 207,000,000 or 228,000,000 by 1975, and more than 300,000,000 by 2000. What form of social service is to insure so congested a population against the compounding of present urban social problems?

Some people have said, in effect, that vastly enlarged government social-service programs are the de luxe superhighway to the

303

future. Not so fast! This is an expensive toll road. The relative numbers of wage earners whose earnings can be taxed to support public programs will shrink as the old-age group lives on, and as a high proportion of young people go to college and remain out of the labor market for additional years. Government social-service expenditures, meanwhile, will hardly shrink. The Forand (King) Bill, a call for socializing medicine initially for the aging part of the population, was a transparent attempt to open wide the flood gates for a whole sea of questionable government activities.

Taxes, personal income, and social-welfare services will remain related; they will not always be on speaking terms. The total tax for social security is scheduled to climb to 9 per cent in 1969, even if no new benefits should be added. Continuing inflation, at perhaps 2 per cent per year, might conceal this tax increase from the stupid or the uneducated, but it will be there nonetheless. While a six thousand dollar income could climb by hundreds of dollars as the result of such inflation, prices would rise in rough proportion. The shorter work week might increase costs of production. The wage earner would pay more income tax from his newly inflated salary even if existing rates should be maintained. These factors are often overlooked. With doubled deductions for social security (and more, if the $4,200 base, raised to $4,800 in 1958, should go still higher), industry will surely raise prices a notch to make possible its own increased social-security contributions. So the purchasing power of take-home pay will be curtailed by an inflationary spiral, one, to some degree, given an extra twist by the desire for economic security. Those trying to live in the sunshine of the inevitably increased benefit payments of social security will find that an inflated economy is no respector of old age. In the productive efficiency born of automation, there may be cheaper products, but, at the same time, heartaches for displaced workers. Since no one can predict the level of defense expenditures or unemployment a decade ahead, further speculation would be fruitless.

What pattern in social welfare can we anticipate? Perhaps through the course of decades the changing population in the United States will have meaning. The economist Frank G. Dick-

304

inson has said that the proportion of voters over fifty years of age will reach a peak in 1970, after which it will decline rapidly. The rising majority of younger voters will, in Mr. Dickinson's opinion, "put a brake on the trend toward the welfare state and lessen the clamor for the guaranteed future, the riskless society." ("The 'Younging' of Electorates," *Journal of the American Medical Association*, March 1, 1958.) Few Americans have thought ahead to so distant a time, and some specialists will dispute the importance of this development on psychological grounds—questioning the significance of age-bracket voting. Those who have seen this kind of voting in states like Florida and California will take the idea more seriously, perhaps.

In the light of present needs and immediate future probabilities, the general public is not ready to accept any proposition that the time has come to do away with either public or voluntary welfare. The consequences of such advocacy are too great. I believe that if the choice were up to existing lay leaders in our communities, the government's public-assistance, cash-payments programs, at least, would be enlarged no further, except in times of recession. But some people, both in and out of social-work circles, clearly look forward to an extension of both public aid and social security in one form or another. The campaign to do away entirely with residence requirements swung into full gear recently, and there was much justice in the outcry that city, township, or county relief was too often administered arbitrarily, with little regard for human factors. But suggested reforms were often schemes to expand aid payments across-the-board at great expense.

Tax-supported health, welfare, and recreation activity has become so firmly entrenched and generally accepted in America that it will never be dislodged, whatever may be said. Much economizing can be done at the state and county level, surprisingly enough. Government welfare's hold on the affections of many voters is such that attacks based on name-calling ("communism," "give-away") only enrage the faithful, who are little interested in charges that independence of spirit is being undermined.

The best line of useful activity for all who have misgivings about the future will be to work for the modification and improvement of existing public-welfare programs and to strive to do away with their worst features. There is ample room for improvement in the social-security and unemployment-compensation systems, and the public would do well to listen to specialists in the field of life insurance and professionals with long experience in meeting the needs of suffering people. Until those who plan our social-security amendments bear in mind the full potentialities of fair-minded voluntary health insurance (and its extraordinary popularity in the population), intelligent planning will be difficult, if not impossible. The savings habits of the public and a multitude of other factors, not always taken into account, bear on the desirability of further social-welfare legislation.

Voluntary welfare will continue to be hard pressed financially. If it knuckles under against its better judgment and adopts pay-as-you-go fees, it will be warped from "the heart in action" into "business as usual." Nor is receipt of tax money a solution to its problem of obtaining better financing. Organized labor could bring immediate help, if it would—and it may. But only the engendering of full faith and confidence in voluntary fund-raising (united or not), and improvement of services followed by honest publicity can bring to the voluntary field the permanent public support it needs for expanding in tune with an expanding nation.

Voluntary welfare's spokesmen must not continue their efforts to persuade government to parallel or outdistance their own services unless they intend for their own agencies to commit suicide.

Social insurance has been undermining public assistance. But the medical-benefits program enacted by Congress in 1956 gave the slipping cash-aid payments system a brand new lease on life. As a result, the abolition of Old Age Assistance and Aid to Dependent Children can only be accomplished in future years by transferring them, with their expensive and politically appealing new medical feature, into the nation's social insurance system. But to do this would mean that the new millions of beneficiaries added to the social security rolls, unlike most of their fellow countrymen, would have paid in little or nothing. The "social insurance" principle would be mortally wounded.

The different and often competitive programs administered by government officials and private-agency executives in years past have not always brought optimum results. Yet it is clear that much has been accomplished by them. Rivalry between individual benevolence, voluntary agencies, public assistance, and social insurance, where present, has been good occasionally for all fields. Duplication of effort has not always been undesirable, for it affords society a measuring stick with which to judge performance.

Government might just as well admit that it cannot enlist the enthusiastic, unsalaried volunteer workers who have been the greatest asset to the voluntary agencies. Red Cross alone claims two million of these. Government, on the other hand, has a giant fiscal base which the charitable agencies cannot match. There is no question that ample room exists in our nation for individual charity, organized voluntary effort, and the two basic types of government programs—public aid and social insurance—provided many adjustments are made. Together, these four basic forms of activity have come to comprise, for better or worse, what I call "the American pattern in social welfare."

As Americans face the future, aware of their heritage from the past, they will want to ponder the desirability of molding these major tendencies in social welfare to match their deepest desires. In the larger sense, it is clear that acts of charity from person to person must continue if our people are to be true to their spiritual inheritance. The churches, service clubs, and fraternal bodies of the nation will want to be ever vigilant in seeing that "doing good," far from moving toward the shallow pools, stays in the mainstream. Voluntary organizations must be strengthened financially, but all major expansion must be justifiable. Here, as elsewhere, results must be in ratio to expenditures of time, effort, and money.

Public assistance programs, designed to meet people's needs by transferring funds from those who have to those who do not, should be kept at the minimum indicated by the shifting fortunes of the economy. Yet our people do not want and will not stand for human suffering in a land of plenty. Local control of such programs, if prevented by federal and state standardizing legislation from inflicting miserly and heartless practices on nonresident strangers, remains desirable. The staffs of our public-welfare departments may be able to play a role in rehabilitation and re-employment, but this will require additional staff training. It may be that the case workers, who come to be surplus in such departments (as OASDI steals public-aid customers), will be more useful in expanded voluntary agencies or in other departments of the government—employment or vocational rehabilitation divisions, for example.

Social insurance, finally, must be made equitable in financing and benefits. There is grave danger that unbridled expansion of benefits, in response to pressure from aging voters, may turn this system into no more than public aid under another name. This is clearly undesirable. The move to bring socialized medicine to the nation through the back door of OASDI amendment is legitimate enough—if that is what the nation insists upon—but so grave a step must come only after prolonged and informed consideration. And discussion of this question will be furthered if criticism and suggestions can be offered without mudslinging by overeager defenders of particular points of view.

These types of social-welfare activity, each designed so clearly to serve the needs of men, women, and children, must be kept in proper balance. There will always be debate on what the balance ought to be. Two things must be said in any case. Too much social welfare activity—or too little—could serve to keep Americans from achieving (or retaining) in their own land a society of which they would be proud. Freedom of the individual to determine his own destiny, as long as society does not suffer as the result of unrestrained action, is something in which we believe. Freedom of opportunity and initiative must be preserved. But, figuratively, freedom to choose the culvert under which one is to starve is not enough of a goal for a humanitarian society.

Many feel that government should provide more social services (perhaps while paying fewer checks); however, there are serious questions of personal freedom of choice involved in anything that smacks of compulsory rehabilitation, career determination, and family reconstruction. This is a little debated problem to be considered by all who desire a new emphasis on the total reworking of "problem families." To know what is best for another and thereby for society is one thing; to impose one's will on another (for his own good, of course) is something else again.

One warning ought to be stated. Centuries of personal security may lie ahead for Americans, if international disputation in a missile age does not forestall them. But centuries of security will be hollow indeed if they come only at the price of a communistic redistribution of property performed at the urgings of a totalitarian government under the idealistic banner of "social welfare." The trend of the twentieth century has been in that direction in many lands. With it came—for whatever reasons—loss of freedom of movement, of speech, and of religion. Does the quest for economic security necessarily involve such personal disasters in the end? The historian can only observe that another quest— the one for liberty, equality, and fraternity—sometimes brought its own disasters for a time. Adequate social services certainly ought to be something that mankind, when governed by responsible and farseeing leaders, can provide without destroying values of enduring merit.

The people of the United States determined, after World War II, to spend enormous amounts of money to preserve the identity of the nation and protect the freedoms of its inhabitants. As a part of this objective, we have tried to remake large parts of the world. Possessed of a long humanitarian heritage, we have sincerely sought to do good through the expenditure of billions of dollars overseas. This has been self-serving social-service work, recognized as such by realistic people at home and abroad. Reformers have seen in such enormous outlays of funds a golden chance to institute parallel experiments in communities, counties, and states across the land. Social-work leaders have rejoiced at being able to point out that even greatly increased costs of domestic experiments in the second half of the century would be no more than footnotes to a national budget geared for semi-

309

permanent cold war and effective national defense. But their argument is unimpressive when weighed against the total needs of our society.

New programs of social service need to be balanced and assessed as carefully in a day of giant defense expenditures as in a day of minimum peacetime outlays. It is no argument for expanding old-age payments, socializing medicine, or nationalizing local programs to assert that the nation "ought to be able to afford" the addition of miscellaneous billions to an already multi-billion-dollar budget. Not everything can be done at once. And some things should never be done. The draining of a marsh in Pakistan as part of national policy does not necessarily strengthen the case for the draining of property owners in order to double public-aid checks. And if our citizens should have to choose between expanding federal social-work activities or increasing the odds favoring national survival, perhaps by building adequate civil defense shelters, they would do well to choose the latter. Physical survival is prerequisite to any individual's welfare.

Through constructive thought and heartfelt action, spiritually motivated, Americans can, even in years of acute crisis, continue to strive to meet all the legitimate needs of children, youth, the aging, and the disadvantaged in our own land. Our people would certainly be making a major error if we should ever come to focus our eyes so intently on satellites in the heavens or political factions in Southeast Asia that misery down the street becomes acceptable.

Our social-welfare objective in the world of tomorrow must have two aspects: We must guarantee at the very minimum the national and physical survival and well-being of our own people. Then, from the store of plenty we will surely build through the years, it may be possible for us to give increasingly substantial and effective help to people in other nations. These twin tasks comprise realistic goals. They are entirely in accordance with traditional American ideals in social welfare. They will stand the best chance of being attained if leaders in the United States will bear in mind the major advantages and the many minor flaws in the American pattern in social welfare. We must appreciate our basic heritage and accept much deeply rooted innovation. A reluctance to be easily satisfied will certainly hasten the day when the organized social welfare activities of America—government and voluntary together—will regularly serve the vital needs of society.

Index

312